pursuit:365

Brains & Beauty
111 Bosses in Lipstick

SHELLY LYNN HUGHES

Creative Director & Typeset: Christina Moore

Book Cover Design: Nicole O'Keefe

First Printing, March 2024

Published by Ho'ola Publishing

pursuit365.com

For my daughter, Ainslee, you are a beautiful soul with a sharp mind, still finding your way in this big, wild world. May this book remind you that you don't have to choose between Brains & Beauty—you were born to embody both. Trust yourself, embrace your unique path, and know that I will always be cheering you on. You have everything within you to become whoever you dream to be.

With endless love, Mom

Shelly Lynn Hughes is a dedicated parent with two children, an accomplished entrepreneur, and the visionary Founder of pursuit:365. Currently residing in Vancouver, British Columbia, Canada.

FOUNDER
SHELLY LYNN
Hughes

In founding pursuit:365, I set out to build something beyond a business — a movement, a platform, and a legacy that celebrates people. The 'brains' behind this venture are not just in strategy and innovation, but in the resilience, adaptability, and creativity that women bring to the table. It's about harnessing our collective intelligence, our problem-solving abilities, and our capacity to see opportunity where others see obstacles.

When I look at the word 'brains,' I see it as a badge of honor — a recognition of our determination to challenge norms and redefine industries. We are not just participants in the business world; we are trailblazers, disruptors, and visionaries. In pursuit:365, I have had the privilege to connect with women (and men) who have rewritten the rules and reshaped industries, proving time and time again that when women unite, extraordinary things happen.

But let's talk about beauty — a concept often misunderstood and narrowly defined. In Brains & Beauty, the 'beauty' we celebrate is not the kind seen in the mirror; it is the beauty of authenticity, kindness, and impact. It's the glow of a woman who lifts others as she rises, the grace in our vulnerability, and the light we bring to our communities through acts of generosity and support. It's the beauty of knowing who we are and embracing our journey — flaws and all.

At pursuit:365, I've witnessed the power of this inner beauty in every story we tell and every person we feature. It's the beauty that radiates from women who have faced adversity head-on and emerged stronger, the beauty of a shared smile in moments of triumph, and the beauty of raw, unfiltered courage.

Together, the brains and beauty we showcase in this book are not separate traits but two sides of the same coin. They are the essence of what it means to be a woman in business today — smart, strategic, soulful, and deeply impactful. This book is a celebration of that union, a tribute to the women who embody both, and a reminder that true beauty is found in the strength, spirit, and stories we share.

— Shelly Lynn Hughes, Founder of pursuit:365

Amanda Da Silva is an Amazon best-selling published author of "Be You Unapologetically" and her new self-published book, "Architecting Your Future by Design." She is also the co-author of best-selling book, "Pursuit 365."

AMANDA
Da Silva

Q: What problem or need does your business solve?

A: At DS Education Group, we focus on helping high school students navigate the intricate university application process from beginning to end. This means helping students identify their passions, understand how these align with potential career paths, reverse-engineer the programs and courses required for university applications and scholarships, and assist with crafting authentic personal statements and compelling supplementary essays, in addition to simplifying all the planning and preparatory tasks involved.

This is a complex, multi-layered process that requires a guiding advisor with a wide breadth of knowledge and experience in the complexities of post-secondary education. My business aims to solve the challenges that arise as students grapple with the overwhelming application process while simultaneously striving for academic excellence. They want to enjoy their final year of high school, partaking in extracurricular activities, engaging in volunteer work, whilst trying to fit into the demanding application timeline without compromising their futures.

Parents have their own set of anxieties, as they're often distanced by years, if not decades from their own university experiences. They find themselves confronted with an educational landscape that has evolved beyond recognition. To address these concerns, my business provides comprehensive support for both students and parents, offering them peace of mind and the reassurance that their children are receiving the necessary guidance.

We deliver immersive and personalized one-on-one sessions during Spring and Summer breaks for students in grades 9, 10, and 11. Students in Grade 12 have the opportunity to participate in a 10-month program designed to guide them through the entire application process. Through regular virtual consultations via Zoom, students have easier access to an online planning platform for university and career preparation. They also receive detailed session notes with actionable steps to take before the accountability meeting the following week.

Q: What sets your business apart from competitors in the market?

A: The personalized one-on-one mentorship model ensures seamless continuity as your advisor remains a steadfast ally throughout the entire process. So, you have an advisor who brings to the table a wealth of knowledge and a vast network garnered from over a decade of specialized experience within the educational sphere, particularly in the university admissions sector.

With a proven track record of professional excellence, your advisor has honed their skills in the independent school system, serving with distinction in multiple Senior Administrative and Leadership roles. Currently, your advisor is a Senior School Vice Principal, University Counsellor, and Teacher, in addition to offering guidance to students across both public and independent high schools through DS Education Group. This unique blend of roles has culminated in a remarkable 100% success rate in helping students secure admission to their 'dream schools' as well as those aspiring to obtain scholarships, including six-figure and full-ride awards across major, entrance, and external categories, tailored to their individual goals.

What truly sets DS Education Group apart is our deep commitment to understanding and aligning with each student's unique dreams and ambitions. Our holistic approach not only addresses academic and application needs but also fosters a sense of personal growth and self-discovery to make sure students are not just prepared for university but for a thriving future beyond academia. DS Education Group caters to the individual and personalizes the experience. It's an online university advising boutique brand with a purpose.

Q: Can you share a story about a particularly memorable customer interaction or experience?

A: One of the most memorable experiences I've had involved a student when they came to me during a tumultuous period in their life. Like many prospective university students, they were riddled with anxiety and deep-seated uncertainty about their future. They were on the cusp of finishing high school but felt utterly directionless, constantly questioning their capabilities and worth. Our initial consultation was supposed to focus on university applications and academic support, but it quickly became apparent that they needed guidance far beyond that.

Over time, our sessions evolved into a comprehensive coaching relationship. We began with structured accountability and regular check-ins, which provided them with a sense of stability that was sorely lacking in their life. Through these interactions, I introduced exercises designed to enhance clarity and focus, not just academically but personally as well.

One particular breakthrough moment occurred when they managed to articulate their dreams for the future—not in terms of career or study, but in qualities they wished to embody: resilience, self-reliance, and purpose. This marked the beginning of a transformational journey. We worked together on developing actionable steps toward these goals, leveraging their academic pursuits as a vehicle for personal growth.

As their confidence grew, so did their academic performance. Slowly but surely, they started to see themselves as the architect of their own future. They started to engage in activities outside their comfort zone, from leading a community project to mentoring younger students facing similar challenges.

The pinnacle of our journey came when they received acceptance into their dream university program. However, the true success wasn't the acceptance letter; it was the profound self-belief that student had cultivated. They had become a person who not only navigated their high school years with grace and resilience but also emerged with a clear vision of who they wanted to be and in what ways they wanted to contribute to the world.

This experience is a vivid reminder of why I do what I do. It's about more than just academic achievements; it's about empowering young individuals to believe in themselves, to find their direction, and to make meaningful contributions to their communities. Witnessing that one student's transformation from a state of doubt to one of purpose and confidence reaffirms my commitment to my work. I will be eternally grateful for my ability to breathe belief into others when they can't find it within themselves and watch them flourish into their fullest potential.

Final Question: Pink or red lipstick?

Pink - actually a Mauve (in between a pink and red)

Nas Nadat is a dedicated Holistic Life Coach & Mentor with a focus on empowering neurodivergent women with ADHD to thrive in their careers. Driven by a passion for unlocking potential, Nas equips clients with the tools to build unshakable confidence, elevate self-esteem, and cultivate the discipline needed to overcome challenges. By addressing mental, emotional, and physical well-being, Nas helps clients achieve not only professional success but also a deeply fulfilling, balanced life.

Q: Can you tell us about your journey as an entrepreneur and what inspired you to start your own business?

A: My entrepreneurial journey stemmed from a lifelong passion for personal development. Since childhood, I've been fascinated by human potential and how we can unlock our best selves. This curiosity led me to explore various coaching modalities and alternative therapies for over two decades. While working in successful corporate careers, I always felt a pull to make development opportunities more accessible. Witnessing the struggles of neurodivergent individuals in the workplace further fueled my desire to create a personalized coaching approach. Having ADHD myself, I understand these challenges firsthand, which allows me to connect with my clients on a deeper level and provide empathy and understanding throughout their coaching journey. This passion culminated in the launch of my business, where I empower people of all neurotypes, particularly those with ADHD and ASD, to thrive authentically in all aspects of their lives. My experience sets me apart by combining coaching expertise with a deep understanding of neurodiversity, allowing me to bridge the gap between personal growth and professional success.

Q: What were some of the biggest challenges you faced when starting your business, and how did you overcome them?

A: Building my business wasn't without hurdles. Initially, the biggest challenge was establishing myself in a saturated coaching market. To stand out, I focused on my unique blend of coaching expertise and lived experience with ADHD. Another hurdle was overcoming self-doubt, which can creep in when you're venturing out on your own. To combat this, I surrounded myself with a supportive network of mentors and fellow entrepreneurs. There were also setbacks, like a time when a marketing campaign didn't yield the results I'd anticipated. However, I viewed this as a learning opportunity. I analyzed the data, adjusted my strategy, and tested new approaches. These challenges ultimately strengthened my resolve and helped me refine my approach, making my business even more effective.

Q: How do you stay motivated and resilient during tough times in your business?

A: Staying ahead of the curve in the coaching industry requires constant learning and adaptation. I actively seek out educational opportunities, attend industry conferences, and connect with other coaches to exchange ideas. Feedback is also crucial. I regularly solicit input from clients to ensure my services remain relevant and impactful. Perhaps most importantly, I prioritize self-care. As a certified naturopathic wellness coach, I leverage mindfulness, meditation, and healthy habits to maintain my motivation and resilience. This holistic approach allows me to approach challenges with a clear mind and a positive attitude, fueling my ability to innovate and adapt in this ever-evolving field.

Q: Can you share a story about a particularly memorable customer interaction or experience?

A: Witnessing my clients' transformations is the most rewarding aspect of my work. I've had the privilege of working with some clients on a weekly basis for years, like one I started coaching in 2017. Seeing them navigate career advancements, strengthen relationships, and achieve personal goals brings me immense joy. These clients have become like family, as I've supported them through life's milestones – marriages, births, and even the loss of loved ones. Moving forward, my biggest aspiration is to create a wider impact. I envision Mission Gravitas expanding beyond individual coaching, offering online courses and workshops to make personal development resources more accessible. Ultimately, my goal is to cultivate a global community where everyone can unlock their full potential and live fulfilling lives.

Q: How do you prioritize tasks and manage time effectively as an entrepreneur?

A: Juggling multiple priorities and achieving work-life balance is a constant exercise for entrepreneurs. To stay on top of everything, I rely on time management techniques like scheduling, batching similar tasks, and setting clear deadlines. However, I also recognize the importance of flexibility. Unexpected situations arise, so I build buffer time into my schedule. Additionally, I leverage technology to streamline processes and automate tasks. For work-life balance, I fiercely protect designated "off" times. Disconnecting allows me to recharge and return to my work refreshed and focused. Prioritizing self-care through healthy habits and hobbies also fuels my overall well-being and productivity.

Q: What advice would you give to other women and what role do you think mentorship and support networks play for women in entrepreneurship?

A: For women considering entrepreneurship, I'd say: Believe in yourself and your vision. The journey will have challenges, but with dedication and perseverance, you can achieve your goals. Don't be afraid to ask for help. Mentorship and support networks are invaluable. Surround yourself with positive, encouraging people who believe in you and your dream. In my experience, these connections provide guidance, celebrate your wins, and offer a shoulder to lean on during tough times. Remember, you don't have to go it alone. Building a strong support system is key to thriving as a female entrepreneur.

Q: Pink or red lipstick?

A: Red – Ruby red, always!

Brooke Abel is the founder of montempe, a leading holistic marketing and brand development house for purpose-led entrepreneurs to build and grow their businesses. Through curated services and digital resources, montempe weaves storytelling, strategies and a growth mindset to turn your passion into profit and freedom. Brooke lives in Australia.

Q: Can you tell us about your journey as an entrepreneur and what inspired you to start your own business?

A: My entrepreneurial journey began very naturally from the desire to offer a product that, at the time, you had to travel the world to find {one-of-a-kind jewellery) and build a career outside of my corporate role that aligned with my values. It was a combination of my passion for the product, my purpose in how my jewellery made my customers feel, my intrigue in business and my creative marketing (storytelling) skills. Along with my university studies and work experience, I built a very successful business and brand, and then I used this experience to build Montempe to help others achieve the same. Once I experienced this level of independence, the joy of my customers, creative control and freedom of entrepreneurism, I never looked back, and neither will you!

Q: In your experience, what are some common misconceptions or stereotypes about women in business, and how do you challenge or overcome them?

A: One of the biggest stereotypes about women in business is that women do not, or cannot, work as hard as men or that they are too 'emotionally affected' to make serious decisions. I find it to be very disheartening that still, in 2024, one's work ethic is gender biased. I believe this misconception is shifting with the rise of successful, strong, and independent entrepreneurs worldwide, but there is still a long way to go. I make it a mission of mine through montempe to uplift, encourage and teach women who desire to start their own businesses that they are capable of everything just as a man is by teaching them the skills they need in business, marketing, branding and most importantly, growth mindset.

6

Q: How do you stay motivated and resilient during tough times in your business?

A: Passion and purpose. Many people will say passion doesn't matter in a successful business, but I strongly disagree. When we are passionate about specific elements of our work, that passion will keep us motivated through challenging times as we have a greater goal and genuine belief beyond the momentary hardship. Purpose is my second motivation, and I would advise anyone to identify their purpose in business and to make it deeper than something tangible like money. It could be to create change within your community, live a certain lifestyle, have freedom of time, etc., and ensure all of your outcomes are aligned in achieving this. With strong growth mindset practices and awareness of your passion and purpose, you can always find a way through any challenges, making the outcome all the more rewarding and your self-belief greater.

Q: What do you believe are the keys to building a strong brand identity and reputation?

A: Authenticity and Storytelling. When starting or growing a brand, it's very easy to look at what others in your industry who have succeeded are doing and think you need to replicate that yourself to succeed - this is the fastest way to failure. When you are authentic in your messaging, energy, and offer, you will attract aligned clients/customers faster and stand out in your industry. People are smart and can quickly see and feel if someone isn't authentic, so be yourself from day one. Secondly, storytelling is critical to building a strong brand identity. No matter your business, people connect to people and their stories - they want to feel connected to similar values and be a part of something greater. You can do this through storytelling - sharing your journey, vision, and why, and your audience will remain loyal to your brand long term.

Q: What problem or need does your business solve, and what motivated you to address it?

A: I build more than brands; I create opportunities for people to live life by their own design. I solve the barrier of freedom that is not present in the corporate system and help others achieve their version of this by not only teaching them how to build a brand and business but one that allows them to share their talents and passion with the world, give back purposefully and create a life they desire whether it be freedom in time, money or impact. This is something I have created for myself through weaving my skills, dreams and passions, and now I have taught and guided hundreds of others to achieve the exact same thing. Life by design can and deserves to be experienced by everyone, not just a select few, and with the right tools, mindset and people (me) by your side, I promise it is possible.

Q: What advice would you give to other women who are considering starting their own businesses?

A: To trust yourself. Trust in your vision, your abilities and your decisions. In business, you need to be your biggest cheerleader in everything you do. This element of self-trust and respect will allow you to make creative, business and financial decisions that others won't understand. I teach all my clients, and I want you to know that there is a greater reason you want to offer a new product or service to the world, and only you can do it your unique way. Once you identify with your passion and purpose as above, everything else can be learned. You've got this.

Q: Pink or red lipstick?

A: I love deep red lipstick - feminine yet powerful, the perfect balance!

Lily Ahonen is the owner of Blond Vagabond Beauty makeup artistry and Marigold Beauty Cosmetics. She is a living kidney donor and holds the international pageant title of Ms. Achievement World 2024.

Q: Can you discuss the role of networking and partnerships in growing your business?

A: Networking is important to be able to build community and create connections. Most of my work has come from word-of-mouth referrals. I believe strongly in working together with others in my field, rather than viewing them as competition. I love collaborating and feel that there is room for everyone.

Q: Looking ahead, what are your goals and aspirations for the future of your business??

A: I offer both a service and retail products. My business Blond Vagabond Beauty currently offers makeup artistry services, and Marigold Beauty offers cosmetic products for sale. I will be adding nail services this year, and my daughter will be joining my business. I am also planning to host empowerment workshops for youth, which would also involve a makeup lesson.

Q: Can you share a story about a particularly memorable customer interaction or experience?

A: One of the most memorable times as a makeup artist, was doing makeup for a photoshoot for my friend who had advanced stage liver failure. It was the top item on her bucket list, to do a "Fight like a girl" empowerment photo shoot in a boxing studio. It was a very emotional day and I'm honoured I could be part of such a profound and intimate time in someone's journey. She passed away about a month later.

Q: What role do you think mentorship and support networks play for women in entrepreneurship?

A: Mentorship is critical for any entrepreneurs. I believe strongly in the phrase "Take her with you" and feel that we should all help each other to rise. I believe that mentors can also learn a lot from their mentees. I belong to a few business communities where I'm able to ask for support and advice. Learning from entrepreneurs who have more experience, and having them take the time to help, is priceless.

Q: How do you prioritize tasks and manage time effectively as an entrepreneur?

A: I make a schedule for every day of the week, and map out my big plan for each following week every Sunday evening. Besides owning a beauty business, I am also a Nurse and Landlord and have to juggle many tasks. I am constantly making lists and revising them.

Q: What do you believe are the keys to building a strong brand identity and reputation?

A: Integrity is very important. I feel that if you are reliable and trustworthy, your customers will take note. Having a good product that you can stand behind is a must. Everyone is welcome at my business. I have done makeup for a diverse population and strive to be inclusive. My business gives back to the community, and this is an important value to me.

Q: Can you share a particularly memorable success story or milestone from your entrepreneurial journey?

A: I was asked to do makeup for Honourable Rachel Notley, our former Premier of Alberta. I didn't know it at the time, but it was a photoshoot for the renowned Maclean's magazine. She was part of the cohort of 50 "makers and breakers" in their March 2022 Power List issue. I went into a bit of a shock when I saw her on the cover of Maclean's on the magazine rack at Walmart!

Q: Can you tell me about your journey as an entrepreneur? What inspired you to start your own business?

A: I've been an entrepreneur since a very young age. I grew up in poverty, so it was necessary to find ways to make ends meet. I used to make cards and sell them in my neighborhood, and I used to offer parking in my backyard, as we lived close to an event stadium. During my college years, buying and reselling items online substantially helped with the costs.

Q: Pink or red lipstick?

A: RED! My dear friend Maarit always said "Whatever bad things happen, just put on some red lipstick, and you'll be ready to face it."

Cathy Cena is....Vivacious, outgoing, and her personality is contagious. She is a people connector, mom, actor, entrepreneur and WIFE.

CATHY
Cena

Q: What advice would you give to other women who are considering starting their own businesses?

A: Believe in Yourself: Have confidence in your abilities and believe that you have what it takes to succeed as an entrepreneur. ~ Pursue Your Passion: Choose a business idea that aligns with your interests, passions, and strengths. Your enthusiasm and dedication will be essential for overcoming challenges and staying motivated. ~ Educate Yourself: Take the time to educate yourself about entrepreneurship, business management, and your industry. Seek out resources, courses, mentors, and networking opportunities to enhance your knowledge and skills. ~Build a Support Network: Surround yourself with mentors, advisors, peers, and other entrepreneurs who can offer guidance, support, and encouragement along your journey. ~Be Resilient: Entrepreneurship is filled with ups and downs, setbacks, and failures. Stay resilient in the face of challenges, learn from your mistakes, and keep moving forward with determination and optimism. ~Embrace Risk: Starting a business involves taking risks, whether it's financial, personal, or professional. Embrace the uncertainty and be willing to step out of your comfort zone to pursue your goals. ~Focus on Your Strengths: Identify your strengths and leverage them to your advantage in your business. Delegate tasks that are outside of your expertise and focus on what you do best. ~Set Goals: Set clear, achievable goals for your business and develop a plan to reach them. Break down your goals into smaller milestones and celebrate your achievements along the way. ~Prioritize Self-Care: Balancing the demands of entrepreneurship with your personal life is essential for long-term success and well-being. Make time for self-care, relaxation, and activities that recharge your batteries. ~Don't Be Afraid to Ask for Help: Don't hesitate to seek help, advice, or support when you need it. Whether it's from mentors, peers, or professional advisors, asking for help is a sign of strength, not weakness. Remember that every successful entrepreneur faces challenges and setbacks along the way. Stay focused on your goals, stay true to yourself, and don't be afraid to pivot or adjust your plans as needed. With determination, resilience, and passion, you can turn your entrepreneurial dreams into reality.

Q: How do you stay motivated and resilient during tough times in your business?

A: Staying motivated and resilient during tough times in business requires a combination of mindset, strategies, and support systems. Here are some ways to stay resilient: ~ Focus on Purpose: Reconnect with your underlying purpose and passion for your business. Remind yourself why you started your business and the impact you want to make. Keeping your purpose front and center can provide motivation and clarity during challenging times. ~ Practice Gratitude: Cultivate a mindset of gratitude by focusing on the positive aspects of your business and life, even during tough times. Recognize and appreciate the progress you've made, no matter how small, and celebrate your achievements along the way. ~ Stay Flexible: Embrace flexibility and adaptability in your approach to business. Be willing to pivot, innovate, and experiment with new strategies or ideas to overcome obstacles and navigate uncertainty. ~ Seek Support: Surround yourself with a supportive network of mentors, advisors, peers, and loved ones who can offer guidance, encouragement, and perspective during tough times. Don't hesitate to lean on your support system for help and emotional support when needed. ~Practice Self-Care: Prioritize your physical and mental well-being by making time for self-care activities such as exercise, meditation, hobbies, or spending time with loved ones. Taking care of yourself is essential for maintaining resilience and managing stress. ~ Break Tasks into Manageable Steps: Break down daunting tasks or challenges into smaller, more manageable steps. Focus on taking one step at a time, and celebrate your progress along the way. This approach can help prevent overwhelm and maintain momentum. ~ Learn from Setbacks: View setbacks and failures as opportunities for growth and learning. Reflect on what went wrong, extract valuable lessons from the experience, and use that knowledge to inform your future decisions and actions. ~ Stay Positive: Maintain a positive mindset and attitude, even when faced with adversity. Cultivate optimism, resilience, and a belief in your ability to overcome challenges and achieve success in the long run. ~ Visualize Success: Visualize your goals and envision yourself overcoming obstacles and achieving success in your business. Visualization can help reinforce your motivation and resilience, giving you the mental strength to persevere during tough times. ~ Take Breaks: Know when to step back and take breaks from work to recharge and rejuvenate. Taking time away from your business can help prevent burnout and restore your energy and focus.

By incorporating these strategies into your routine, you can cultivate resilience, maintain motivation, and navigate tough times with grace and determination in your business.

Q: How do you balance work-life commitments as an entrepreneur?

A: Balancing work-life commitments as an entrepreneur requires intentional effort and effective time management. Here are some strategies to help achieve balance: ~Set Boundaries: Establish clear boundaries between work and personal life. Designate specific work hours and stick to them as much as possible. Similarly, create designated time for personal activities and prioritize them. ~Prioritize Tasks: Identify your most important tasks and commitments both in your work and personal life. Focus on completing high-priority items first and delegate or defer less urgent tasks when possible. ~Schedule Downtime: Make time for self-care and relaxation by scheduling regular breaks and leisure activities into your calendar. Treat these activities as non-negotiable appointments and prioritize them just as you would a work commitment. ~Delegate: Delegate tasks and responsibilities to trusted employees, contractors, or family members to lighten your workload and free up time for personal pursuits. ~Practice Time Management: Improve your efficiency and productivity by using time management techniques such as prioritizing tasks, batching similar activities together, and minimizing distractions. ~Communicate Openly: Communicate openly with your team, clients, and loved ones about your work-life balance needs and limitations. Set realistic expectations and be transparent about your availability and boundaries. ~Set Realistic Goals: Set realistic goals for both your work and personal life. Avoid over-committing yourself and be willing to adjust your goals as needed to maintain balance. ~Learn to Say No: Don't be afraid to say no to commitments or opportunities that don't align with your priorities or values. Learning to set boundaries and decline requests respectfully is essential for maintaining balance. ~Take Care of Yourself: Prioritize your physical and mental well-being by getting enough sleep, eating healthily, exercising regularly, and practicing stress-reduction techniques such as meditation or mindfulness. ~Evaluate Regularly: Periodically evaluate your work-life balance and make adjustments as needed. Be flexible and willing to adapt your approach based on changing circumstances or priorities.

By implementing these strategies and prioritizing self-care, you can achieve a healthier balance between your work and personal life as an entrepreneur.

Q: What advice would you give to someone who is considering starting their own business?

A: Start with a solid idea, create a business plan, be prepared to work hard, build a strong network, focus on the customer, stay flexible, manage finances wisely, stay resilient, never stop learning, and prioritize self-care.

Q: Pink or red lipstick?   A: FUSCHIA (PINK)

Beth Chisholm: Sound and Energy Coach &
Entrepreneur.

Hi, I'm Beth Chisholm and I'm a Sound and Energy Coach. My journey as an entrepreneur is a testament to resilience, passion, and a deep commitment to healing. I didn't set out to build a coaching business at age 54, but when I discovered it was possible to heal from my past traumas, I felt a calling to share my experiences and knowledge with others. This desire to support and empower women on their healing journey inspired me to start my own business.

My path toward founding Kamiyah Coaching, a business focused on holistic wellness and personal development, was deeply intertwined with my healing journey. After witnessing the shooting death of my friend, I was desperate for freedom from the anxiety and fears that plagued me daily. Nothing gave me lasting relief until I discovered Emotional Freedom Technique, also known as Tapping. For the first time in 8 years, I could finally breathe! I had discovered tools that worked. Even better, I could use them anywhere and at any time.

What sets Kamiyah Coaching apart from its competitors is my holistic approach to healing and personal development. Drawing from my experiences and extensive training in various healing modalities, I offer a unique blend of techniques tailored to individual needs. As I guide clients towards holistic well-being and lasting change, it's my emphasis on empowerment, self-awareness, and inner transformation that makes a distinct difference in the level of service I provide. Moreover, my genuine passion for helping others shines through in every aspect of my business, creating a supportive and nurturing environment for growth and healing.

In the rapidly evolving landscape of holistic wellness and personal development, I am particularly excited about the growing emphasis on integrative approaches to healing. I see a trend toward combining traditional and alternative modalities to address the holistic needs of individuals, which aligns perfectly with the philosophy of Kamiyah's approach to coaching. The increasing recognition of the mind-body connection in mainstream wellness practices opens up new avenues for exploration and innovation in the therapy field.

One of my client success stories centers around a woman named Ley. When she first came to me, she suffered from regular panic attacks, debilitating fear, anxiety and constant triggers. After partnering together, she no longer has panic attacks and is remarkably calm, and at peace, there's no pressure, and no anxiety. In her words: 'A massive weight has been removed from my shoulders; the anxiety has gone!!! GONE!! GONE, GONE!!!!' Giving hope and freedom is why I launched my business and continue to do what I do.

Technology is vital to the success of Kamiyah Coaching, acting as both a bridge and a catalyst for growth and connection. It allows me to reach a global audience, breaking down geographical barriers. Through online platforms and video conferencing tools, I can conduct healing sessions, workshops, and group circles, offering the same personalized support as in-person meetings. This accessibility is crucial for clients without local holistic wellness resources. Additionally, technology enables me to create and share valuable content—blog posts, videos, and online courses—that educates and empowers individuals on their healing journeys, attracting potential clients and providing ongoing support and inspiration.

At Kamiyah Coaching, my strategies for attracting and retaining customers are based on authenticity, personalized service, and genuine connection. I believe that building trust and fostering meaningful relationships are the foundation of a successful coaching business. By openly sharing my healing journey, tailoring my coaching programs to meet the specific needs and goals of each client, adopting a holistic approach that addresses the mind, body, and spirit, and committing to continuous learning and professional development, I create a supportive and empowering experience that helps clients feel seen, heard, and valued, ultimately fostering lasting transformation and loyalty.

To other women considering starting their own business, I offer this advice: trust yourself and your intuition, believe in your abilities, and don't be afraid to ask for help when needed. I cannot emphasize enough the importance of finding mentors and building a supportive community, as well as being resilient in the face of challenges. Embrace your unique perspective and strength, and recognize them as assets in your entrepreneurial journey.

Oh, and I prefer pink lipstick, hot pink lipstick!

Dawn Chubai: Director King Willow Management Inc. , Principal, Live Selling School and Dawn Chubai Media Services.

Q: Can you tell us about your journey as an entrepreneur and what inspired you to start your own business?

A: I was always leveraging my skills and talents to offer services to others even while I was employed, but it wasn't until 2003 that I incorporated King Willow Management Inc. to house Dawn Chubai Media Services (dawnchubai.com) and most recently Live Selling School (LiveSellingSchool.com) to my business model. In 2023 I decided to leave the "comforts" of full-time employment working Nationally as a Broadcaster and TV Home Shopping Host to exclusively focus on the value I could bring with my range of services. It's exhilarating to experience my client transformations both personally and in their businesses. With Dawn Chubai Media Services, I enjoy working with Brands to help them earn valuable media opportunities with effective audience-centric pitches and presentation skills that offer significant brand exposure and ultimately support their business growth. My Live Selling School goes a step further and provides a solution to the limited reach and engagement of traditional brick-and-mortar stores by implementing Live Commerce strategy and training. As Brands work toward navigating the future in retail, I help them expand their customer base beyond geographical constraints, increasing Brand visibility and enhancing customer engagement (and sales!) With Live, Video, and Social Commerce.

Q: What inspired you to start your own business?

A: It all started in 2003 when I saw a Real Estate Agent on TV who not only struggled to present himself confidently on camera but in the process, most likely lost a certain amount of credibility. I would later hear that this appearance did not generate a single sales lead for him, which I expect was his ultimate goal in dedicating advertising dollars to this media appearance. I was not the most confident when I started in TV, but I knew if I could do it…I could help others. I have since worked with a range of industries, from CEO's to Chefs across the country. And now with my Live Selling School, I am uniquely qualified to help retail brands, their sales personnel and ambassadors do what I was able to successfully do as a TV Home Shopping Host (with over $30 Million in personal sales) in the Live, Video and Social Commerce space…authentically SELL through the screen and ultimately ease their anxiety about their future viability in the digital world.

Q: What are some of the biggest challenges you've faced as a woman entrepreneur, and how have you overcome them?

A: I wish I could blame the fact that I am a "woman" for any delayed success, but the reality, any challenge I may have encountered would come from my own limiting beliefs. Once I let go of what I "thought" everyone believed was necessary to succeed as an Entrepreneur, whether it was education or even experience, I came into my professional power. Knowing what you are good at and how it can solve another's problem is all that matters. If you don't have all the tools in your toolbox to execute that business plan, get help. But as my first boss in the TV biz said to me when I fumbled my way through an audition with no experience, "Everything is trainable except for personality". I have enjoyed a highly successful career on TV screens across Canada as a result. Had I not said yes to auditioning in the first place, I would never have realized that the transformation I experienced was possible for others.

Q: What are some trends or developments in your industry that you're particularly excited about?

A: The over-arching "theme" of my business is mastering the art of communication and customer conversion. Developments in E-commerce trends have created a need to incorporate authentic voices to balance the lack of personal connection due to technology and the diminishing trust that consumers feel, especially with the use of AI. From earned media that allows Brands to share authentic stories that drive brand awareness to taking the next step to using Live Selling Strategies on owned channels, the competitive edge is there for the innovation-ready, growth-ambitious and yes, even the crisis-affected.

Q: What sets your business apart from competitors in the market?

A: The old saying of "those who can't do…teach" doesn't apply here and I invite you to research anyone who offers training or coaching to establish why they might be qualified to work with you. I "do", "have done" AND I "teach".

I have taken everything I have learned and accomplished over the last 25 years both on Television and in Sales and helped my clients authentically and effectively represent themselves and their products both in person and "through the screen". When looking to make that impression using mediums that exist forever, trial and error can have costs that go beyond money. From reputation management to adapting to new retail landscapes and technology, look to someone who has successfully navigated both.

Q: Looking ahead, what are your goals and aspirations for the future of your business??

A: As an innovator in a growing space, my future is clear and my aspirations are large. I have already worked to scale my 1:1 and group coaching business with a video course developed for Sales Reps, Brand and Ambassadors and Influencers who want to up-skill before they are out-skilled. In addition to collaborating with retail brands (both big and small) to execute strategies that drive connection and conversion, I also foresee opportunities to collaborate with YouTube, Shopify and even Netflix, where Livestream Shopping and other creator commerce strategies either exist, are evolving or on the verge of activation. To achieve scalability, credibility and authority in business, you must be first, best or different. I believe my offerings as an Entrepreneur now, and in the future of retail, tick all of those boxes.

Q: Pink or red lipstick?

A: Red !

Dr. Divi Chandna, MD, is an Intuitive Coach, teacher, author, and speaker.

DR. DIVI
Chandna, MD

Q: What are some of the biggest challenges you've faced as a woman entrepreneur, and how have you overcome them?

A: One of the biggest challenges is simply believing that you are important, regardless of your sex. I remember when I was training in medicine, the sexual bias to male trainees was so obvious, especially in areas like surgery and internal medicine. I experienced that first when I was 21 years old and I was in an operating room with male physicians and there was a feeling in my body that I would describe as shrinking, not being seen or acknowledged. Now, if I feel that way, I am very aware of it and I simply recognize that I am believing something that is not true. I am just as important as any man – and it is up to me to believe it first. Just that awareness shifts it.

Q: How do you maintain a work-life balance while running your own business?

A: For myself, my work life balance is crucial. I have one son, who is currently 19 years old. During my entrepreneurial journey, I have been aware that it never ends. I don't see myself as a certain age or with limitations. While he was growing up and living at home full time, I put him and my family first. I always knew that as he got older, and was more interested in friends and basketball than his mom, I would have more time and space. Now that he is in University, I have been able to expand my business more. I hold no regrets or thoughts that I am old. I feel like I'm 25 years old every day – and if I have that as my mental construct, anything is possible!

Q: What advice would you give to other women who are considering starting their own businesses?

A: Just do it! As more of us get out there, the idea that it is a "man's world" shrinks. It is not the same world as when I was little. I owe that to all the women who preceded me and opened their own doors. You are only as limited as your mind says you are. Our minds can be changed in a second!

Q: What advice would you give to other women who are considering starting their own businesses?

A: This one I have struggled with as I used to believe in the idea of "competition". What I started to realize is that everything comes from my thoughts. If I believe there is competition - there will be. But when I have that thought, I am shrinking away from my own gifts. I truly believe that each of us are gifted with our own gifts - even if there are thousands of people doing the same thing. When we are hyper-focussed on our gifts, and our talents, we increase the energy and that increases people knowing of us. When we are focussed on others and afraid, we are diluting our energy and thereby diluting people who find us. Keeping the focus on ourselves is the key!

Q: How do you stay motivated and resilient during tough times in your business?

A: I try to stay out of the story. When tough times occur, human nature is to try to figure out what is going on outside of us that is causing it. So for example, we might think: ' there is a recession' or ' interest rates are high' or ' there are less people who want this" and so on. Our mind LOVES to figure out why. When tough times occur, I remind myself- there is ebb and flow in everything. The ocean comes and goes from the beach (high tide/low tide) - this is just a bit of low tide. Let me sit tight and remember that there is a VAST ocean out there that will come in. This may sound silly and counterintuitive to most people, but I look at tough times as a time to DIVE deeper. Because I run a Spiritual business, I think of tough times as a learning opportunity for me to learn something more about myself. I remind myself I am part of this vast Universe, with infinite beautiful things. That vast Universe and the creator is in me. There is NO LACK. There is only a lack of focus. Let me dive into a Spiritual text, let me learn more about me, let me listen to my intuition, let me meditate more. These are the things I take pro-actively on. I look at tough times as a chance to level up, to figure out what in ME needs to be shifted to allow in more magic from the Universe. That takes some inner work, but if I listen to my intuition and slow down, I will always find the answer!

Q: How do you stay motivated and resilient during tough times in your business?

A: I try to step out of the story. When challenges arise, our natural instinct is to look for external reasons to explain them. We might think, "It's a recession," "Interest rates are high," or "There's less demand." Our mind loves to rationalize. Instead, I remind myself that everything has an ebb and flow. Just like the ocean's tides—high and low—this tough moment is simply low tide. It's a phase, and I know there's a vast ocean out there that will inevitably flow back in.

This approach might seem counterintuitive to many, but I view tough times as an opportunity to dive deeper. Running a spiritual business, I see challenges as a chance to learn more about myself. I remind myself that I am part of a boundless universe, filled with infinite possibilities. There is no real lack, only a lack of focus. So, I use tough times to reconnect with my inner self—reading spiritual texts, meditating, and listening closely to my intuition.

For me, challenges are a call to level up. They're a nudge to look within and identify what needs to shift so I can welcome more magic from the universe. It takes inner work, but when I slow down and trust my intuition, the answers always come.

Q: How do you measure the success and growth of your business?

A: I measure success and growth based on how it all FEELS. If I feel inspired, uplifted and forward moving, then I am on the right path! My success is not based on my bank account (though there is that measure), but for me, it is that constant moving upwards and that feeling of being in flow. It is that feeling of alignment with the Universe and right place-right time. Those feelings and being in that flow state then creates the bank account!

Q: Pink or red lipstick? A: Red

Christine Daer is a Certified Life Coach and creator of Power In Aging, a group coaching program for women in midlife. She is also an Angelic Reiki Master Practitioner, Ageless Grace Educator and proud Mama of two boys!

CHRISTINE
Daer

Q: What problem or need does your business solve, and what motivated you to address it?

A: We help women to feel empowered to choose themselves and reimagine their lives as they journey through midlife. Our goal is to inspire intentional and mindful choices to nourish the body and soul. I felt very drawn to the area of midlife aging as it was something I was personally going through. We are all aging, but there is a stigma around hitting 50, as well as ageism, and I felt there was a large hole in the coaching industry when it came to supporting women going through middle age and all of the physical, hormonal, emotional, mental and spiritual changes we encounter. I knew that if I was feeling "stuck", uninspired and no longer sure of my purpose or passions, that other women must also be questioning their self-worth and wondering what is next for them. The secret is knowing that what is next is entirely up to us and that we can really create the life we want. We are far more powerful than we realize. Most women just need the wake up call to come home to themselves again and reignite their spark.

Q: How did you come up with the idea for your business, and what was the process like from concept to execution?

A: I knew that I wanted to build a beautiful community of like-hearted women that supported and inspired one another and that would be the foundation. I am always my best "avatar" so I started creating what I would most want and need in a program, and then built it from there. I knew there had to be a wealth of wisdom to serve our community so I started with a Guest Speaker series once a month, with a wide range of valuable topics and expert speakers. We also started with online workshops in the beginning and are now also using webinars and masterclasses to introduce Power In Aging to more people. Our main focus has been building our Online Membership program and community. It's been a labour of love but I'm thrilled that we have just completed our first year and are launching boldly into our second! I have previously been in other online membership communities myself and knew what I loved and didn't love, so I decided to build an online membership program with all my favourite aspects put together. We consider it a unique triad approach combining monthly group coaching sessions, member support meetings and self-paced online development work. This allows for the busy women (that we all are) to accommodate their schedules while also learning accountability to 'show up', for both themselves and their community.

Q: Can you share a significant milestone or achievement your business has reached, and what did you learn from it?

A: We have just celebrated our 30th Guest Speaker event as well as our first year of our Online Membership Program - Yay! When I look back, I'm still amazed how all of these ideas running around in my head somehow managed to jump onto my laptop, and then just like magic, became a reality! I have learned that resilience is key - and a practice - and to just keep going, even when others doubt you, and especially when you doubt yourself. Listen to that positive inner voice telling you to keep going. The best things in my life have taken the most work, but the lessons and growth along the way have been gifts that I don't take for granted. I've also learned that where you place value won't always align with that of others but you must always remain true to you.

Q: What advice would you give to someone who is considering starting their own business?

A: If you are looking to start your own business, my best advice would be to do something that makes you want to get out of bed every day and makes your heart sing. Many people think you have to be practical and make decisions with your head, but I have always led with my heart. If you look at time as a gift, then you will start to appreciate the way you decide to spend that time and know it needs to count. You need to also make intentional choices where you invest your energy, so make sure your business choices align with your values and will allow your light to shine brighter!

Q: Looking ahead, what are your goals and aspirations for the future of your business?

A: We are making a few tweaks to our current membership program as we are always looking to improve and make things flow better. We will also be introducing a few new group coaching course options this year, more specialized and specific to both intuitive life coaching, as well as functional health and wellness coaching. We are planning to launch some independent empowerment courses for women in midlife as well, which we are really excited about.

Q: What is your mission and what are you inspired to share with the world?

A: My mission is to practice living on a higher vibration every day, and then to help show other women how that is possible. It may look different for each person, but at the end of the day, we all want that optimal feeling of joy, and living our truth and purpose. If we make intentional choices in every moment we are on our way from "ordinary to extraordinary". Every thought, every action and every relationship is an energy exchange. It's about how you spend, receive and share that energy. Ultimately, it is up to you. It is a choice and it is a practice. We all have the power to make better, more intentional choices!

Q: Pink or red lipstick?

A: Pink! I know red is a fiery and passionate colour but it's never suited me. I'm a pink gal all the way for lipstick! Pink is also a very healing colour for me.

Kamal Atwal, Mompreneur, CEO of ICON Debt Solutions, Your RESP Specialist

Q: Why did you start your own business?

A: I started my business back in 2005 because I wanted to combine my big entrepreneurial dreams with being a hands-on mom. By 2001, I already had two kids and knew I wanted to be there for the important moments—like school drop-offs and pick-ups—and really spend quality time with them after school. A regular 9-to-5 job just didn't fit with that, so I decided to start something that would give me the freedom to do both.

Q: How important are mentors and support networks for women in business?

A: Having a strong support system and good mentors is super important, especially for women in business. These networks help you see things from different angles and can offer solutions when you're feeling stuck. Mentors, in particular, bring a lot of experience and can give advice that helps you avoid mistakes and grow faster. They're great for bouncing ideas off of and getting strategic input when you need it.

Q: What big challenges did you face as a woman starting your own business, and how did you deal with them?

A: Starting a business as both a woman and a mom definitely came with its own challenges. One of the biggest was not really having any examples or role models to follow—I didn't personally know any women who had done something similar. That made it feel pretty lonely at times, and I often had to figure things out on my own, which could be overwhelming. But I was determined to make it work. I just faced each challenge as it came, kept learning, and adjusted as needed. I really believed I could make it through, and that pushed me forward.

Q: Any advice for other women thinking about starting their own business?

A: My main advice is to build your business around something you're really passionate about. That passion will keep you going, especially when things get tough. Also, it's important to really know your field—be prepared and flexible enough to adapt when things change. Being open to evolving your strategies will help your business survive and grow over time.

Q: How do you balance work-life commitments as an entrepreneur?

A: I stay balanced by sticking to a schedule that helps me stay productive but also takes care of my well-being. I start each day with some exercise and time for myself, which helps me stay focused and positive. I also pay attention to my diet, making sure my meals are planned out to keep me energized. I try to tackle the most important work in the mornings, which frees up my afternoons for other responsibilities. This way, I stay organized and make time for both my business and personal life.

Q: How do you stay innovative and adapt to changes in your industry?

A: I don't get too caught up in specific industry trends; instead, I focus on what's working today. I always ask, "What do people love right now? How do they like to communicate?" By staying in touch with what people are into, I adjust my strategies to meet them where they are. Whether it's using new platforms or tweaking my services, my goal is to stay connected with my audience and keep my business flexible.

Q: How do you keep going when times get tough with your business?

A: When things get tough, I rely on my strong belief in my business and the goals I've set. I stay focused on what needs to get done, while keeping in mind the bigger picture and long-term goals. Being consistent in my actions helps me stay steady, even when challenges pop up. It's about trusting that you're on the right path and reminding yourself why you started in the first place.

Q: Pink or red lipstick?

A: RED LIPS ALL THE WAY!

Geeta Dayal, a renowned entrepreneur, educator, mentor, and celebrated BIPOC makeup artist, garnered a Hollywood Makeup Artist and Hair Stylist Guild nomination in 2022 for her exceptional contributions. Her journey found purpose with the births of her niece Ava in 2006 and daughter Charley in 2014, propelling her commitment to being a positive female role model for fellow women entrepreneurs.

GEETA *Dayal*

Q: Can you tell me about your journey as an entrepreneur? What inspired you to start your own business??

A: It all began when I was very young. I would line up my dolls and stuffed animals on the bed, pretending they were my employees and I was their boss—maybe I just enjoyed giving them instructions!

As I grew older, the arrival of my niece Ava in 2006 and my daughter Charley in 2014 inspired me even more to be a positive role model and an entrepreneur. I wanted my girls to see me as a strong, independent woman and to set a good example for them and other aspiring entrepreneurs.

Q: In your experience, what are some common misconceptions or stereotypes about women in business, and how do you challenge or overcome them?

A: One misconception about women in business that I have personally encountered is the assumption that my husband is the brains behind or funding my business when people find out I am married. I find this assumption very insulting. What has worked for me is being direct and clear from the start, asserting that this is my endeavour. This approach helps set the right expectations for our working relationships more quickly.

Q: What role do you think mentorship and support networks play for women in entrepreneurship?

A: I believe mentorship and support networks are crucial in entrepreneurship. It's essential to surround yourself with strong, determined individuals who can guide and mentor you. Having people who have already walked the path you're on can help elevate your business.

Building a strong tribe around you is key. Networking is incredibly valuable because you never know who you might meet and how you can mutually benefit each other.

Q: What are some trends or developments in your industry that you're particularly excited about?

A: I'm thrilled about how artificial intelligence and data analytics are transforming the medical spa industry. By predicting skin conditions, tailoring treatments, and monitoring progress, these technologies will revolutionize how medical spas deliver services and operate.

Q: Can you discuss a failure or setback your business encountered, and how did you bounce back from it?

A: In June 2021, a near-fatal car accident dramatically changed my life. The experience and my journey since then have been profoundly humbling. Before the accident, I never showed weakness or asked for help; I was always the one going the extra mile for others. For nearly three years, I've been undergoing various forms of physical and emotional therapy. Accepting that I can no longer do the things I once loved has been a major challenge. Learning to ask for help and realizing I don't always need to be the strongest person in my circle has been difficult for me.

With the support of my therapists, I started to see—and believe—that I had more to offer beyond being a celebrity makeup artist. This realization led me to dream and create a plan B. Now, I'm at the beginning of my comeback journey and in the process of opening a Medical Spa. Our team of highly trained professionals will cater to the film industry and others in the Tri-Cities, Fraser Valley, and Lower Mainland.

I have an incredible team of women guiding and supporting me through this venture, and I'm excited to open our doors this summer. My disabilities will not define my achievements. If I can't physically do the work, I'll lead and grow the business with a capable team, guiding them toward successful careers.

Q: Looking ahead, what are your goals and aspirations for the future of your business?

A: Looking ahead, my goals and aspirations for my business include growing the Medical Spa to the point where it is running smoothly and has waitlists. In three years, I aim to open another location in a neighbouring city, and within five years, establish a third location. I want to provide a space where my team can build vibrant and sustainable careers.

Q: Pink or red lipstick?

A: Always red lipstick!

Jaina Jordan is a Clinical Hypnotherapist , NLP Master Practitioner, Life Coach, and Speaker who lives in Frankfort, Illinois, United States.

Q: Can you tell us about your journey as an entrepreneur? What inspired you to start your own business?

A: I was going through a difficult time in my personal life and started down the road of personal growth. I found a coach who helped me transform my life and realized that's what I want to do for others. I started studying different coaching modalities and was fascinated with NLP (neurolinguistic programming) and hypnotherapy. I couldn't get enough knowledge on the subjects, so I decided to find a mentor and instructor for certifications. I'm a lifelong learner and will continue to perfect my craft. Helping people get freedom in areas including overcoming self-limiting beliefs, relationships, family dynamics, and even releasing food and behavior fixations will never get old!

Q: What advice would you give to other women who are considering starting their own businesses?

A: I'm mainly speaking to moms here...communication is key! Let your family know what you're doing and why. My kids are all teens, so they get why I wanted to start my business and are amazingly supportive. The more you can explain your passion and purpose to your family, the better. I've explained to my kids what hypnotherapists and life coaches are and how I can use these tools for other people's lives to help them overcome issues in their lives.

Q: What were some of the biggest challenges you faced when starting your business, and how did you overcome them?

A: I had a difficult time at first. I'm the wife of a CEO entrepreneur. My husband built his cyber security business from the ground up when our twins were born, 17 years ago. He has now recently taken his company public and travels quite a bit. I was a stay-at-home mom, from the moment we brought the twins home from the hospital. The biggest challenge was learning how to flow between wife, mom, and business. I'm kind of a black and white sort of person, so it was a learning process to look at things as a whole, rather than in parts. In overcoming these challenges, I worked with a coach who really helped me see things as flowing rather than scales tipping like a balance. Sometimes I'll need to be home...work from home or just set aside work for the day (if I'm not seeing clients). Sometimes, I'll be at my office for a while and then come back home to take care of things there. Thankfully my office is 4 min away and I can conveniently go back and forth as needed. My family is really supportive of my work, and my kids have really stepped up to help even more than they already were. At first my heart was a bit torn between work and family. Now, there's no more heartache, I see it's only grown. :)

Q: What role do you believe technology plays in the success of your business?

A: Most of my clients are seen over video calls, so technology is crucial to my business. Additionally, many leads come from social media, and promotional prints are made easy with the help of Canva.

Q: How do you balance work-life commitments as an entrepreneur?

A: As previously stated, I don't really see things as a balance anymore. It's more of a flow. Who do I need to be more of today, or even in this moment? I check in with my kids throughout the day as they attend an online school from home. I'll text them before a client session just to make sure they're good. They already know what they can do and where they can go when their schoolwork and house work is completed. Establishing guidelines, expectations, and training my children to be excellent communicators is crucial. Even down to putting things on the shared grocery list through the iPhone Reminders App is really helpful. *also, thank the Lord for Instacart! lol

Q: What advice would you give to someone who is considering starting their own business?

A: Just do it! and don't stay stuck in "launch" mode forever. Everyday, live by the 2% rule, "do 2% more than you did yesterday."

Q: Looking ahead, what are your goals and aspirations for the future of your business?

A: I love collaborating with other women entrepreneurs in complementary careers who share the same love I have to help others heal. That being said, a shorter term goal is to run retreats with these wonderful like minded people for women to rest, reset, and restore. I love coaching and seeing people's eyes light up with new self-awareness and realizations. Intensive hypnosis VIP weekends are on the map as well!

Q: Pink or red lipstick?

A: PINK!

Randi Winter embodies a life of passion, purpose, and pizazz. She co-founded The P2P Life to create enriching travel and life experiences, driven by her enthusiasm and dedication to making a difference in the world every day.

RANDI *Winter*

A: Success means different things to different people based on their circumstances. My biggest achievements have impacted many while also inspiring individuals on a personal level.

I've played a key role in companies, projects, and collaborative book efforts, including Muslims Who Saved Jews During WWII (The Eye Contact Foundation), DiabetesandMe.org (Type 1), and co-founding The P2P Life, an inclusive travel and lifestyle company offering unparalleled expertise and privilege (Paradise2Perfection, Planned2Perfection, Passionate Travel, Travel and Cruise with a Cause), among others.

As a dedicated "Lost Canadian" volunteer, I advocate against outdated Canadian laws and amendments that contribute to statelessness, particularly affecting children and creating a two-tiered citizenship structure. These discriminatory laws, along with proven adjudication errors, have denied citizenship to first- and second-generation children of Canadian citizens while accepting millions of immigrants without connections. Sadly, politicians are using Lost Canadian children as political pawns. Justice delayed is justice denied.

The fact that a handful of people recognized flaws and legal misinterpretations, persevering to redefine and establish fair citizenship legislation, is humbling. We each have different skills but share one common purpose: ensuring equality.

Q: What roles do mentorship and support networks play for women in entrepreneurship?

A: Mentorship is a mutually enriching experience. I am constantly amazed by the diversity and shared values we hold. The more you give, the more you receive in return—through trust, sharing knowledge, and learning to act rather than react.

Q: Tell us about your journey as an entrepreneur and what inspired you to start your own business.

A: It's often said, "The riches are in the niches." Be a focused expert in one area. I take a broader view, analyzing everything from a 50,000-foot perspective. I see interconnectedness across diverse enterprises and volunteer efforts.

My experiences, teaching, and lifelong learning have taken me from passion projects to careers in business, travel, and writing at both national and international levels. I have countless eclectic interests and passions. I work with others, not for them.

Follow your heart. Life's true value cannot be measured financially.

Q: What problem or need does your business solve, and what motivated you to address it?

A: Our approach to inclusive, experiential travel sets TheP2PLife.com apart, creating unique experiences in luxury, romance, philanthropy, and purpose-driven travel.

Time is our most precious, non-renewable resource. People often don't fully grasp what drives travel or how to maximize their experiences. AI won't replace us; it will simply optimize for mutual benefit. That's why our WOW factor includes perks and privileges from personal connections. #traveldreams2memories

Q: What sparked your personal style?

A: My mother was a Barbizon model, which sparked my love for fashion. I modeled in New York and Vancouver, supporting local designers and contributing to Vancouver Fashion Week. My hair, glasses, and accessories reflect my personality and invite interaction.

Q: Can you discuss the role of networking, partnerships, and giving back in creating real change in business and large-scale causes?

A: My passion for travel, writing, and philanthropy is grounded in collaboration. We never know where our next lead, client, challenge, or solution will come from. The synergy of the right 1 + the right 1 = infinite possibility, and this always inspires me.

Everything I do involves giving back—whether it's a percentage of profits, time, writing, mentoring, or advocacy. I aim to amplify voices that may not have a strong platform or cause recognition. This is my WHY.

Heidi Nordlund is a certified Ayurvedic Doctor and Yoga Therapist, Medical Intuitive and Spiritual Healer. She uses Herbs, Breath work, Meditation, Past Life Karma Clearing, Tibetan Cranial and channeled energy Healing to help those ready to heal at all levels and thrive.

Dive into Entrepreneurship with Passion and Purpose!

Are you ready to jump into the thrilling world of entrepreneurship? Let your passion be your guiding star! Find a venture that truly lights you up and brings joy to your heart. This isn't just a business—it's a tangible expression of your dreams and desires. Starting a business is more than just a financial endeavor; it's a chance to create something meaningful and impactful. So dream big, create boldly, and above all, be your authentic self!

Stand Out by Being Uniquely You!

In a world where it seems like everything has already been done, how do you stand out? Simple: be uniquely you! No one else can offer exactly what you do. When you pour your heart and soul into your business, your genuine passion shines through. This authenticity is what sets you apart and attracts people to you. People often tell me my Namaskar Healing business is extraordinary because I genuinely care about my clients' health and well-being. When you love what you do, miracles happen, and your unique touch makes all the difference.

Embrace the Power of Technology

In today's digital era, technology opens up endless opportunities for growth and connection. Imagine a world where borders blur, and connections form with just a click. From the comfort of your living room, you can connect with amazing people all over the globe. Phone calls, social media, and virtual meetings all bring us closer together, creating a network of support and collaboration. Whether you're in Canada, North America, Europe, Australia or India, I'm just a click away. My journey has been one of continuous learning and discovery, thanks to technology's ability to bridge distances and connect me with masters and great teachers from around the world.

My Journey: From Pain to Purpose

Growing up, I faced numerous health challenges, including scoliosis, headaches, and various ailments. Before discovering Yoga, Ayurveda, Tibetan Cranial, and Spiritual Healing, my days were filled with painkillers and despair. Embracing these ancient healing methods transformed my life and fueled my passion for guiding others on their healing journeys. Through my Namaskar Healing business, I aim to break down barriers to health and happiness, tackling everything from depression and digestive issues to chronic pain and inflammatory conditions. My journey from pain to purpose has been a rollercoaster ride of resilience, revelation, and radiant health.

Listen to Your Body's Whispers

Wellness starts before symptoms scream for attention. Those tiny aches, a bit of congestion, bloating, or chills are your body whispering about imbalances. Don't ignore them! I used to overlook my body's signals, lost in the depths of meditation, thinking I was spiritually advanced. But I was suffering! Everything changed when I learned advanced muscle and energy testing. These practices transformed my health and business, helping me align with my greatest good. By listening to your body and seeking support when needed, you can prevent minor issues from becoming major problems.

Join Me on a Healing Journey

Together, we can reshape your health story, turning discomfort into vitality. Let's embark on this healing journey and let your Soul Light shine bright! As you chase your entrepreneurial dreams, remember your business is your legacy—nurtured with love, passion, and dedication. Cherish it and watch it grow beyond your wildest dreams. The world is ready for your greatness. Step forward with confidence and make your mark!

Dance Through Life

Embrace the vibrant hues of life—whether it's the boldness of red or the softness of pink. Dance through life with open arms, savoring every moment with joy. Revel in the colors, variety, and all the wonders life has to offer. Life is a beautiful journey full of diverse experiences. Embrace it all with an open heart and an adventurous spirit.

With Love and Light,
Heidi Nordlund

Jennifer Dawn is a transformation coach specializing in business & intuitive development. Jennifer is passionate about helping people take the guesswork out of business and fuel their excitement about being their own boss.

JENNIFER
Dawn

Q: How do I measure the success and growth of my business?

A: Unlocking the full potential of my business by blending conventional strategies and spiritually rooted practices, cultivating an environment of positivity, self-empowerment, ongoing enhancement, and true purpose alignment.

Q: Can you tell me about your journey as an entrepreneur?

A: My journey as an entrepreneur has been a transformative rollercoaster ride that has brought me immense growth and fulfillment.

I am so thankful I listened to the nudges that I received over 6 years ago. I remember the day that I knew I had to say yes to entrepreneurship and goodbye to 3 decades of management.

Q: What inspired you to start your own business?

A: I knew that I would feel more fulfilled and happy working for myself than working for others. I had a strong desire to help others, but I didn't know how I would do that. I am happy that I took the leap of faith and allowed everything to flow and click into place.

My business is international, and I am very grateful to be able to help people in a variety of ways with a variety of modalities, including Coaching and regression therapy.

Q: What advice would you give to other women who are considering starting their own businesses?

A: It is so important to surround yourself with "Life-Enhancers!" Life-enhancers will support and encourage you.

Energy & mindset are very important in the development of your business. When we feel good, motivated and supported, we can focus on what we need to and achieve our goals and dreams.

Q: Looking ahead, what are your goals and aspirations for the future of your business??

A: I am excited about the future of my business. I find it so rewarding seeing positive changes for the people I work with and that is part of what inspires me to create and develop more ways to help people.

A few of my goals include the release of my book, "Dad's Pennies from Heaven" with Hay House at the end of this year, and a film adaptation of "Dad's Pennies from Heaven." I feel honoured to spread the message that my dad shared about his experience with dementia and how this information can help those who have Alzheimer's or dementia, and their loved ones and caregivers.

I will be creating a new course this year called "So You Pick Up on ▯ Now what?" This course will help one to understand what is happening as their intuitive abilities are developing.

Q: Can you share a particularly memorable success story or milestone from your entrepreneurial journey?

A: Visions can become reality! I had a vision for what I wanted to accomplish with my first solo book. This vision started in 2020. I had 3 parts of the vision and just a week ago, I completed the second part of my vision.

The 3 parts of my vision were to have my book published by Hay House, the support of the Alzheimer's Society of BC and my book turned into a major motion picture. Before I even started writing my book, I had these 3 pieces in my mind, but didn't know how it would happen. I trusted that I would be guided and that things would click into place after I did the work and that is exactly what happened.

My solo book takes readers on a journey about my father's experience with dementia and the unknown truth he shared about dementia in his final days. I am a spiritual medium as well, so I blended my beliefs, practices and experiences into the book, including what it is like for me now that my father continues to communicate with me from the other side.

I am so excited that my book will be published by Hay House and that it will be released soon. The only part left of my vision is that my book becomes a movie. I feel very strongly that this final piece of the vision for "Dad's Pennies from Heaven" will become a reality!

Q: What advice would you give to other women who are considering starting their own businesses?

A: The advice I would give to other women who are considering starting their own businesses is to start! There never is a perfect time to start. If you procrastinate, you will have a higher chance of killing your dream of being your own boss. I also highly recommend that a focus is put on the environment that one is going to be working in.

Questions to ask oneself are:

1. Does my home environment support me in becoming an entrepreneur?

2. Do I have a support system that will encourage me vs discourage me?

An entrepreneur can thrive and grow when the physical environment is supportive and the people that the entrepreneur surround themselves with is as well.

Q: Pink or red lipstick?

A: I love to channel my inner Barbie and wear a bold, Barbie-pink pucker!

Heidi Morrison joined exhalo Spa as a Master Aesthetician and was quickly promoted to Communications Director with her 20 years of industry experience. Her expertise in fostering strong connections between colleagues and clients is matched by her strong leadership and commitment to enhancing the spa experience. Heidi's passion for beauty and wellness, dedication to both personal growth and professional excellence is a valuable asset to exhalo Spa.

HEIDI *Morrison*

Q: How do you approach leadership and team-building within your company?

A: As a communication director at our spa, fostering a culture of teamwork, collaboration, and respect is paramount to our success. Here's how I approach leadership and team-building within our company:

Lead by Example: I firmly believe that leadership begins with setting the right example. I strive to embody the values of our spa in my daily interactions with team members, clients, and stakeholders.

Open Communication: Transparent and open communication is key to building trust and fostering a supportive environment within our team.

Recognition and Appreciation: Recognizing and appreciating the contributions of our team members is essential for morale and motivation. We usually do a Friday shoutout that allows each staff member to thank, or commend one another for something small or big, and it fosters a stong team.

Empowerment: Empowering our team members to take ownership of their work and make decisions fosters creativity and new ideas between generations and to me that's a win/win.

Professional Development: Everyone should continue to invest in themselves. We provide opportunities for training, workshops, and certifications to help them enhance their skills and stay updated with industry trends.

Q: How do you stay motivated and resilient during tough times in your business?

A: I stay motivated by focusing on the positive impact our products and services have on people's lives, especially our local community.

Resilience comes from adapting strategies, seeking inspiration from trends, and maintaining a passion for creativity and innovation.

Q: What are some trends or developments in your industry that you're particularly excited about?

A: Having been in the beauty industry for 22 years, I'm thrilled by the increasing focus on sustainability and eco-friendly products.

The shift towards clean beauty and cruelty-free formulations is promising. Additionally, advancements in technology, such as virtual consultations and personalized skincare solutions, are revolutionizing the way we interact with clients.

Green Circle Salon, Eminence Organic Skin Care , Keune Hair Care are all brands we use and trust because their CSR(corporate social responsibility) practices impact our entire world one product at a time.

Q: What strategies do you employ to attract and retain customers?

A: At exhalo Spa, we prioritize personalized experiences, loyalty programs, targeted promotions, and engaging social media content to both attract and retain customers.

We also emphasize exceptional customer service and regularly gather feedback to ensure their satisfaction and loyalty.

Q: What do you believe are the keys to building a strong brand identity and reputation?

A: I believe authenticity, consistency, and aligning with our team's values are paramount in building a strong brand identity and reputation for exhalo Spa.

Clear messaging and genuine connections with our audience are key to earning trust and loyalty. Continuing to support other local businesses and share the love of health in wellness in our communities - I love my job!

Q: Pink or red lipstick?

A: No competition - Pink, light pink. The way nature intended it to be. There is room for both the bold babes and the natural beauties at the table!

Kelly Graham Tick is a RMT, educator, storyteller, lover of life, people, animals, and planet, duchess of nurturing touch, hugger of peeps and talking trees, wisdom seeker, soul doula, cuddler of babies, hand holder of the olders, resounder of respite, proud mama of amazing humans, plants and fur babies, compassionate extraordinaire, and Founder of One Caring Human Non-Profit Society.

KELLY
Graham Tick

Q: What are your businesses and organizations, and what led you to start them?

A: The first business I started was right after I turned 40. I had been inspired to go back to school to finally become a Registered Massage Therapist.

I was the teenager who was drawn to helping others who were hurting, and started offering massage to my friends and family members through my 20's, and though I looked into massage school back then, tuition was out of reach for me.

After jobs in travel and municipal government, a friend asked me to come to a college info session with her... at a massage school. Though I had just become a single parent and my dad passed months prior, I instantly knew I needed to be there.

It is a step I have never regretted, and has led me to discover my passions, creativity, and how I want to serve the world.

I began to work with the elderly and the dying, and as a teacher, I ran outreaches with my students at care homes. I began to see the failings of the Canadian healthcare system, in terms of how we care for our seniors and their caregivers.

The covid lockdown really highlighted the devastating effects of loneliness. More than 80% of the Canadian deaths in the first 3 months of covid were seniors living in long-term housing. And because no visitors were allowed, many of them died alone.

After 18 months of enforced isolation, the care home was allowed to have visitors again. The residents spoke of the horrible isolation, friends dying of loneliness, and many confessed that they would rather die than live like a shadow.

The realization that if just one caring human had been able to visit these folks, to offer presence and kind touch, it would have changed the outcome and saved lives, was the reason for the second business I founded. It's an organization called One Caring Human. The purpose is to provide compassionate presence and therapeutic touch to the elderly and the dying in care homes, hospice, and in the communities of the lower mainland of British Columbia, Canada. We aim for ongoing funding so we may offer this care at no cost and to improve the quality and meaning of life for these populations. Through this organization, I also hope to create intergenerational collaboration, visibility for those who are rarely seen, and leave a legacy of compassion in our culture.

Q: Who has inspired you on your journey?

A: I have been inspired by countless people and animals, and by nature. Lakes and forests have held me in my worst times, through grief and pain, and in my joy and celebration. Because of this, I strive to be a buoyant force of nature for others. Teachers are everywhere if we choose to listen. Some of my favorite teachers have been the patients I've had the privilege of working with, the many writers and artists that speak their own truth and spark the truth in others, my family, and my dear friends.

Q: What are the values that drive you, and how do you find time to get so much done?

A: My core values are love, care, nurturing, human dignity, and continuous learning. It is upsetting for me to hear about or witness someone's dignity being ignored or trampled on. So, being proactive toward a culture of exceptional care is important to me. I feel like I've stepped into the action phase of my life after being a rampant procrastinator. I had huge imposter syndrome.

When I decided to feed myself first, emotionally and spiritually, I miraculously found more time in my days. I began sharing my truth and ideas with others, in small ways at first, and then bigger ways as my confidence grew.

I have found that learning to be confident is a practice, just like learning an instrument, language, or art. I get up in the morning at least 2 hours before I have to do anything. I ritualize my coffee. I feed my soul everyday, by either writing or reading poetry or meditating or standing barefoot in the grass. I feel more alive and connected to the whole, to mystery and magic when I do this for me.

Q: Looking ahead, what are your goals and aspirations for the future of your business?

A: My long-term goal is to contribute to creating a Wellness Village in every community. A place where everyone feels welcome, a place where people feel creative and cared for.

A place for us to find family in each other, to learn to grow food and have meals together, for our individual and collective health to be a priority. A space where medical care is offered alongside other integrative health options. Where we learn how to care for our bodies, our minds, and each other, to nurture connection and communication. Where community is built at the same time as birdhouses.

Art together with architecture, and where home is a feeling as much as a physical place.

It's time for the village to help raise our children again, to care for the dying again. Where everyone can contribute and play and grow and be accepted and loved and nurtured, from birth to death.

Lofty? Maybe. Necessary? I believe cooperative systems can change how we view healthcare and death, so that we may know ourselves and our communities, and begin to live fully once more.

Q: Pink or red lipstick?

A: I don't actually wear lipstick. I prefer Burt's Bees grapefruit scented lip balm.

LEILANI
Kopp

Q: Can you tell us about your journey as an entrepreneur, and what inspired you?

A: My journey as an entrepreneur began unexpectedly, stemming from my volunteer work with Cancer Surgeons. My background in Film/T.V. as a Makeup/Hair artist, was all about glamour. What started as a passion project helping Cancer patients, out of a bedroom, styling wigs and helping with skincare and Makeup soon evolved into a full-fledged company driven by my desire to make a meaningful impact in the lives of those affected by illness. As one of few in Canada specializing in Paramedical, Corrective Makeup, my dedication, innovation, and commitment to excellence, was the driving force behind Sweet LeiLani Cosmetics. From navigating highs and lows of entrepreneurship, leveraging my unique experiences and skills to create products and services that bring comfort, support, and hope to individuals and families facing health challenges. Sweet LeiLani Cosmetics was ahead of the curve in what Clean Beauty would mean to the everyday women today.

My journey from a bedroom to navigating the retail landscape to adapting to the online realm to becoming a expert formulator for Clean Beauty. I believe I exemplify the power of passion and purpose in a world of business. Staying true to my mission by empowering others to prioritize their health and the health of the planet. Others have told me that my dedication to better beauty and my unwavering commitment to customers well being has set a remarkable example in the beauty industry for generations to come.

Q: What problems does your business solve and what motivated you to address them?

A: Sweet LeiLani Cosmetics is dedicated to solving problems with clean plant based beauty products, inspired by a deeply personal journey, that was motivated by my volunteer work with patients undergoing Cancer treatments. I witnessed firsthand the importance of safe and effective skincare during challenging times. This drove me to create a line of clean beauty products that prioritize purity, safety, and efficacy, providing a solution for individuals seeking gentle yet powerful skincare solutions. By harnessing the healing power of natural , plant based ingredients and avoiding harmful chemicals. Products that offer a holistic approach to skincare that promotes overall well-being and confidence. With a commitment to transparency, sustainability, and social responsibility, Sweet LeiLani Cosmetics aims to empower individuals to make healthier choices for themselves and the planet. As an advocate for redefining what clean beauty means, I strive to alleviate skincare concerns and enhance the lives of those facing health challenges, embodying, compassion and care that first inspired my entrepreneurial journey.

Q: What sets your business apart from your competitors?

A: My mission as a formulator of clean plant based ingredients I am a passionate advocate, for change in the Beauty Industry

We live in a world that bombards us with superficial standards. This is not just about skincare and makeup routines it extends beyond outside beauty. It's embracing a lifestyle that prioritizes both inner and outer well being

In a world where there is more intention behind consumer purchase than ever, we have a compelling purpose, mission, vision and social environmental impact behind the Brand.

The fact that I have decades of experience in Film, specialize in Paramedical Makeup,I am a speaker, educator and an expert formulator for Clean Beauty puts us ahead of our competitors

People believe in us, they trust us, and they know by supporting us by purchasing my products it allows me to continue my pro bono work. I'm in the trenches working with people, not just donating money. Customers tell us they have switched to our Brand because of what we do as well as what we stand for.

These products change people's lives, it fills a need, we make a promise and we deliver that.

Q: What strategies do you employ to attract and maintain customers?

A: There is a clear shift towards a healthy conscious lifestyle, and consumers have a keen eye for sustainable socially conscious Brands, they want to be aware of eco-friendly, ethical production methods. They believe in Brands that are being honest about intentions, showing transparency and authenticity in what your business practices are and how your company cares about our planet for their futures.

Sweet LeiLani Cosmetics is an advocate for a holistic approach that encompasses self-care practices. With my background I bring together experts, including derms, pharmacists, and doctors to collaborate and share insights on skin health. Our education platform is like no others, we have a resource of materials like no other Cosmetic Company.

Q: What roles do you think networks play for women entrepreneurs?

A: Networking is a crucial aspect of entrepreneurship for women, providing opportunities for growth, collaboration, and support. Several roles come into play when it comes to networking for women entrepreneurs.

They bring diverse and multifaceted roles to networking, contributing to the strength, and resilience, while navigating through their journey. Networking encompasses connections, mentors, advocates, resource providers, community builders, and innovators, that empower each other to thrive in the ever-evolving world of entrepreneurship

Q: Pink or red lipstick?

A: Pour yourself a drink, and a swipe of red lipstick. This bold hue exudes timeless elegance and sophistication! While conveying strength and self assurance. Let's continue to break barriers, shatter glass ceilings, and pavan the way for future generations of women entrepreneurs to thrive and succeed.

Allyson Matos is a photographer and lifestyle blogger capturing events, BTS, travel, and reviews!

ALLYSON
Matos

Q: How do you stay motivated and resilient during tough times in your business?

A: I started Allyfotografy Media Co. over a decade ago during a period of deep uncertainty in my life. It was a time when I felt utterly lost and searching for direction. Creating this business became my beacon of hope, a way to channel my creativity and passion into something I was proud of. My business is not just a means to make a living; it's a testament to my resilience and determination. Knowing that I've built something from the ground up fuels my motivation to keep pushing forward, even when it gets tough. It can be hard to navigate tough times in business but I try to see them opportunities for growth.

Q: Can you tell us about your journey as an entrepreneur and what inspired you to start your own business?

A: My journey began with an entirely different focus. Graduating with a degree in Criminology, I never envisioned myself as an entrepreneur. However, life often takes us down unexpected paths. Photography entered my life almost serendipitously, initially as a means to explore my creative side amidst a period of feeling directionless. What began as a hobby swiftly evolved into a full-fledged passion. Within just a year of picking up the camera, I found myself immersed in the world of photography, capturing everything from portraits to weddings. One evening after friends and family encouraged me to start a business, Allyfotografy was born and I never looked back.

While my journey started with capturing moments behind the lens, it soon transitioned into something deeper. I discovered my knack for content marketing, business strategy and videography; new areas where I could blend my passion for storytelling with a desire to help others succeed in their business ventures. This is when I really found my path.

I wake up each day filled with gratitude for the opportunity to do what I love. The ability to weave narratives through my work and empower fellow entrepreneurs is a privilege I cherish to my core.

Q: What sets your business apart from competitors in the market?

A: What sets me apart in this industry is my unwavering commitment to storytelling and authenticity. I believe that at the core of every successful business is a compelling narrative waiting to be told. That's why I lead with storytelling, diving deep into the authenticity of each person or brand I work with.

My approach is unique in that I don't just capture moments; I capture stories. By understanding the essence of each individual or brand, I craft personalized marketing plans that resonate on a deeper level. This isn't about cookie-cutter strategies; it's about harnessing the power of authenticity to connect with audiences in a meaningful way.

What truly sets me apart is the comprehensive range of services I offer. Whether it's photography, professional videography, or user-generated content, I provide a one-stop solution for all visual and strategic needs. I also offer full 1:1 coaching and strategy sessions, empowering clients to take control of their narrative and drive their businesses forward.

I've always made the promise that I'm committed to making these services accessible to all. From aspiring entrepreneurs to established brands, I believe that everyone should have the opportunity to unleash their creativity and thrive in their business. That's why I offer my services at an affordable price point, ensuring that cost is never a barrier to unleashing the power of storytelling in business.

Q: What were some of the biggest challenges you faced when starting your business, and how did you overcome them?

A: One of the most significant hurdles was the overwhelming sense of having to wear all the hats as a solopreneur. Juggling everything from photography, videography, administration to marketing and business strategy was, and still can be, a daunting task.

Also, battling with imposter syndrome was a constant internal struggle. Despite my passion pushing me forward, there were moments when I questioned my abilities and felt like a fraud in my own field. Overcoming this required daily reminders of how far I've come and the value I bring to my clients and community.

While there were many individuals willing to lend a helping hand when I started out, I also faced obstacles from those who sought to gatekeep and withhold support. Navigating this landscape taught me the importance of resilience and perseverance. Instead of allowing these roadblocks to deter me, I sought out amazing fellow entrepreneurs on this journey who many I am still very close to.

Another challenge I struggled with was maintaining boundaries. I poured my heart and soul into my work, often at the expense of my own well-being. Despite my best efforts, there were instances where my dedication wasn't reciprocated, leading to burnout and exhaustion.

However, I refused to let these challenges define my journey. Through perseverance, self-reflection, and a willingness to adapt, I found ways to overcome each obstacle. Whether it was seeking support from like-minded individuals, prioritizing self-care, or setting boundaries to protect my energy, I learned to navigate the ups and downs of entrepreneurship with resilience and grace.

Q: What do you believe are the keys to building a strong brand identity and reputation?

A: I believe that building a strong brand identity and reputation requires a combination of courage, empathy, perseverance, and authenticity.

Community also plays a pivotal role in building a strong brand identity and reputation. Honest communication, transparency, and building genuine relationships with your community are essential. I also tell my clients to listen, something I have to remind myself daily.

Telling your own story is a powerful tool in building a strong brand identity. Our stories are what make us human, and sharing them authentically allows us to connect on a deeper level with our audience and community. By leaning into your story, vulnerabilities, and experiences, you invite others to join you on your journey. I feel that when we can show up as our true most vulnerable selves, it allows others to do the same. This has been the most impactful for me and why I love what I do.

Q: Pink or red lipstick?

A: I pick Red! To me, it symbolizes confidence and empowerment!

Erin Sample is an Entrepreneur of Simply Immaculate Cleaners and a passionate advocate for both the disabled and victims of domestic violence.

ERIN
Sample

Q: Have you found any specific advantages or opportunities in being a woman in your industry?

A: Being a deaf woman and survivor of domestic violence has definitely thrown some curveballs my way. But you know what? I've learned to see the bright side of things! Here are a few perks I've discovered along the journey:

Empathy and Understanding: Being a woman has given me this amazing ability to really understand where people are coming from. It's like I have this superpower of empathy that helps me connect with others on a deeper level.

Resilience and Determination: Surviving tough times has made me super tough! I've got this inner strength and determination that helps me tackle any obstacle that comes my way. Nothing can knock me down!

Perspective and Insight: My experiences have given me this unique outlook on life. I see things from a different angle and come up with some pretty cool ideas because of it. It's like having a secret weapon in my back pocket!

Advocacy and Empowerment: Being a woman in my industry means I get to stand up for what's right. I'm all about lifting others up and making sure everyone has a voice. Together, we can make some real change happen!

Collaboration and Connection: There's something special about teaming up with other awesome women in my industry. We share experiences, swap stories, and support each other through thick and thin. It's like having a built-in squad of amazing friends!

Sure, there have been challenges along the way, but being a woman has brought me so many cool opportunities and moments of growth. I wouldn't trade it for the world!

Q: In your experience, what are some common misconceptions or stereotypes about women in business, and how do you challenge or overcome them?

A: So, as a deaf woman in business and a survivor of domestic violence, I've come across some pretty interesting misconceptions. Some folks think that deaf people, especially women, don't have what it takes to succeed in business because of communication skills. And then there are those who think survivors like me are all emotionally unstable and unreliable. Pretty wild, huh?

But you know what? I'm not letting these misconceptions hold me back! Nope, not at all. Instead, I'm showing off my strengths and unique perspectives. I'm all about using cool communication strategies like writing stuff down and using awesome technology to show just how capable I am in any business setting.

Oh, and let's not forget about educating others! I'm spreading the word about deaf culture and accessibility needs, so folks can understand better. Plus, I'm all about showing off my resilience and professionalism, proving that survivors like me can kick butt in the workplace! Sure, there are some tough times, but with a bit of counseling and support from my peers, I'm not just surviving – I'm thriving! My goal? To shake things up, break down those stereotypes, and create a workplace where everyone feels included and valued. It's all about leading by example and inspiring others to do the same!

Q: Have you encountered any gender-based biases or discrimination in your industry, and if so, how have you addressed them?

A: Being a deaf woman in my industry has definitely had its moments! I've faced some challenges, especially with communication barriers and people making assumptions about what I can do. But you know what? I've found ways to deal with it.

First off, I've become pretty good at standing up for myself and making sure people understand what being deaf is all about. Education is key, right? I've also come across some gender-based discrimination, where people have questioned what I can bring to the table just because I'm a woman. But guess what? I've shown them what I'm made of! I've made it my mission to showcase my skills and knowledge, proving that gender doesn't define my abilities. And you know what else? I've found some awesome people who get it – supportive networks and allies who are all about diversity and inclusion. Together, we're challenging stereotypes and making our industry a more welcoming place for everyone. Sure, there are still hurdles to overcome, but I'm not backing down! I'm all about equality and smashing barriers. With a bit of perseverance, a lot of education, and some kick-butt collaboration, I'm on a mission to create a workplace where everyone – no matter their gender or ability – feels valued and included. Cheers to breaking down barriers and having some fun along the way! Cheers to breaking barriers and making waves in the business world!

Q: How do you build and maintain a strong team, and what qualities do you look for in potential hires?

A: Building and keeping a solid team is like crafting a recipe for success! I mix in a good dose of teamwork, sprinkle some effective communication, and stir in heaps of mutual respect. The result? A deliciously strong team bond! When it comes to finding new team members, I'm on the lookout for folks with a can-do attitude, a sprinkle of adaptability, and a generous helping of positivity. Diversity is the secret ingredient, adding flavor and depth to our team dynamic. At the end of the day, we're cooking up something special together, and I'm excited to see what tasty treats we'll whip up as a team! In my kitchen, everyone's voice is heard and valued. I make sure to listen to my team's needs and desires, giving them the space to share their opinions and pitch their own creative ideas. After all, the best recipes often come from collaborative cooking sessions!

Q: What role do you believe technology plays in the success of your business??

A: With technology on our side, we're not just cleaning; we're orchestrating a symphony of efficiency. Digital scheduling tools ensure seamless coordination, keeping our team in perfect harmony. Communication apps bridge any hearing gaps, allowing us to stay connected as if we're all in the same room. FaceTiming or virtual meetings bring us face-to-face with clients, fostering trust and rapport, despite any hearing hurdles. Moreover, technology equips us with state-of-the-art cleaning gadgets and eco-friendly solutions, enabling us to make a positive impact on the planet. It's not just about tidying up; it's about contributing to a cleaner, greener future. My being deaf, technology is on my side, empowering me to lead my team with confidence and ensuring that we deliver exceptional results with every clean. Together, we're leveraging the power of technology to create sparkling spaces and happy smiles!

Q: Pink or red lipstick?

A: Au Naterel! But if I really have to…….. Pink

Marilyn R. Wilson is a freelance writer, interviewer, published author, speaker and poet.

A: At age 50, I was feeling adrift. I needed a new challenge. While I was scrolling through Craigslist, I noticed a New York fashion magazine looking for submissions. I lacked any experience or industry knowledge, but on a whim submitted three story ideas. No one was more surprised than I when two were accepted. Even more surprising was my reaction to my first interview. While I listened to the designer share their life story, I realized I loved interviewing, and I was willing to do whatever it took to continue.

What followed was a roller coaster ride of highs and lows that led me to co-owning a local fashion magazine, contributing to others both local and international, publishing two books (so far), and contributing to five collaborative books. At the start it was a dive into the deep end where I had to swim as hard as I could. To deal with societal bias against older women, I worked harder than I ever had, built my own doors when none were open, and just kept putting one foot in front of the other.

Q: Can you share a particularly memorable success story or milestone from your entrepreneurial journey?

A: After the magazine I co-owned folded in 2012, I went to a very dark place. It took six months before I found a new direction – writing my first book. Easy, right?. What I didn't expect was the brutal self-doubt that plagued me throughout the writing process. There were moments I almost walked away in despair. I clearly remember the moment I finished that first draft. I breathed a sigh of relief as I hit send, forwarding the manuscript to my publisher. There were goosebumps the day I received a box of my books; in my excitement, I gave the postman a signed copy. However, my highest moment was standing on stage at my book launch celebrating with my publisher and the community that stood beside me. I reached my dream of publication only with their support. The memory still brings goosebumps, and it happened just a few weeks after I turned 60. It truly is never too late.

Q: What advice would you give to someone who is considering starting their own business?

A: Whether you are a more traditional entrepreneur or a creative who has to function as one to sell their work, this road demands huge commitment. If you want a job you can walk away from at the end of the workday, where you receive predictable compensation, holiday pay, and a pension, then you should work for someone else. That said, there is nothing more fulfilling than following your passion, especially if it uplifts others. Just be ready to commit fully, and work like a beast.

Q: How do you stay motivated and resilient during tough times in your business?

A: Staying motivated and resilient has been a struggle for me since day one. Three things have helped. The first is being surrounded by a supportive community. The second is having a mentor to guide me on how to best achieve my goals. Even after 17 years, I still need both of these in place to keep me on track.

The last piece didn't fall into place for me until I read the book Atomic Habits. Inspired by one of the suggestions the author made, I developed a habit of showing to work up every day. Each morning, after my first cup of coffee, I head to my computer, sit down and write. It doesn't matter if I work for thirty minutes or four hours – this time is non-negotiable.

Q: How do you stay innovative and adapt to changes in your industry?

A: The literary world is constantly changing, especially in how books are sold and marketed. To stay on top, I have a mentor with her fingers on the pulse to advise me. I joined several writing/author groups where we share tips. I read every day – both non-fiction and fiction – and take online classes. To challenge myself as an artist, I explore other types of writing such as poetry and fiction.

Q: How do you measure the success of your business?

A: For me, success is creating work I am proud of. Whether I am giving wings to the words shared with me by others, or my own musings, my hope is what I publish will land where it is most needed. I hope it will inspire and help raise someone struggling from their dark place. Even if only one person's life is made better, I consider that a success.

Q: What is the best advice you've ever been given?

A: It came during an interview with Canadian tap icon William Orlowski (now deceased). He was struggling with Dystonia which really limited his work as an artist, dancer and choreographer. Yet he continued to stay upbeat, still working, and was full of ideas for new projects. As I struggled with self-confidence and procrastination, I asked him what advice he could give me. His answer was short and uncomplicated, but to this day it still stands as the best advice I have ever received. "There is no secret, just do and be brave." Love and still miss you William.

Q: Pink or red lipstick?

A: I don't wear lipstick, just tinted gloss. In terms of color in general, I like red over pink.

Alexis Gail Ellis is upcoming director in national pageant. Currently she is a national beauty queen.

ALEXIS
Gail Ellis

Q: Can you tell me about your journey as an entrepreneur? What inspired you to start your own business?

A: My entrepreneurial journey is deeply rooted in my experience as both a pageant participant and director. I've always loved the world of pageantry, but I felt there was a need for a system that embraced diversity. I wanted to create a pageant that was inclusive—open to all sizes, genders, and ages—allowing everyone to showcase their inner beauty and confidence.

Q: What are some trends or developments in your industry that excite you?

A: One of the most exciting trends in pageantry is the growing recognition that beauty is found within. Our system reflects this by welcoming everyone, regardless of who they are. I'm thrilled to be building a pageant system that celebrates individuality and promotes empowerment.

Q: What problem or need does your business solve, and what motivated you to address it?

A: In many traditional pageants, there's a lack of inclusivity. I wanted to create a space where everyone, regardless of background, can compete and feel empowered. My goal is to inspire participants to find confidence within themselves and feel a sense of achievement through pageantry.

Q: How did you come up with the idea for your business, and what was the process like from concept to execution?

A: The idea for my pageant system came from my desire to see more representation in pageantry. I envisioned a national pageant in Canada with no appointed titles, where winners could represent the country at the international level. The process has been a journey of building a strong foundation through word of mouth, and I'm determined to see it grow.

Q: What were some of the biggest challenges you faced when starting your business, and how did you overcome them?

A: The biggest challenge has been building awareness. Starting out, I had to rely heavily on word of mouth to spread the message about the pageant system. We began with virtual events before moving to live competitions, which helped build momentum and trust within the community.

Q: What role do you believe technology plays in the success of your business?

A: Technology is crucial in pageantry—from the mics to the lighting, sound systems, and scorekeeping. A smooth technological setup ensures that everyone has an enjoyable and professional experience, which is key to the success of any event.

Q: What advice would you give to someone who is considering starting their own business?

A: Research is essential. Know your business model and understand what will attract people to your brand. Timing is also important, especially in the pageant industry, where participants need time to secure sponsors and prepare for both national and international stages.

Q: How do you prioritize tasks and manage time effectively as an entrepreneur?

A: Time management is vital in pageantry, especially when coordinating events. You need to ensure that participants have enough time to change outfits, do their hair and makeup, and feel prepared for each stage of the competition. It's about creating a smooth flow without overwhelming anyone.

Q: What do you believe are the keys to building a strong brand identity and reputation?

A: Honesty and punctuality are the pillars of success in pageantry. You must ensure that your judges are unbiased and that participants are good representatives of your brand. Being transparent and running your pageants on time builds trust, which will encourage more people to participate.

Q: How do you measure the success and growth of your business?

A: Success for me is seeing a thriving national competition with strong representation across all divisions. I envision a future where Canada is well-represented on international stages, showcasing a diverse and empowered group of individuals.

Q: Can you discuss the role of networking and partnerships in growing your business?

A: Networking is essential in this industry. A good director needs to be honest and choose the right people to represent the pageant system. Forming partnerships with others who share your values helps build a strong, reliable network.

Q: Looking ahead, what are your goals and aspirations for the future of your business?

A: My goal is to establish a new pageant system in Canada, where each province holds its own competitions, leading to a national winner who will represent the country internationally. I want this pageant to inspire and empower all genders, allowing them to shine on a global stage.

Q: Pink or red lipstick?

A: Red.

Karen Dosanjh: Mother. Award-Winning Marketing Executive. Author. Film Producer. Historian. Mentor to Many.

Q: Have you found any specific advantages or opportunities in being a woman in your industry?

A: I believe that women possess superpowers in terms of having a high level of emotional intelligence (EQ: that they bring to the business world. Having a high IQ or expert knowledge is a given to be successful in any field or industry. However, having high EQ can be a key differentiator for women and what sets us apart as leaders and change agents in business. Some of the core characteristics of EQ include empathy, communication, interpersonal skills, self-awareness and relationship management. I would encourage women to tap into your EQ leadership superpowers which is your ability to influence decisions, motivate teams towards a collective vision, and drive cultural shifts within an organization – big or small.

Q: What role do you think mentorship and support networks play for women in entrepreneurship?

A: I believe that it's not enough to get up and go to work or run your business every day just to make money. It's important to think about what legacy you want to leave behind. Ask yourself, what impact are you having on your community? How are you helping mentor others within your sphere of influence? Are you using your voice to create positive changes for others? All of these things have been equally important to me and are close to my heart. It feel it's simply not enough to do well for

46

yourself and for your family. Empowered women have a duty to help empower other women. So with that, I lent my time and talent to write a book that preserves South Asian history and heritage in Canada. I also regularly volunteer as a mentor to young women in business to guide them through careers in business and tech. I also use my voice and platform to speak out on many issues impacting women in the home, at work and in the community. Inevitably when women within a community rise, the entire community can benefit from their success.

Q: What are your thoughts on the importance of diversity and inclusion in organizations?

A: I believe we are making progress in terms the "conversations" about diversity and inclusion in business but we have a long way to go in order to see a real shift change. According to a 2022 Compass Rose report, women make up only 18% of top executive positions in corporate Canada. Women of colour only hold 6.4% of those C-level positions in corporate Canada which speaks to the lack of recognition, advancement, and opportunities for women of colour. As the first woman of colour to hold a VP position in my company, I want to see changes for the next generation of women starting their careers and have made it my mission to speak out on this topic whenever I can to affect real change in the future.

Q: What role do you believe technology plays in the success of your business?

A: Artificial Intelligence is revolutionizing the way we work and how we run our businesses. As a Marketer, we need to be at the forefront of technological evolution and are uniquely skilled to adapt to today's changing digital landscape. I have worked through many technological advances including the beginning of the Internet & email communication, to the rise of social media for business, the digital transformation and e-commerce boom and much more. Today, I leverage generative AI to develop digital content, manage data analytics, and to elevate my business brand. Having worked in tech for three decades, I have learned that you must fully embrace change and swiftly move with it. I believe that if you don't embrace and adapt AI strategies into your current job and/or your business you will soon be left behind with the floppy disks of the past.

Q: Can you share a particularly memorable success story or milestone from your entrepreneurial journey?

A: I was recently named a BC Business Women of the Year in the Entrepreneurial Leader category. When I went to go pick up the magazine, there was my face staring right back at me on the cover. Over the years, I remember seeing white, male CEOs grace that coveted cover and never in a million years did I imagine myself on it being recognized for my career accomplishments. When I saw myself on the cover of BC Business, my eyes filled with tears because in that moment I knew it was no longer about me. I knew that I was representing my community as a Canadian-born woman of Punjabi heritage. I thought of all the young people who would see that cover and think of it as the norm and as a place for them one day too.

Q: Pink or red lipstick?

A: Red!

Christina Bonner is the owner of Studio She™ - Maryland's first Hair Extension Salon.
Studio She™ Academy also trains Hair Extension Specialists from around the globe.

CHRISTINA
Bonner

Q: Can you tell me about your journey as an entrepreneur? What inspired you to start your own business?

A: My journey as an entrepreneur started at 20, driven by both necessity and my own insecurities about my fine hair. Discovering the transformative power of hair extensions wasn't just a revelation, it was an opportunity. I began braiding, sometimes for 12 hours a day, falling more in love with the craft and the confidence it gave others with each braid. That passion for empowering transformations fueled my entrepreneurial spirit.

Q: What are some of the biggest challenges you've faced as a woman entrepreneur, and how have you overcome them?

A: The hair extension industry, while focused on a traditionally female product, is surprisingly male-dominated. Navigating this as a woman, especially while establishing my own brand, presented unique challenges. During factory visits abroad, I encountered skepticism and dismissiveness simply because I was a woman in a male-dominated business landscape.

To overcome this, I prioritized respect for cultural differences while also becoming more astute. Hiring translators wasn't just about language, it ensured clear communication and prevented misunderstandings that could arise from cultural biases. This strategy protected my interests and helped build trust in environments where I was initially perceived as an outsider.

Q: How do you maintain a work-life balance while running your own business? What strategies have you found most effective for networking and building professional relationships as a female entrepreneur?

A: Work-life balance is deeply personal. The pandemic, while challenging for many, offered me a chance to redefine my own balance. It forced me to slow down from the relentless 12-hour days and discover that rest actually increased my productivity and decision-making abilities. Now, I prioritize weekends and personal time, understanding that recharging ultimately makes me a better entrepreneur.

For networking, I go where my ideal clients are: gyms, pilates, yoga classes, even medspas! Building genuine connections in these spaces feels natural and has led to invaluable relationships. I also seek out female friendships with those who inspire and challenge me intellectually – a mutually beneficial exchange of knowledge and humor!

Q: How do you stay motivated and resilient during tough times in your business?

A: Tough times are inevitable in business, often bringing self-doubt and the temptation to quit. However, I remind myself that these challenges forge resilience and separate those who are truly dedicated from those who aren't. My faith and remembering "my why" – the core reason I started my business – are my anchors. I focus on the road ahead, learning from the past but not dwelling in it.

Q: How do you prioritize tasks and manage time effectively as an entrepreneur?

A: My approach to task management is to tackle the least enjoyable ones first. This prevents procrastination and ensures they get done. I'm a big advocate for "task dumping" – writing down everything, then prioritizing and color-coding tasks by monthly, weekly, and daily urgency. This system brings order to chaos and allows me to allocate time effectively.

Q: What role do you believe technology plays in the success of your business?

A: While human connection remains crucial, technology empowers my business to scale and reach new heights. Automation tools streamline operations, CRM systems manage customer interactions, and video conferencing facilitates global communication. Platforms like Trello enhance project management and team collaboration.

Data analytics provided by these technologies offer invaluable insights into customer behavior and campaign effectiveness, allowing for data-driven decisions. This tech-driven approach optimizes processes, reduces costs, elevates customer experiences, and ultimately strengthens our competitive edge.

Q: What advice would you give to other women who are considering starting their own businesses?

A: Embarking on the entrepreneurial journey demands passion, dedication, and the courage to embrace imperfection. Remember, perfection is elusive, and striving for it can stifle progress.

Believe in yourself: Confidence is paramount. Recognize your self-worth and potential – it's the foundation for overcoming challenges and achieving your vision.

Do your homework: Thorough market research is essential. Understand your target audience, analyze competitors, and identify your niche.

Develop a clear vision: Outline your business plan, including financial projections, marketing strategies, and a realistic budget.

Find a mentor: Seek guidance from experienced entrepreneurs who can offer invaluable advice, support, and insights based on their own journeys.

Embrace the mess: Don't let the pursuit of perfection paralyze you. Be willing to learn, adapt, and iterate as you go.

Starting a business is a transformative experience. Embrace the challenges, celebrate the victories, and never underestimate your ability to achieve remarkable things.

Q: Pink or red lipstick?

A: Pink ;)

Sabine Deans, a former military spouse, earned numerous accolades for her volunteer work as a Family Readiness Group Leader and with the American Red Cross. Her extensive experience coordinating travel and events for military families prepared her to excel as a travel agent. Known for her tenacity and professionalism, Sabine combines her background and volunteer experience to offer fast, thorough, and high-quality travel planning. Whether organizing business trips, leisure vacations, all-inclusive packages, or cruises, Sabine ensures her clients receive top-notch service. She is a certified travel agent dedicated to meeting every travel need.

SABINE
Deans

Q: How do you maintain a work-life balance while running your own business?

A: Maintaining a work-life balance as a business owner is all about being organized and clear with boundaries. I create a structured schedule that defines my availability, and I ensure that my clients are aware of these hours. This helps me manage expectations and avoid overextending myself. While I generally stick to these hours, I make an exception for clients who may be traveling and need more flexibility. In addition to managing my work time, I prioritize taking breaks and spending quality time with family and friends. These moments of relaxation are essential for recharging and staying energized, both personally and professionally.

Q: What strategies have you found most effective for networking and building professional relationships as a female entrepreneur?

A: One of the key strategies I've found effective for networking is attending travel industry conferences, seminars, and workshops. These events allow me to connect with like-minded professionals, learn from industry leaders, and stay updated on trends. Beyond formal events, I'm also very active in my local community, which is a huge part of my networking approach. Supporting other female entrepreneurs, attending local meetups, and being involved in community initiatives have helped me build strong, lasting relationships. These connections have been invaluable for my professional growth and have created opportunities for collaboration.

Q: What advice would you give to other women who are considering starting their own businesses?

A: My biggest piece of advice for women thinking about starting their own business is to make sure your "Why" is powerful and meaningful to you. This sense of purpose will be your guiding force, especially when challenges arise. Connecting with other entrepreneurs can also be incredibly helpful. Building a network of like-minded individuals provides encouragement, advice, and opportunities to learn from one another's experiences. And finally, remember that consistency is key to success. Progress may not always be immediate, but staying committed and consistent in your efforts will eventually pay off.

Q: How do you stay motivated and resilient during tough times in your business?

A: During challenging times, I always remind myself of the reason why I started my business in the first place. This helps me refocus and reignites my passion to push through obstacles. Additionally, having a strong support system of fellow entrepreneurs is crucial. Surrounding myself with people who understand the ups and downs of running a business provides encouragement, advice, and inspiration. Their support helps me stay motivated and resilient, even when things get tough.

Q: Pink or red lipstick?

A: It depends on the occasion! Both have their moments, but a bold red can be a great confidence booster when you need to make a statement, while pink is perfect for a more playful, everyday look.

Dr. Lillian Nejad is a clinical psychologist and author who founded two digital tech businesses in the mental health space, Skills for Life and Contain Your Brain.

DR. LILLIAN *Nejad*

Q: Can you tell me about your journey as an entrepreneur? What inspired you to start your own business?

A: I never set out to be an entrepreneur! It wasn't even on my radar when I began my career as a clinical psychologist. But when I look back on my career, I think I've always had that entrepreneurial mindset. In every role I held, I could always see the gaps: what's missing, who is missing out, and what can I do about it.

When the pandemic hit, the boundaries to gain access to traditional therapy became much more obvious and pronounced. So the question was, how can I help people access psychological information, resources and care in a more inclusive and equitable way?

Both Skills for Life, an online platform with mental health self-help programs and resources, and Contain Your Brain, an app that helps people worry less helped fulfil this brief. Skills for Life programs address the most prevalent problems—anxiety, stress and sleep and have reached over 15000 people, far more than I could have seen one on one—in my whole career! And our app, Contain Your Brain offers a modern, secure, and evidence-based approach for worrying less at home and at work—that is accessible, user-friendly, and affordable.

When it comes down to it, what inspires me is giving people access to the tools they need so they can build the lives they want.

Q: What are some of the biggest challenges you've faced as a woman entrepreneur, and how have you overcome them?

A: The mental load that women carry in their daily lives is REAL. Then add a business, or two or three to the list of things to think about, plan, organise, and develop—well it is not possible to juggle all the balls to perfection! Really ever.

So for me it's about remembering why I decided to do this, accepting that I can't do everything all at once, being strategic about how I spend my time and energy, and collaborating with people who have the same vision and values that I do so I don't have to go it alone.

I'm a big believer in partnering with people who have different skills and the same values, because great things can happen!

Q: How do you maintain a work-life balance while running your own business?

A: The notion of work/life balance is flawed. Work is part of life.

So I strive for WHOLE life balance.

To strike a balance that feels right to me, I reflect on my most central values—fostering and maintaining positive relationships, pursuing challenges with optimism and acceptance, and squeezing as much fun in my life as possible!

It's not always easy, especially in the start-up phase of business, when there is so much to do and so many hats to wear! I think I approach it with flexibility, knowing that sometimes my values are competing with one another and it's okay to place one before another as long as it's a conscious and deliberate choice I am making.

Collaborations and partnerships have also been key to helping me reach a healthy life balance. It's important to be able to delegate tasks and share the load because running a business might be fun, exciting, and fulfilling, but it's not easy! The more support you have, the better.

Q: What are your thoughts on the importance of diversity and inclusion in entrepreneurship?

A: Diversity and inclusion in entrepreneurship, are not just crucial for innovation and progress, but also for access and equity. All people deserve equal access to opportunities to learn, change and grow in their personal and professional lives.

We can't know the true power and impact of female entrepreneurs if they don't have the same access to financial backing and support. Only 7% of funding from venture capitalists go to female founders. WHAT!?

Not only do we need to ensure that women and all people with diverse backgrounds and abilities are given the resources they need to succeed, we need to question and modify the structures, processes and procedures to access these resources. The existing systems were created in the absence of diverse voices and perspectives, without consideration for inclusive practices, and without respect for varying needs and circumstances.

We all have to work together to create pathways that makes sense for ALL aspiring entrepreneurs.

Q: What are some trends or developments in your industry that you're particularly excited about?

A: The digital health space is already transforming the delivery of mental health care. With ethics, excellence and equity as my guiding principles, I am excited to help shape the future of mental health with digital tools and resources that are safe, accessible and effective.

Q: Pink or red lipstick?

A: RED!! And pink, brown, orange, nude, purple…

Talia Beckett Davis is the Founder of the Organization of American and Canadian Women in Public Relations, and President of Pink Pearl PR, an agency specializing in luxury female marketing.

TALIA BECKETT *Davis*

Q: Can you tell me about your journey as an entrepreneur? What inspired you to start your own business?

A: I started my agency Pink Pearl PR to help female entrepreneurs showcase their products and services on a global scale. After working with some amazing clients over the years, I felt a calling to give back to the public relations industry, so I launched Canadian Women in Public Relations and American Women in Public Relations (Women in PR North AmericA:.

As the organization continued to grow, so did my knowledge of the PR profession, my connections with media and public relations professionals, and my industry influence.

Q: What advice would you give to other women who are considering starting their own businesses?

A: The time is now to build your business online. I believe that the biggest difference between entrepreneurs that have customers and clients knocking at their doors and entrepreneurs that cannot get anyone to buy is that they are not taking the time to make themselves visible.

Everyone has something unique about them, but they need to showcase it the right way to build a successful business. Your audience is also unique and if you want to attract quality leads, you need to know what your customers want from you. The simplest way to do this is to ask them. Create a poll or online survey and provide an incentive for them to participate. Then, give them what they have asked for.

It's also important to narrow your focus when you're first starting out. If you are overwhelmed by distractions, try focusing only on one single task at a time, ignoring everything else. When so much emphasis is on doing, achieving, producing in the entrepreneurial landscape, many entrepreneurs forget to really stop and listen so they can focus. Listen to your customers and clients. Listen to your followers. Listen to your peers and especially to your team. The most successful people know how to listen and follow through.

Q: Can you discuss the role of networking in growing your business?

A: A little while ago, I attended a luncheon and noticed that half of the attendees were multitasking, checking phone messages and not being present at the event. This is not an unusual occurrence, and it made me stop to remind myself why I was attending these networking events in the first place. I was using my time to network and make meaningful connections, but networking with a group of strangers can be intimidating. If you use your phone at a networking event, do it with a purpose, and use it to connect and follow with new potential partners. After you have attended an event, follow-up with your connections and work on building that relationship. Your immediate goal should not be to get something from this person, but rather to learn how you can potentially collaborate, and that will grow your business.

Q: What are your tips for building an effective team?

A: If you want to develop an effective team, you must engage with them consistently. An engaged employee is more involved in your business and more likely to take on a leadership role.

As a leader at your organization, you need to learn more about each team member's natural strengths and appeal to them. Look for the things that they're naturally good at without trying. For example, you might have an individual on your team who is a natural facilitator. You can use this person's natural skills by putting them in a capacity where they facilitate communication with the rest of the team.

If you want your team to take action, you must explain your overall vision. Craft a clear statement of your organization's vision and impart this to all team members. Teach them what it means and how it looks in action. Ask team members to reinterpret this vision to make sure they understand it and reward behaviors that show their understanding.

Q: How do you empower employees to be successful?

A: The best way to allow people to learn is to set them free. Give your team members a task and let them run with it. Check their results and offer feedback. If you micromanage, your employees won't feel empowered. Empowerment drives engagement and development. In addition to taking an interest in your team members' professional well-being, consider their personal well-being. Make sure they're doing well in terms of their personal life, health, and any challenges they're facing outside of work. Support your team members and have their backs when they face trouble. Make sure you are always there for your team, and they know it.

Q: How do you prioritize tasks and manage time effectively as an entrepreneur?

A: To manage my time effectively, I use the 1-3-5 rule. Choose 1 large task and get started on that first thing in the morning. Choose 3 medium sized tasks and 5 small tasks. As you finish each one, cross it off your list so you can see how much you have accomplished for the day. Forget about multitasking and use the time blocking method on your calendar to plan your work week. Delegate your small, mundane tasks to an assistant to gain more time in your day. You can focus on the bigger tasks while she focuses on the smaller tasks.

Q: Pink or red lipstick?

A: Pink of course!

Dr Avi Charlton is a low carb doctor and keto doctor GP practicing in Melbourne, Victoria. She graduated from medical school in Melbourne University.

DR. AVI *Charlton*

Q: Can you tell me about your journey as an entrepreneur? What inspired you to start your own business?

A: My journey as an entrepreneur began with a personal struggle that illuminated the profound impact of nutrition on health. Despite my extensive background as a general practitioner spanning over 20 years, I grappled with my own weight issues. This journey sparked a deep curiosity in exploring the science of weight loss and nutrition further.

Around 7-8 years ago, I embarked on a personal weight loss journey that transcended mere numbers on a scale. It was a transformative exploration of the intricate relationship between food choices and overall well-being. Through rigorous research and personal experimentation, I unearthed the transformative benefits of adopting a low-carb lifestyle. Not only did this lifestyle shift lead to visible weight loss, but it also ushered in improvements in energy levels, mental clarity, and overall vitality.

Alongside dietary changes, I employed exercise as a key component of my journey, incorporating activities such as running, weight lifting, and completing two full marathons.

Inspired by my own journey and armed with newfound knowledge, I felt compelled to share this transformative approach with others. In October 2022, the Melbourne Low Carb Clinic was born, rooted in the principle of providing personalised nutrition and lifestyle plans tailored to individual needs.

Q: What problem or need does your business solve, and what motivated you to address it?

A: The Melbourne Low Carb Clinic addresses the pervasive issue of deteriorating health resulting from poor nutrition and lifestyle choices. Traditional weight loss approaches often fall short, leaving individuals grappling with frustration and despair. Our clinic offers a solution grounded in evidence-based practices, emphasising the transformative benefits of a low-carb lifestyle. By empowering individuals to make sustainable lifestyle changes, we not only facilitate weight loss but also pave the way for improved overall health and reduced risk of chronic conditions such as diabetes, Alzheimer's, and cancer.

Q: What sets your business apart from competitors in the market?

A: What sets the Melbourne Low Carb Clinic apart is our unwavering commitment to patient care. Each consultation is characterised by empathy and dedication, ensuring that every patient feels heard and understood. We believe in the power of personalised care, taking the time to delve deep into the root causes of health issues and crafting tailored solutions.

Q: How do you balance work-life commitments as an entrepreneur?

A: Balancing the demands of entrepreneurship with family and personal commitments is an ongoing journey. As a parent to two teenage boys aged 15 and 12 and managing all household responsibilities, effective time management and clear boundaries are paramount. Delegating tasks, prioritising rest to recharge, and continuous learning are essential strategies in maintaining a healthy work–life balance.

Q: Looking ahead, what are your goals and aspirations for the future of your business?

A: Looking ahead, the future of the Melbourne Low Carb Clinic is brimming with promise. Our goal is to expand our reach and impact, spreading awareness of healthy nutrition and motivating more individuals to embrace positive lifestyle changes. Through talks, seminars, online platforms, and community outreach, we aim to empower individuals to take charge of their health and well-being, one step at a time.

Additionally, I have recently delved into the realm of breathwork and functional breathing. This journey was sparked by a desire to explore holistic approaches to health and well-being. Breathwork has been a revelation, highlighting how essential proper breathing techniques are for reducing stress, enhancing mental clarity, and improving overall physical health.

With this newfound passion, I am eager to integrate breathwork into my practice. I plan to host workshops and breathwork sessions designed to help individuals harness the power of their breath. By teaching functional breathing techniques, I aim to support patients in managing anxiety, improving their respiratory health, and achieving a greater sense of well-being. This holistic approach aligns seamlessly with the clinic's mission to foster sustainable, healthy lifestyle changes, empowering individuals to lead their healthiest, most balanced lives.

Jasmine Daisy is a dominating force inside the ultra high ticket sales & High performance Coaching world.

JASMINE *Daisy*

Q: Can you tell me about your journey as an entrepreneur? What inspired you to start your own business?

A:Entrepreneurship came from a deep realization that I had 2 options: 1. Continue working for someone else, continue to make them wealthy & get a teeny tiny cut of doing 100% of the work OR 2. Risk everything I was conditioned to believe was "as good as it gets" & go all in on something I wholeheartedly believed in. I chose to risk it all.

Q: What are some of the biggest challenges you've faced as a woman entrepreneur, and how have you overcome them?

A: The single greatest challenge I've faced as an entrepreneur is continuing to push through when I felt like giving up. I overcame this each and every time by reminding myself what going back to work for someone else looked like.

Q: How do you maintain a work-life balance while running your own business?

A: I don't. Until my business fully runs on its own, without my input or assistance, I don't have work/life balance, & it's worth every gruelling second.

Q: What strategies have you found most effective for networking and building professional relationships as a female entrepreneur?

A: Being genuine in any approach to networking has been paramount in having the high calibre quality of business connections I have & continue to build. Accepting that not everyone likes me & choosing to ONLY surround myself with like-minded people has changed my very existence.

Q: What advice would you give to other women who are considering starting their own businesses?

A: Understand that it can & will most likely take years to grow a thriving business. Be prepared to get into debt before making actual profit. Don't quit your day job until you've built enough cash flow from your startup business.

Q: What role do you think mentorship and support networks play for women in entrepreneurship?

A: Choosing a PROVEN mentor who has the life you want is the single EASIEST way to start making incredible income. Your net worth will ultimately be affected by your network. Choose your associations wisely.

Q: How do you stay motivated and resilient during tough times in your business?

A: I remove emotion & choose to only think analytically. I choose to pivot no matter how difficult. I focus on my wins & learn from my losses.

Q: How do you prioritize and manage your goals and tasks as an entrepreneur?

A: It's going to sound overly simplistic & I assure you it IS: I time block 6 days a week & refuse to deviate from my schedule.

Q: What problem or need does your business solve, and what motivated you to address it?

A: My business partner & I have made & lost tens of thousands of dollars in TESTING. Through learning about what DOES & DOES not work over the past 2 decades, we have refined the entire process of launching, monetizing & scaling brick & mortar or online business with our "6 P's to 7 figures" Formula.

Q: What sets your business apart from competitors in the market?

A: We refuse to offer a "1 size fits all" approach to mentorship. Each and every client that works with us receives a completely hand tailored, unique business plan based on their specific business needs. Our results are testament to our individualized approach.

Q: How do you stay innovative and adapt to changes in your industry?

A: I never stop investing in my education.

Q: What strategies do you employ to attract and retain customers?

A: Primarily organic and word of mouth. Besides this, ad campaigns on all of our social platforms, cold outreach & a plethora of quality content creation.

Q: What role do you believe technology plays in the success of your business?

A: Simple: the majority of eyes on our business come from FREE social media attention. There are no longer excuses that can be made from not posting & engaging with your audience.

Q: Can you share a story about a particularly memorable customer interaction or experience?

A: One of my very first coaching clients quadrupled revenue across multiple locations in under 30 days.

Q: How do you measure the success and growth of your business?

A: By the revenue we generate every quarter and most important: client successes.

Q: Pink or red lipstick?

A: Red

Allyson O'Brien is a multi-certified Clinical Aesthetician with nearly 20 years experience specializing in Oncology Esthetics™, advanced skincare and nutrition. She is the founder of Allyson O'Brien | Nutrition & Advanced Aesthetics. Her love of glowing skin brought her an opportunity with cancer patients on their journeys since 2013 and is an Educator for Oncology Training International. She is currently working towards her Nutrition degree to combine skin health and gut health treatments to better assist her clients with tricky skin conditions. She is a celebrity facialist, consultant and has extensive experience in spa management, operations, and education. Her goal...glowing skin for all.

ALLYSON O'Brien

Q: How do you measure the success and growth of your business?

A: The happiness and satisfaction of my clients who visit my studio truly reflect the success of my work. Their positive feedback and referrals are incredibly rewarding and demonstrate that I am meeting, and often exceeding, their expectations. While it's important to track growth through business metrics and reports, the real indicator of success lies in the relationships I build and the trust my clients place in me. It's the people who walk through my door that reveal the true impact of my efforts and the potential for growth in any small business, regardless of the industry. Their support is a testament to the quality of service I strive to provide every day.

Q: What advice would you give to other women who are considering starting their own businesses?

- Take constructive criticism(s) and use it to your advantage.
- Accept failures and wins equally. They are teachers for success.
- Build a team with strengths you don't have. The more experience, the better. Don't be intimidated because your staff may be more knowledgeable in certain areas of your business than you. Utilize them to build the business. Staff will feel more uplifted when they realize you appreciate their craft and education.
- Take the time to breath, reflect, and enjoy a glass of wine after a day (good or bad)
- Humble yourself. Do not lead with your ego. Ego can be the devil in disguise and make you choose things that will lead to a negative path.
- Patience is key. Sometimes businesses do not flourish until the 3 to 5-year mark.
- It is YOUR story to write, so make it the best one you can possibly think of.

Q: What were some of the biggest challenges you faced when starting your business, and how did you overcome them?

A: Well, I own a home-based business, which has more challenges than your typical business. One of the biggest challenges I faced was establishing a professional image and gaining credibility with new clients. Working from home can sometimes be perceived as less serious or illegitimate compared to a traditional brick-and-mortar business. To overcome this, I invested in creating a professional website and business cards, and always presented myself and my business in a professional manner. Networking and word of mouth also helped me gain credibility and attract potential clients. Overall, any business requires determination, adaptability, and perseverance, but with the right strategies, you can overcome these challenges and establish a successful and reputable business.

Q: How do you prioritize and manage your goals and tasks as an entrepreneur?

A: When faced with an issue or situation, I often ask myself how it will impact me. To navigate this, I apply my "333 Rule": I consider the effects of the situation over three weeks, three months, and three years. This approach helps me evaluate its significance and timeline, allowing me to address it effectively.

I've utilized this rule throughout various chapters of my life and career, and it has proven invaluable in keeping me focused. It encourages me to reflect on the unfolding events and determine the best course of action to take. This structured perspective not only clarifies the importance of the issue but also empowers me to manage it with intention and purpose.

Q: What role do you think mentorship and support networks play for women in entrepreneurship?

A: Mentorship and support networks play a crucial role in the success of women in entrepreneurship. As in any traditionally male-dominated field, women often face unique challenges and barriers when starting and growing a business. Having a mentor who has already navigated these challenges and can provide guidance and advice can be invaluable for female entrepreneurs. Additionally, support networks provide a sense of community and connection, allowing women to share their experiences and learn from one another. These networks also provide access to resources, funding opportunities, and potential partnerships, which can greatly benefit women in their entrepreneurial journey. Ultimately, mentorship and support networks not only help women overcome obstacles but also empower and inspire them to reach their full potential as entrepreneurs.

Q: How do you approach leadership and team building within your company?

A: I am currently a solo aesthetician, but the goal is to my own skincare and wellness clinic and hire a team, I believe that effective leadership and teambuilding are crucial for success. As a leader, I strive to lead by example and create a positive, collaborative work environment. I believe in setting clear goals and expectations for my team and providing them with the necessary resources and support to achieve those goals. I also encourage open communication and foster a culture of respect and inclusivity within the team. To build a strong team, I value individual strengths and encourage teamwork. I also believe in recognizing and celebrating the achievements and contributions of each team member. By promoting a strong sense of trust, respect, and ones that want to grow themselves and the business together. I believe that I can foster a motivated and high-performing team that can drive the company towards success.

Q: What strategies do you employ to attract and retain customers?

A: My charming personality of course! That is not enough? Dang. In all seriousness, my personality (I am a transparent person), coupled with my ability to build strong relationships, is just the tip of the iceberg. But don't just take my word for it. I believe in being authentic, utilizing my education, owning my expertise and when I don't have all the answers, I am honest about it and make sure to find the information for my clients. After all, no one knows everything, and it's important to show respect for both your craft and your customer. That's why my loyal clients have been with me for over a decade and continue to trust in my knowledge and transparent approach to each and every treatment I offer.

Q: Pink or red lipstick?   A: A great blue-red does the body good. Red symbolizes energy, action, confidence, courage, and change.

Anita Cotton is a business builder, a serial entrepreneur, a board member, a business coach, a mentor, an advocate for women.

ANITA
Cotton

"The people who are crazy enough to think they can change the world are the ones who do." ...Steve Jobs

Isn't it time to change your world?

'This time when you build another successful enterprise bring them all with you!' screamed the nagging voice in my head. Its time to see the bigger picture!

I've worn many hats, some fit really well, and others not so much, but what if there was a way to share those hats and lessen the load and create success for everyone. What would that look like?

I'd been cultivating this project for sometime, but it wasn't until I attended a Gala and business conference with Shelly Lynne Hughes that the pieces came together. I was honoured to be in the company of such inspirational business builders, and it was then, that the vision became clear.

Remember Field of Dreams? Kevin Costner says "if you build it they will come" so he does the most outrageous thing. He turns his corn field into a baseball diamond so the White Socks would appear to play that one forsaken game....BUT, how is this relevant to you and me?

Well, we all have a field of dreams but the game we are playing is different, the rules, the team players, even the curve balls being thrown can dramatically affect your success and trajectory.

The movie revolves around the reconciliation of regrets, challenges, forgiveness and clearing the path that blocks forward movement. What is blocking you? Is it you, the game you are in, the team or lack there of, the need for support or the system / stack that is broken?

Are you stuck in- in the box thinking? I say, "You have to be an outlier & you don't have to go it alone"!

Clear the path, get off the edge, change your thinking - Embrace a new way to play the game and success can happen.

Field of dreams tries to resolve generations being passed over and becoming relics.

Translation: AI is a fast moving train, are you on it or becoming a relic?

The magic in the movie is the sentiment for the past - then resolving to progress in the present.

Translation: We are creatures of habit but if you want to succeed, its time to shake it up!

You wake up everyday with KPI's to hit.

You utilize every tool, hack, and SEO strategy to garner market share for

Your products

Your services

Yourselves

Here's the problem: The word 'YOUR'.

You are creating 'entities' for yourselves, not successful communities because that was the norm, but its 'in the box thinking at its finest!'

The pyramids were built by a team of innovative thinking visionaries.

Together they assessed the build and determined the strategy for their amazing feat and built the impossible.

At GiveHer Network we've taken what we know works, and ditched what doesn't. Our critical thinkers, innovators, business builders, and yes, AI, have built the first ever inclusive collaborative model where you can ramp up the pace and trajectory of your success right alongside your fellow entrepreneurs that also align with our hands up, hands out philosophy.

Q: What advice would I give to other women just starting out?

1. Get on our waiting list.

2. Have a sense of humour.

3. Know your business. Assess your personal readiness.

4. Take the Myers-Briggs test.

5. Include a 'super voting power' clause in your contracts!!!

6. Accept mentorship. Listen, take action, pay it forward. Mentorship embodies the ethos of giving back.

7. Nurture relationships. Honesty is paramount, keep your word. Build trust in the community by adhering to these values.

8. Never stop learning, be a sponge!

How do you maintain motivation and resilience during challenging times in your business?

Know the difference between them!

Motivation initiates action - Resilience sustains it.

Motivation ignites enthusiasm - Resilience ensures its continuity.

Motivation originates from personal aspirations and provides the initial impetus and energy.

Keep a visionary outlook. Adopt a pragmatic approach when confronting financial metrics.

Resilience is the ability to rebound from setbacks, learn from failure and sustain long term determination.

Have a little cry, a great bottle of red with a friend, put on your big girl pants, your red lipstick and get back on that horse!

Your lipstick colour can shift how you feel and perform

So, Pink or Red?

Depending on whether you're in the boardroom or the bedroom. (humour)

Be yourself. Be bold!

How do you want to feel today?

Pink is: Soft and Understated. Daytime and Casual. Fresh and Youthful. This is the, Ill negotiate colour.

Red is: Bold and Confident. Classic. Great day or night. Glamorous and Sophisticated. This is the, Don't mess with me colour!

I think confidence is the best accessory, so its a red day for me, how about you?

Belinda Djurasovic is the CEO and Founder of Brass Village.

BELINDA
Djurasovic

A: Reflecting back, I think it came about from a lifetime of overcoming adversity, speaking to as many women as possible to hear their stories (I was always the office chatterbox), my own spiritual development, and having a strong calling to support other women. I truly believe in what I teach, as I followed my intuition and took action on the nudges I was receiving – starting the website before I even knew what my program would be, and acting, thinking, and feeling like a business owner before even having any offerings or programs. I just let it all unfold and grow organically.

I have always felt a strong calling to serve others. Through introspection, I realised that I consistently went the extra mile for friends who needed support through various seasons of life, whether in relationships or careers. I had a genuine interest and a knack for helping them uncover the possibilities within themselves. Everything I had cultivated within myself, I wanted other women to experience—helping them realize their own power and teaching them how to cultivate and nurture the feelings within to achieve true fulfillment.

Q: How do you maintain a work-life balance while running your own business? Replay within 24 hours.

A: While still lying in bed, I start each day with a short meditation to connect with my heart space, express gratitude for the day, and release any beliefs or energy that aren't mine and no longer serve me. With a young child, I don't always have the luxury of time in the mornings, so I stick to self-care commitments that are super nurturing and achievable.

Throughout the day, I prioritize mini-breaks—whether it's practicing nervous system resets, enjoying a cup of tea in the sun, or simply listening to my body and responding when it needs care. I believe in showing up 100% for my clients, and I know I can't give them the best service unless I feel my best.

For decades I used to struggle with daily anxiety, and everything always felt more hectic, busy, and difficult than it needed to be. Now, by staying regulated, setting boundaries with others, and prioritizing my energy above all else, I actually achieve much more. I can handle the never-ending mum duties, my daughter's needs, work, running the household, and more—with flow and ease. Most of the time!

Q: What advice would you give to other women who are considering starting their own businesses?

A: Learn and be motivated by other women in your industry and just start. Don't be held back by overthinking the 'how's' or worrying if your website and social media are perfect. When you are in a financial position to do so, you can hire experts and coaches to help you where you need it. I stayed in part-time employment, and that has been really good for my mindset, as it's taken the pressure off while I build my business and its offerings.

Q: What were some of the biggest challenges you faced when starting your business, and how did you overcome them?

A: Mindset! You are not your thoughts; observe them, but don't let them hold you back. All those fears, judgments, and limiting beliefs women have about themselves can be released, allowing you to evolve and feel unstoppable. When I first launched my business, I didn't get the support I expected from some family and friends – it took a mindset shift to realize they weren't even my ideal clients, so why would they understand my services? Your people will find you, and 9 times out of 10, they won't be from your inner circle, so don't look to them for validation.

Q: Looking ahead, what are your goals and aspirations for the future of your business?

A: I am incorporating more energy work and intuitive practices into my coaching, workshops, and online offerings to teach women how to build these skills within themselves. This allows them to dig deeper, develop a more powerful mindset, heal more effectively, and achieve more by empowering themselves to look within. By offering all offerings as an online option, I can now reach women anywhere in the world, especially with my self-led retreat offerings and women's circle self-care sessions. These sessions are individually tailored with exercises that women can do on their own or with friends, making retreats and workshops more accessible than ever. I would love to see that expand out and grow.

I have been creating online courses and will continue to expand these offerings to teach other women how to become a powerful force within themselves. This includes learning how to get what they want by understanding how to operate from their heart space rather than their headspace, deepening their intuition, and cultivating unshakable self-worth. My goal is for everyone to feel supported and part of my village—held, seen, and heard. However that looks for them.

Q: What strategies have you found most effective for networking and building professional relationships as a female entrepreneur?

The most honest, supportive, and helpful connections I've made with other female entrepreneurs have come from being my most genuine, raw self. I don't compete with anyone or judge anyone else's work. Instead, I am completely honest and open, sharing my struggles and asking for help and advice when I need it. In the networks i'm a part of, I never approach conversations with a sales pitch or the intention to sell down the line. I build connections the same way I would when making new friends—focusing on connection over sales.

Being in a more spiritually-led business, I find that the communities I'm part of are made up of women who have a genuine desire to serve others and who always offer help. We're all working toward the same goal: living a fulfilled life and supporting the rise of women's courage while nurturing their soul's journey.

Genicca Whitney is a Manifestation Mentor & Business Strategist, She lives in Vancouver, BC, Canada with her two daughters.

GENICCA
Whitney

I accidentally became an entrepreneur. I was 19, without a University or College Degree, and after working with a direct sales company for 2 years, right out of high school, I had this uncommon urge to start my own business. I've been self-employed for almost 20+ years now and I've learned a lot about myself, the world and what it takes to grow a thriving business.

If there is anything that has supported my entrepreneurial journey over the years, it has been the introduction to the Law of Attraction, when I turned 18 years old. I was mentored by two incredible leaders who introduced me to this life-changing concept and since then, I have become a student of the Laws of the Universe. Learning how to transform my mind and how to use my energy to manifest my wildest dreams - has completely changed my life.

I became a student of manifestation with a big vision to build an empire of empowered women who were just like me: hungry, curious and committed to becoming the change our ancestors needed. When I realized that I could consciously create a life I never had, I made it my mission to break generational curses, manifesting the commissions from my direct sales job to buy my immigrant parents a house by the age of 19.

I strongly believe that entrepreneurship is the most incredible journey towards activating human potential and that by mastering our mindset, improving our self-concept and understanding how to work with energy, we can transform our reality faster than we ever imagined possible.

I love the spark people get in their eyes when they dream beyond the box. I love guiding them from their 3d reality towards their imagination, 4d consciousness, where absolutely everything is possible.

Once they give themselves permission to dream, I lead them towards the next elevation of consciousness, which is the 5th dimension. In this level of consciousness, I teach them, step-by-step, how to become, create and experience everything they ever wanted to be, do and have, in this lifetime.

This is where I reveal my 5d manifestation method, which is an extremely magnetic formula that bridges the gap between Point A to Point B, in the most simple and potent way.

It is because of what I've been able to achieve over the years - buying my parents a home at 19, becoming a serial investor at 20 and manifesting 6-figures as a new mom to two new babies - through the Law of Attraction, that I committed to mentoring women from all walks of life, to master the art of manifestation & conscious business creation.

It is my mission, as a Filipino immigrant, to empower women to strategically manifest the lifestyle and the business beyond their wildest imagination - even without any proof that it is possible.

There is nothing more that I love than connecting with those who are ready to break free from the soul-sucking rules that keep us trapped, in lack and in fear. It is my purpose to help you discover their highest potential and to show you how to become magic in heels, while building the most breathtaking life, business & brand that you are obsessed about & aligned with.

My soulmate clients and students have manifested illogical miracles like unexpected raises in their 9-5, podcast hosting opportunities, trips around the world, significant cheques out of nowhere, soulmate partners fueled with love - and the brand & booming business... of their wildest dreams.

In my world, it doesn't matter where you came from, what you do or don't have or how much you know. My 5d manifestation method works when you decide to become a student of your own potential and you are willing to do whatever it takes to become everything you ever wanted.

You go first, the Universe follows.

Virginia Ede is the compassionate heart behind a business dedicated to animals, nature, and the profound healing energies they offer. With a background in people-oriented industries like hospitality, public relations and entertainment, Virginia felt a deep calling to shift her focus toward a more meaningful, soul-centred path. This led her to create a space where gentle complementary therapies and the healing arts are not only practiced but embraced, particularly in connection with animals. Driven by a desire to make a difference in the world, Virginia's approach is rooted in authenticity, empathy, and a deep commitment to the well-being of others. Her work fosters healing from the heart and soul, offering a nurturing space for transformation and empowerment.

I have always possessed a deep passion for animals, Nature and natural healing energies; so after working in a variety of people oriented industries such as hospitality and entertainment, developing my own business became a very natural and extremely desired life progression.

After years of working to live, it was time to finally follow my heart and begin living my work. My desire was to live a life that would make a worthwhile difference in this world of ours.

It is therefore the most wonderful characteristic that I have discovered in business today that women are now decisively stepping out of our predetermined feminine roles into our very individual niches. It has become a journey that permits women being heard as well as seen and finally able to receive assistance, guidance and support in a non-judgemental network of like minds and like hearts.

This kind of encouragement can form the difference in the lighting of our entrepreneurial fire, setting us on our own adventure and permitting us the ability to create a vision that is a world apart from the norm. We have become so much more than the pigeon holes that we were assigned to. With this in mind, my advice to anyone considering starting their own business is to first connect deeply with your 'why.' It is about understanding what drives you and what you're truly passionate about. When your work aligns with your heart's calling, it becomes more than just a business – it becomes a way of life.

Not being afraid to step outside of societal expectations or the 'norm' to create something uniquely yours. Authenticity will always be your greatest asset, and when you lead with your true self, you'll attract the right people and opportunities. Always, and in all ways!

Also, be prepared for challenges as they're a natural part of the journey. Remain resilient by remembering your purpose, and surround yourself with a supportive community that believes in you and your vision. That is what has always guided me on my journey.

And most importantly, take care of yourself. Running a business is demanding and it's easy to get caught up in the hustle. Ensure that you make time for self-care, stay connected to what grounds you, and always remember that your well-being is the foundation of your business's success. If you love what you do and are true to yourself, the rest will follow.

My world and deep dedication is complementary therapies and working with animals in the healing arts, which steps outside of the square of expectation and beliefs, generating positive distinction. My training in gentle complementary therapies revolves around the healing connection of the heart and soul rather than mere mental attitudes.

This develops a deeper communication within the being and sets about a conduit for shifting choices and decisions that may not be conducive to overall wellbeing. Although this directive is viewed by many in the world as 'Woo Woo', there is nothing frivolous about the outcomes that come as a result.

In fact, when there are tough times, and there will always be those when 'stepping outside of the square' in innovative business adventures, I always come back to my core values: compassion, authenticity, and being of service. I tend to remind myself why I started this journey - to help others and to connect deeply with nature and animals. Working with them, I see the impact of my efforts firsthand, and that fills me with resolution and gratitude. I also make space for self-care, which includes spending time in nature, grounding myself, and reconnecting with the healing energies that inspired my business in the first place. Surrounding myself with a supportive community helps me stay strong, and when challenges arise, I view them as opportunities for growth and learning. Ultimately, knowing that I am doing work that resonates with my soul keeps me extremely motivated as well as resilient.

In truth, I believe what sets my business apart is the authentic desire to assist and 'be of service' in empowerment, healing and wellbeing. What makes me different is that I don't view other 'like' businesses and approaches as competition. We are all here to assist in making life easier, healthier and happier and if I or someone else can assist, then I am truly living my works.

After working in fields that didn't resonate with the change and growth that I was experiencing and the unhappiness and frustration in living a life that I felt wasn't my own, a huge fire in my belly was initiated that moved me.

I became more aware of just how much I disliked the inauthenticity of the values of the people I was working for and there had to be something more. My mantra became "Do what you love and love what you do" and that drove me forward in my development and training.

My particular vocation addresses the need for authentic, heart-centred healing approaches in a world that often overlooks the deeper connections between mind, body, and soul. Many people, including women who are stepping into their own power, feel disconnected from their true selves due to societal expectations, stress, or past trauma. My work focuses on restoring that connection—both within themselves and with nature—through gentle, complementary therapies and the healing arts. I was motivated to address this need because I've experienced firsthand how transformative this kind of healing can be. After years of working in industries that didn't align with my values, I realized how important it is to live authentically and help others do the same.

This work is my way of contributing to a healthier, more balanced and harmonious world. As I grow and expand, my brand identity tends to change as I become more developed in my uniqueness. Compassion, authenticity, resilience, courage, integrity and continued growth are what make us all strong in the building of what empowers us.

Reputation is about being true to who you really are. Walking, talking and living your walk and talk, knowing that every day that you are developing to be the best that you can be, and do the very best that you can do. Being authentic, genuine and compassionate - That is my brand.

And with my complexion – definitely a dark pink lipstick would be my ultimate selection!

Danielle Brisebois-Duncan is a single mom of four children, two of whom she has full time and two who are grown. She is an entrepreneur and business owner of BlueRavenCanada Vintage Jewelry. She currently resides in Powell River BC.

DANIELLE
Brisebois-Duncan

I have always loved jewelry. Even as a little girl I can remember sitting on the couch holding my mom's hand and being mesmerized by how her wedding ring would sparkle in the light. I would twist her hand in all directions and watch the different colours play off the diamonds. I thought that ring was the most beautiful thing in the world.

As I grew older I became more interested in jewelry. If anyone asked me what I wanted for my birthday or Christmas the answer was always the same, jewelry!

I had amassed quite a collection by the time I was in my early thirties, but I had gone through some very difficult times. I was on the television show Intervention because of an addiction to Percocet. I thank my family and the show so much for getting me the help I so desperately needed. I wouldn't be here today without them. After my three months in rehab I separated from my husband and ultimately got divorced. While we were separated I was in Calgary for several months and had nothing. I wound up pawning everything I had. Including all my jewelry. I had to start from scratch.

I eventually built up my collection but after my grandma passed away my mom gave my sisters and I a few pieces of her collection. Not knowing anything about them and thinking they were junk I stuck them in my jewelry box and there they sat for years, until one day my mom came over and we started talking about how she still had a ton more of my grandma's collection. That was when the lightbulb came on!

I came up with the idea for my business the day my mom and I were talking about my grandma's jewelry collection. I went into my jewelry box and took out the pieces that she had given me so many years earlier and I looked at them. I mean I really looked at them, and they were beautiful! I couldn't understand why I didn't recognize the craftsmanship and pieces of art that they were when I just shoved them in my jewelry box years ago. I knew right then and there this was what I wanted to do.

I asked my mom to bring over the rest of her collection and everything started from there. I didn't know the first thing about business. I started on Ebay and hated it. I moved to Etsy, I got myself a business license and started building a social media presence on Facebook and Instagram. I started networking with the most amazing people. I have found women in business really stick together and want to see other women succeed. Now I'm in the process of building my own website. I am still very new and I learn something new everyday but I am proud of what I have achieved in my short career as an entrepreneur.

Being an E-commerce based business I don't think I would exist without technology. I literally have an app for everything. I can do product research, I can get help writing better descriptions, I can check what a stone is if I'm not certain, I can network, the possibilities are endless.

I believe diversity has a huge role in business and in life. Without diversity you only get to see the same things over and over again. It's like eating vanilla ice cream everyday all day. When you add in diversity you get to see things you have never seen before. Things from different cultures and places. It opens a whole new world of beauty and charm to the world of business. I would love to see more diversity in entrepreneurship!

The role I think mentorship and support plays for women in entrepreneurship is almost essential. I have had so much help from some of the most amazing, talented, intelligent, experienced and successful women out there. Even though my business is still going at a very slow pace due to personal reasons, I can still reach out to any of the aforementioned women and find the absolute best advice out there. I have learned I don't know everything lol, and that I do have to ask questions about just about anything and everything. Getting a second opinion from a successful woman who has already been in my position is the most valuable thing I have right now. Whether you have known one of these amazing women all your life (like my Godmother) who is one of the smartest businesswomen I know and is someone I can go to anytime with any financial questions or it's someone you met in a FB group. They are all incredible and have different areas of expertise. I also find they want to help. They're not just saying it, they truly want to see you succeed. My advice would be to look for those FB groups and join as many as you can that relate to you and your business. You can never have enough great advice and even greater women who have your back!

Looking ahead at the future goals and expectations for my business, I am thinking way ahead. I am also thinking huge! I am taking an online course right now that is going to take this business to a whole new level. I am going to really get this business to a place where I will have to hire someone else to run it. I am going to be one of the biggest online vintage jewelry brands out there! I am going to build my brand one day at a time through the power of social media and I will have my own website very soon. After that I am going to go to school to either do freelance copywriting or social media marketing and that will be my second business. I can use all of what I learn in school to help make take this business to the top and also have my second business as a freelancer to make sure all of my dreams and aspirations come true. I know it's a lot to take on but I'm not afraid of work and I am going to give my children a better life than what they have now. You have to start with a dream then make a plan and then put that plan into action! I have just started the action stage, so I hope to see some of you as clients in both businesses soon! Staying motivated and resilient is a challenge, being a single mom with two daughters still at home and having one of them as my other full time job is difficult. She was born with a genetic mutation and she had a stroke at birth, leaving her completely blind, she can't walk, talk, has a seizure disorder and is fed through a feeding tube. With that being said that is how I stay motivated. My girls are my world. They give me all the motivation I could ask for and more. I also have two older children a son and a daughter who I also want to make proud. When things get tough I think of them and all and everything comes into focus and nothing can stop me!

Pink or red lipstick?
Red

Daniela Fisher a proud mom and wife to a beautiful family, founder of Naturally Given.

DANIELA
Fisher

Q: Can you tell me about your journey as an entrepreneur? What inspired you to start your own business?

A: My journey as an entrepreneur started when I was 20 years old as my mom invested in Canada to open an Argentinean food factory and retail store called, Tango Café in Langley, BC.

I had no clue on how to operate a business or any aspect of it. In short, I had to learn fast, and understand every aspect of it with my mom's guidance while she was travelling back and forth from Argentina to Canada.

I also worked in the film industry for 17 years doing acting, dance shows, and modeling as I went to school for TV & Film Production before opening the family food business,

As well, I got my Real Estate License did project marketing for a while before giving birth to our children.

These experiences have given me a great foundation on how to create a business from scratch and it forced me to push through my fears and develop confidence, grit, and taught me to believe in myself.

Furthermore, I had to learn to deal with the 'not good enough' and 'fear to fail' patterns, and I love that saying, "success is about falling nine times and getting up ten". No matter what, I taught myself to never give up!

All of the above has shaped me into who I am today, and has given me a clear path forward, but I felt there was still something more meaningful to come my way…

On June 7th, 2016, Naturally Given was born.

Our purpose is to "fearlessly elevate humanity to its highest frequency of love" by offering services and products that restore balance within the emotional, physical, mental, and spiritual body.

Naturally Given just felt right, because it was aligning within my soul's gifts and bringing me "internal fulfillment".

Wow…things are looking up now! – I said to myself!

I believe that by unlocking the power of our minds and working towards a greatness mindset, can help us discover our meaningful mission where we get to then use our soul's gifts to serve our highest good and therefore understand that we are enough and worthy, just as we are!

It is our passions and strengths that will always drive us to make a significant impact in the world.

I envision my life as a big puzzle, and every day I am excited to find the next piece to make it whole!

Q: Can you discuss a failure or setback your business encountered, and how did you bounce back from it?

A: When things get tough, that's exactly when you do not give up!

Several times during the development of my business, I wanted to just quit!

Because of course, it was easier to quit than dealing with the uncomfortable - not good enough - and failure patterns. This process awakened me to the fact that I had the ability to transform challenges into opportunities and when I did so, magic happened. I also had to learn to be more patient and take things one step at a time.

Our thoughts are our only limits! So, we can say, that FEAR is a contractive energy which hold us back from success, comparing to GRIT which is an expansive energy which allow us to fly high.

I had to choose to "think different" and really believe with every ounce of my being that I was worthy of an abundant life in all aspects, and that by pursuing growth with a burning desire, I could push past the fear, and become authentic which led me towards a successful journey.

Q: How do you maintain a work-life balance while running your own business?

A: I am a goal-oriented type of personality, so I always write down my goals at the beginning of the year as well as I create my vision board and positive affirmations to have crystal clear clarity on what I need to improve, manifest, and / or balance more of in my life on that year. My goals are set in all aspects, such as family, work, health / wellbeing, relationships, and abundance.

Every day, I make time for my family, work, and self-care which includes not just looking after myself but also doing something that I love.

Sometimes I have more time than others, but I enjoy meditating while I am inside the salt room which also has the red light, so doing three things in 20 minutes is efficient. I really love writing my gratitude list daily or every other day. I enjoy listening to motivating spiritual podcasts or reading positive self-help books when I can. I like to practice grounding as often as possible and work out / dance training at least 5 times a week and eating healthy foods. Taking minerals and vitamins are very essential to run at our optimal. I love having energy and feeling ALIVE!

One of my absolute favourite things to do is to light up an incense, roll on essential oils, turn on a candle, and do my Angel oracle cards. And I do have to add that looking after my plants is very therapeutic and healing.

Q: What advice would you give to other women who are considering starting their own businesses?

We were all born abundant. How exciting is that?

What stops us from manifesting our dream life is our Abundance blockages that we have created through negative patterns that have been programmed in our subconscious mind. But the great news is that we can create transformation quickly by just identifying our blockages and replacing them with higher frequency thoughts which will guide us towards a greatness mindset and will automatically lead us towards success.

Everyone has a different definition of success; for me, success means achieving internal fulfillment by discovering my life purpose and serving my highest good through our soul's gifts.

Never let anyone dim your Light. You must believe in yourself and who you really are, a gifted human with free will to choose Love over Fear. And remember, that you are enough and worthy just as you are, and everything you need to know is within you.

Q: Pink or red lipstick?

Both as I like to use red lip liner and bright pink inside the lip.

Sandra Flora — Owner, Designer, Decorator @ Sandra Flora Home Design, Vancouver BC.

Q: What were some of the biggest challenges you faced as a woman entrepreneur and how have you overcome them?

A: One challenge I face in my business is not being taken seriously as a female entrepreneur in networking meetings. While thankfully this has not occurred often, regardless it has taught me the importance of knowing how to respond by another's condescension or frustration. How have I navigated these situations?

I have learned to be prepared for meetings. People are much more likely to meet your level of professionalism and business insight both when you demonstrate you are educated in your field and when you articulate yourself with confidence. In addition, you absolutely need to build a toolkit of strategies for how to respond in the moment. Very few people are great at responding how they'd like when they are put on the spot, so my advice is to practise how best to react when confronted about your business decisions. It has been immensely helpful for me to have sought out mentors who meet with me, propose scenarios, and offer input for different ways of responding. I've also benefited from a business life coach whose insight and advice has added to my toolkit of strategies for how to react to and diffuse intimidating interactions.

Q: What advice would you give to other women who are considering starting their own businesses?

A: Before you start a business, you have to know the business well. Great ideas need to be built on a foundation of knowledge and ongoing inquiry-based learning. At the top of my list for how to gain this insight, I would tell an aspiring entrepreneur to do their research, which can largely be done online through searches, asking questions or analysing business platforms that currently exist. This knowledge can also be attained by reading self-help books from the library but of even more value, I suggest visiting comparable businesses in person. For instance, if you are interested in opening a hair salon, pop into a few local salons where you live and ask if you can take the owner out for coffee to pick their brain. More seasoned entrepreneurs are almost always happy to offer a wealth of practical information about costs related to start-up inventory, maintenance and staffing, and to share about challenges they have faced and strategies that have worked for their business.

Once you have familiarised yourself with the business, next write out a business plan, set some specific goals and establish concrete steps for how you will fulfil those goals. When (not if) you encounter obstacles or difficulties around starting your business, persevere! Resilience is a core characteristic for any entrepreneur just starting out.

Finally, don't tackle starting your business in private; instead, surround yourself with like-minded people, supporters who commit to encouraging you and pushing you, but who will also remind you to take care of yourself. You don't want to get burned out, so remember to take an hour, or a day, to recharge, because it will serve you in the long run!

A: Technology plays an enormous role in running and growing my business. Most of my advertising is online, whether through social media or online through the local newspaper. Social media offers me the platform to display some of the projects I've worked on, as long as a client consents to having photos of a room or home posted publicly, and then prospective clients can take a look and gauge whether my decorating is of interest to them and their needs.

Q: Can you share a story about a particularly memorable customer interaction or experience?

A: This question really gets to the heart of what I love about my business. A couple years ago, I was hired by an elderly woman's adult children to help their mom downsize. At the time, Marie was 89, had recently lost her husband of 67 years, and had a large house full of decades of cherished objects and memories, but it was time for her to make a transition to something more manageable. Though she wished to move to a condo, her children were really encouraging her to move into an assisted living facility. But Marie was nervous about getting pushed into a decision that wasn't her own, and so I offered to tour a few facilities with her.

In spending time with this client, I came to really know what mattered to her, and she settled on one facility—on her own terms. However, Marie was still distressed and saddened about divesting a life's worth of furniture, decor and photos, with only a fraction to be distilled into one room. I told her that we would approach it like a dollhouse; I said, "We're going to take your home and make a replica of what is familiar and miniaturise it to fit in your room." This was a relationship of trust, where I helped Marie mentally let go of a lot, but where she entrusted me to recreate "home" in her new place of residence. I assured her that she would wake up every day surrounded by those things that she cherished most.

I worked with Marie to understand what was most meaningful to her, and photos of her husband, children and grandchildren were at the top of her list. Spanning half of one wall of her bedsit, I placed mixtiles of black and white photos of her family and life created from those that we chose together. In the center of that wall, I hung her family crest, then along the other half of the wall I created an artful collage of paintings, framed needlepoint, and other beloved items gathered from her home. Of the objects that Marie wished to hold onto was a queen-sized quilt, but it was much too large for her new twin bed, so I hired a fantastic seamstress who beautifully reworked the bedspread to fit this smaller bed.

For this client it wasn't difficult to go above and beyond, to know that I was helping to make her last few years comfortable and familiar, and in fact, I visit Marie as often as I can , bringing her a chai tea and banana chocolate chip bread, which I know she loves. Through this project I've acquired additional business from residents in Marie's facility that want something similar.

Working with people is so much more about earning a paycheque—I get to be a part of helping people feel really comfortable in their most intimate spaces, and as a bonus, I get to build relationships with many lovely people.

Q: Can you discuss the role of networking and partnerships in growing your business?

A: As an interior decorator, I rely heavily on growing a network and establishing partnerships with many people in my community. As my business has grown, I've been hired by local realtors to help people get their homes ready to be sold, offering tips about staging, making rooms neutral by depersonalising and decluttering, and ideal for professional photography. Often the most important part of the job is ensuring the curb appeal is good, so that prospective buyers will walk into a home already with a good first impression.

Other networking relationships I've worked to build are with local businesses. Supporting local business is very important to me. Instead of ordering large quantities of uncomfortable furniture that is mass produced overseas, for instance, I can send a client to use my 20% discount at a boutique store down the road, and everyone is happy.

Those in my network include a team of contractors whose expertise I draw off on behalf of my clients. You might suppose that an interior designer would be my competitor but in fact I have built mutually beneficial relationships with several; often an interior designer doesn't want to go shopping with people for furniture or textiles, for example, and that is something I'm happy to take on. Likewise, when I have crafted a plan with a client that requires a new paint job, I connect them with a contract painter from my team.

I strive towards a holistic view in business, to be a part of a network of talented entrepreneurs who rely on one another, who each get to play a tangential part in a project, rather than outsourcing labor and goods to places farther afield that will have an impersonal approach to clients' needs.

Q: Pink or red lipstick? A: Pink

Accredited as a Brain Coach, Neuro Linguistic Practitioner and Cognitive Behavioural Therapist; whilst utilising the modalities of Transactional Analysis and Positive Psychology, Susie empowers women to break free from their challenges and limitations. Those that past conditioning has gifted, without awareness, illuminating how we are all masters of imitation!

SUSIE *Ford*

Q: Can you tell us about your journey as an entrepreneur and what inspired you to start your own business?

A: When hit with adversity, by coincidence I was living in my parents' home, there I stayed for twelve months of rehab. It was at that time through adult eyes, I came to see clearly my own damage, what had impacted me in the positive and the negative, due to past conditioning.

More realisations and clarity came of the detrimental beliefs and patterns of behaviour that I had absorbed, the course of my life I had chosen and the love I deprived myself.

This inspired me to guide others, so they understand why the frustrations, anger, resentments, negative talk of self, judgements, and more, are in their lives now. Then gaining self-awareness, realisations and clarity around what they have absorbed as their own DNA, and how to navigate steps to change.

Q: How did you come up with the idea for your business, and what was the process like from concept to execution?

A: There was no question I had to follow the path I had already been on, generational beliefs and patterns of behaviour. Through research I developed processes that enabled me to see souls who without help, may never in this lifetime recognise their detrimental gifts. The ones that have been absorbed into their subconscious mind, and unconsciously being played out daily.

Calling the business; "Let's Just Be Fabulous" had to be to ensure others felt just that, plus I had used these words for years!

Now working one-to-one, couples, various workshops, and speaking events in private sector and corporate; I continue to bring awareness to the emotional challenges we all experience; gifted from our parents, or a significant influence from early childhood, without awareness.

Q: Can you share a significant milestone or achievement your business has reached, and what did you learn from it?

A: I was operating for a few years before being approached by a couple who wanted to do some work, couples had never been a given thought until then. What unfolded had such an impact on me, honouring the layers of generational challenges that had affected these two souls. Witnessing the change, I would recommend all couples do this, so they obtain a deeper level of understanding, empathy and patience for each other.

Q: What advice would you give to someone who is considering starting their own business?

A: Ensure what you are considering is your passion! Then it won't seem like work, instead the joy of every step of success, will give you more empowerment to achieve and stay on track!

Q: What problem or need does your business solve, and what motivated you to address it?

A: I work with women who are challenged with the impact of detrimental past conditioning, which they experience as voids in their lives. These are portrayed in the workplace, socially, and homelife, as anger, resentments, frustrations, depression, negative self-talk, judgements, anxiety, and more.

After gaining awareness of my own past conditioning the choices I made without awareness, plenty not that fabulous, it all made sense! I had been writing about this subject for years, not knowing where it would land, then it was crystal clear!

These realisations escalated my passion and clarified my purpose, it was a knowing that I had to bring this clarity to why many are repeating detrimental conditioning.

Now through solution-based education, women's lives can dramatically alter, if they choose to consciously take steps to change unconscious beliefs, and behaviours. .

Q: Can you discuss the role of networking and partnerships in growing your business?

A: I wouldn't have been able to build my business without the networking element. Potential clients need to obtain trust before they commit and it is vital to understand their needs in all aspects, to ensure you can fulfill theirs, that takes connection. Partnerships bring growth, support, suggestions and or collaborations.

Q: Pink or red lipstick?

A: Pink Lipstick!

Estrellita Gonzalez is a business owner who operates a skincare clinic, Derma Bright Clinic,and a wellness centre, Holistica Wellness, in Vancouver, BC. She also operates an online store, My Skin Salon and is a Wellness Educator.

Q: Can you tell me about your journey as an entrepreneur? What inspired you to start your own business? How did you come up with the idea for your business?

A: I started my first company when I was 24; we provided construction cleaning services. It was the first of many. On entrepreneurship, I had been influenced by my Dad and Aunt, who both worked for themselves. The feeling of freedom and self-accountability I saw in them resonated with me.

I started Derma Bright Clinic in 2012 through a series of coincidences. Prior, I had been visiting a holistic doctor to set a health baseline. This included proactive tests like heavy metals. This test revealed I had off-the-charts lead in my body. I was shocked! As I researched this, I won a book, "Not Just A Pretty Face, the Ugly Side of the Beauty Industry", which delved into toxic processes and ingredients in beauty products, including the possibility of lead in lipstick!

Learning there were harmful ingredients in beauty, skin and personal care products surprised and angered me. As I was completing a marketing project for a US esthetics manufacturer, I could see technology was going to play a big role in skin care. I combined these 3 coincidences to create a skin care concept that would include: tech- based treatments using healthful (i.e. organic) ingredients and professionally-trained team; I would run and market the company. Derma Bright Clinic was the result!

Q: What were some of the biggest challenges you faced when starting your business, and how did you overcome them?

A: There are several challenges I encountered as I started this journey. Mostly I didn't know what I didn't know! Starting a small business requires juggling many roles, some of which I wasn't good at. At first you have to do a lot of things yourself. Another challenge is financing and cash flow management, tough when you are brand new and have no history with banks. As a result I had to self-finance my business. I also lacked accountability. This is one reason I have worked with coaches along my journey.

Q: What advice would you give to other women who are considering starting their own businesses?

A: In May I reached out to my first business coach. She asked how I was doing. I said great, I am celebrating 12 years in June. She said that was fabulous and that I should congratulate myself as only 4% of businesses make it to 10 years! What!? I was shocked! So my advice to anyone wanting to start a business, consider buying an established (at least 10 years) business (or franchise). You have much higher odds of making it then doing it yourself. You could also get purchase financing much easier as it is established, with a proven track record.

Q: How do you approach leadership and team-building within your company?

A: My professional and educational credentials include Human Resources and Business Management. For me, leadership is based on a person's values. What's important and drives you will contribute to the kind of leader you are. Your team needs to understand your values plus the business goals and objectives. People perform better when they understand where the business is going and what their role is in getting there. With team-building, I aim to be fair and not play favorites. They are each unique and contribute something different to the organization. I work with each member to determine what that is so there is a sense of autonomy for them in the roles they play and how they contribute to the company.

Q: How do you maintain a work-life balance while running your own business?

A: I consider myself a Wellbeing Promoter. My businesses are centred on wellbeing. So it's critical that I take care of myself! I do this with a program that includes: exercise, meditation, eating well, having healthy relationships and spending my time doing things I enjoy. I have cut out "the fluff" and focus on things that expand me: reading, travel and courses. My philosophy is that we are here to expand, create and enjoy life so I aim for this every day.

Q: Looking ahead, what are your goals and aspirations for the future of your business?

A: My business has been on an expansion path since 2012. Every year I plan activities to take my business to the next level. This will continue! I do this personally as well. In 2022 I launched another company, SimplyDivineRetreats.com, which is all about travel, wellbeing and retreats. It is another aspect of the Wellbeing Promoter.

Q: Pink or red lipstick?

A: I wear both! Pink is my day lipstick and red is my evening or when I am wearing red. As long as they are free of lead, I am wearing lipstick!

Diane Rolston specializes in coaching female business leaders to have more confidence and success while living a balanced life. When she's not coaching, speaking on stages, recording the Dynamic Women Podcast, and showing business owners how to hire, train and have success with their own virtual assistant... you can find this mother of two hanging with her family or on the soccer field.

Q: Why are you so passionate about what you do?

A: I'm passionate about coaching high-achieving women and entrepreneurs to realize their potential and unleash their dynamic selves. I do this because I've felt the same pains and struggles. I often share this lesson when coaching, delivering a keynote, or training: "Stop measuring your life according to your success."

Society defines success in a way that keeps us chasing it, only to find it feels fleeting once achieved. This constant chase leaves us unsatisfied. Instead, measuring satisfaction along the way to success is a game-changer. It allows you to feel satisfied not only when you reach your goals but every day in between.

I love using coaching tools to help you get ahead, like scoring your satisfaction, which helps you answer a crucial question: What do you want? Once you have that answer, you'll know what brings you energy and resonance. I then support you in connecting the dots with a simple formula, boosting your confidence and propelling you into action.

Since my mission is to empower more women to be dynamic and successful, I'm also passionate about donating my books and proceeds to Women's Shelters.

Q: How do you balance work-life commitments as an entrepreneur?

A: You'll never balance work and life because there are ten different areas of life to juggle, and work is just one of them. Once you realize this, like my clients, you'll feel a massive sense of relief and easily spot which areas are out of balance. This clarity helps you effortlessly allocate your time where it matters most.

Since I have two school-aged children and want to continue multiplying my business results yearly, I realized early on that I couldn't do it all myself, so I hired help. I systematized and streamlined my business using virtual assistants, and I now have a team of VAs from the Philippines who I match with business owners in my VA Made Easy Program.

Q: What are some of the biggest challenges you've faced as a woman entrepreneur, and how have you overcome them?

A: I've faced and overcome the same challenges I see in my clients; whether I'm coaching them 1:1, in a group program, or virtually, they're universal. The sad thing is, you've been led to believe these lies. Here are two of them:

"You have to dim yourself." I'm sick of successful, confident women feeling pressure to fly under the radar because society cuts them down when they're at the top. It's okay to achieve, be strong, and unapologetically yourself. You don't need to dull your sparkle. Even if others feel intimidated or jealous. We're not doing anything wrong; we're raising the bar!

"You can't afford to delegate or hire help." You can't afford not to. Leveraging your time, money, and skills is essential. By doing so, you can earn more revenue, focus on your core competencies, have more fun and, most importantly, gain time for the things that truly matter. Besides, my virtual assistant team is more affordable and highly competent than you might think. And what if the person you hired made you enough money to pay for themselves? It's a no-brainer.

Q: What sets your business apart from competitors in the market?

A: As I shared with Jack Canfield in my interview, I not only provide proven strategies, ideas, and a clear plan to help overcome obstacles with the best solutions, but I also practice what I preach. I don't just teach how to be dynamic, prioritize satisfaction, or delegate work to scale your business—I actively run a successful business using these concepts, strategies, and systems.

Also, not many have my experience level, or they've fallen behind on the latest in life, business, and technology. They're on the sidelines, not in the game. I'm different because I still run a balanced and successful business while raising two children. I'm not perfect, but I've been through the same challenges my clients face, and I guide them through efficiently and effectively. I also provide significant transformation by helping clients clarify their goals, and when needed, I connect them with vetted virtual assistants to simplify their lives and businesses.

I invite you to see me at events, on stage, or online to see what sets me apart. Also, it's important to note that when you hire me, you get me, not someone who works for me: you get my coaching, consulting, and business expertise. These are why I have over 1000+ five-star reviews.

Q: What is something special you are working on?

A: I'm creating a one-woman show using my stand-up comedy, coaching and keynote speaking to provoke women to wake up their most dynamic selves.

Q: Pink or red lipstick?

A: Pink is for every day, and red is for when I want to be in my power.

Erian Baxter is currently Co-owner, with Bob Putnam, of Deep Cove Kayak, Coast Outdoors, Cates Park Paddling Centre, Deep Cove Collective and Jericho Beach Kayak. Previously she founded The Block Clothing Store and Bebop Vintage. She fosters her creativity with Conspire2Inspire inspirational jewelry. She is a volunteer board member of The Seymour Art Gallery, and the Deep Cove Community Association, and the proud mom of three amazing children with her husband, Kevin.

ERIAN *Baxter*

Q: Can you tell me about your journey as an entrepreneur? What inspired you to start your own business?

A: I'm a serial entrepreneur so I've had a few starts over the years yet the common theme has been an enthusiasm for sharing my passions with others. My first passion business was Bebop, a vintage clothing store with my business partner and friend, Sally, located in Vancouver and opened way back in 1981. Next came The Block, again in Vancouver and opened in 1984, a clothing store and cappuccino bar that originally carried young Canadian designers as I had developed a passion for the great styles we have in Canada. Now it's Deep Cove Kayak, Coast Outdoors, Cates Park Paddling Centre, Deep Cove Collective and Jericho Beach Kayak, all of which I co-own with my business partner, Bob Putnam. We grew all of these from our original purchase of Deep Cove Kayak from my mother, Ingrid Baxter, who was the founder. With all of these enterprises we share our passion for getting people out paddling and cross-country skiing, as well as building community and inspiring deeper connections to the outdoors and one another.

Q: What role do you think mentorship and support networks play for women in entrepreneurship?

A: I have found that women thrive when they are supported by other women, so finding networks and mentorship is key.

I purposely build community amongst women for this very reason. For 22 years now I've been hosting a Women on Water (WOW) kayaking evening and this has proven so satisfying as I see friendships and connections being made all the time amongst my ladies.

Q: What advice would you give to other women who are considering starting their own businesses?

A: My advice has always been to research it to a certain extent, but not over think it, speak to some others that already do it, make sure you're passionate about it and then take the leap!

Q: How do you build and maintain a strong team, and what qualities do you look for in potential hires?

A: We look for a positive attitude first in our people as that's crucial to their success with us. We know we can teach any knowledge or technical skills they might need but their own approach to life comes from their earlier learning and a positive one ensures they will thrive with us.

Q: Can you share a particularly memorable success story or milestone from your entrepreneurial journey?

A: Recently our company was nominated and won Business of the Year. This was an especially rewarding milestone as it really recognized all the efforts our entire team puts in to making every thing we do matter. We were fully acknowledged for both our excellent customer service as well as our community building which meant so much to us all.

Also, recently I was pleasantly surprised by being nominated personally for a prestigious award, who knows if I will actually receive it, however even be nominated for it affirms for me the approach I take in my life is inspirational and that's mostly how I'd like to be recognized. I have a saying that is special to me, "conspire to inspire" that is at the core of my way of being. It's such an important saying for me that it's the name of my next passion business as I'm now encouraging others with special sayings hammered on to silver pendants!! *Note, Erian recently received the King Charles the Third Coronation Medal for making a difference in her community.*

Q: What sets your business apart from competitors in the market?

A: We've grown our business along with our key people so I believe one way we are different than others in our field is the knowledge, passion and commitment our key staff have to our purpose of inspiring deeper connections to the outdoors and one another. Our staff also have full knowledge in their respective areas and happily share that with our customers, providing confidence to our customers as well.

Q: Looking ahead, what are your goals and aspirations for the future of your business?

A: We want to continue to maintain our high standard of service and knowledge as well as continue to create ways to gather people in the outdoors. Staying active and getting outside is so good for all of us it's a pleasure to keep on creating opportunities and access for all our existing customers while attracting new one too.

Final Question: Pink or red lipstick?

PINK!!!

Renee Lodge is a Licensed Investment & Insurance Specialist, located in the lower mainland of British Columbia. Her clients and teammates span across the country from BC to Ontario. Her specialty and passion is to educate Canadians about How Money Works, and to wipe out Financial Illiteracy. She thrives on helping families become the Best Version of their financial selves that they can be, and to have each life she touches have an an incredible relationship with their money.

RENEE
Lodge

My entrepreneurial spirit was ignited after meeting many successful, driven, and Excited business people in the financial industry. Knowing these business owners in the investment space gave me a window into their passion for making people's lives better. Their work ethic, focus and life goals, were aligned with how I applied my own work ethic while working for someone else…. So what if I tried this? How could I fail if I applied my strong moral character and work ethic working for myself!? I was excited, not scared! One would think it may have been nerve wracking to leave a very well paying Job as a Pharma Sales Director, but that wasn't the case at all. I decided to embrace this challenge to run my own financial firm as I embraced all challenges, with integrity, excitement, and positive action!

Today, the financial field is filled with wonderful women! Why? Because women love seeing other women succeed, whether as a client or as a teammate. I believe one of our advantages as women is that we genuinely love empowering, uplifting, and encouraging one another. I've had the professional and personal benefit of knowing many Wonder-Women as Mentors and Leaders! Bound by our experiences as daughters, sisters, wives, mothers, mother-in-laws, grandmothers…. We truly GET each other, share our success journeys, and want the Best for one another! THIS is our SuperPower.

We make decisions often from the heart, even in business. I believe we have the gift of nurturing people a fair bit differently than our male counterparts, and this is a bonus, not a hinderance! Using our hearts as well as our heads to help each other is truly beneficial.

There is monotony, frustration, and challenges in every woman's business. No one is immune! Remaining grateful is of utmost importance and helps break the frustration. Become grateful for every minute of every single day! Managing my own Self-Talk has been a key ingredient to staying resilient throughout those tough times. Surrounding myself with like-minded, uplifting business people, who are focused on similar goals that I'm focused on, is huge. I am proud to say that I am exceptionally good at removing negative things and negative people from my life. Another SuperPower! Creating a positive environment is a daily discipline, and one that I have come to cherish!

Being a broke single mother was one of the most challenging times of my life. It wasn't for a long period of time, but it was long enough for me to know I never wanted to be in that place ever again. I always had high paying Jobs and the ability to live a great lifestyle. Then I went through divorce. Divorce was the last place I thought I would ever be. I was devastated emotionally, mentally, physically, and, especially financially. A friend gave me a book on how money actually works. I devoured it! I had been making so many mistakes with my money, and had been going in the wrong financial direction for a long time. It was time to make some big changes.

When I found this industry, or this industry found me, I knew I wanted to help those who suffered from financial illiteracy, especially women. I realized how little I knew about the science of how money worked, and the relationship one needed to have with their money…. Why were we not taught this in school? Why were most people suffering from this disease they called Financial Illiteracy? Why were so many drowning in debt? Why were people not investing like this book talked about?

I had to learn as much as I could and pass this onto others. That's when I knew….. this was my calling.

I made the decision to change my life. And has it ever changed!

Today, our team is helping hundreds of families across the country stay on track and achieve their financial goals. These families may not have achieved their financial hopes and dreams if I had not stepped into their financial lives. THIS is how people are blessed by your decision, by your responding to that tug in your heart to start that business. You can positively affect so many lives.

There are a lot of considerations going into business for oneself. Regret was one of the largest factors that danced in my mind when I was deciding to move forward, or to stay in my job. I look back now and see how many people's lives have been so positively affected by my decision to step into this business, and it's incredibly heartwarming. I'm not sure where they might be today if we had not stepped into their lives.

Our goal is to continue to grow our Advisor team size, and our client base by empowering people to have a relationship with their money. Yes, you can love on your money, versus love your money. We can do amazing, wonderful things when we are financially free to help those we love, and help the causes that are important to us. It is a privilege to serve those we do, and to continue to positively change the lives of our fellow Canadians.

Tanya Benlow is a dynamic Business Strategist based in Australia, passionate about mentoring individuals to unlock their full potential and build thriving online empires.

TANYA
Benlow

Q: Can you tell me about your journey as an entrepreneur? What inspired you to start your own business?

A: I owned and operated three restaurants in my early 20s, working as a chef by trade. Unfortunately, I lost my last one, which left us broke. I then changed my career, working with a large manufacturer. However, I suffered a serious spinal injury that led to two major spinal fusions and multiple additional injuries. I was told I'd never walk again and would be in a wheelchair for the rest of my life.

I changed careers again, moving into education and training for the next 20 years. But then, I had another serious accident at work, which ended my working career. This pushed me into entrepreneurship. It was a line-in-the-sand moment when, in early 2019, I decided my career was over, but as a workaholic, I needed to learn how to generate an income from home. I didn't want to rely on a disability pension, as this was my second major permanent disability classification.

I spent the last 10 years working with large-scale businesses, helping them train and educate their workers to run lean operations. I realized I had the transferable skill set to do this online. However, I first needed to learn and understand how the online space works. So, during the year I was in recovery from four surgeries in 2019, I upskilled by taking four online courses simultaneously, learning how to build and scale online businesses through automation. Once I realized I had been generating around $6 million a year in new business for employers, I decided to do this for myself instead. Plus, everyone was getting into the online space.

One of the programs I took focused on how to build and scale your social media and personal branding. Another taught me how to build and scale Facebook groups. Now, I mentor others to do the same and add high-ticket items to their businesses to generate a high-impact income online or in person.

The first year of this journey was full of self-discovery. I realized I wasn't a nice person, especially to my husband, as I had been a high-profile manager. Once I began reading entrepreneurial books, I recognized that I wasn't happy and needed to find myself. So, during the first six months, I let go of the realization that I wouldn't be returning to work. I committed to doing whatever it took to build my business and generate an income because I didn't want to rely on a pension.

I made my business about sharing the journey of becoming an entrepreneur. When I launched "The Hot Seat" for entrepreneurs on social media, I interviewed people I had met across Australia. Especially once COVID hit, many businesses either shifted or closed. I interviewed some amazing people, and then the show went global. This built my authority, gave me the courage to speak, and helped me overcome the fear I initially had.

Speaking or delivering training in a corporate environment is very different from starting online. I was terrified when I first started doing live talks, particularly on topics like aged care, where I discussed my experience with my mum. I also shared talks on total and permanent disability, insurances, and navigating Workcover claims. It was both scary and fun. In 2019, I learned so much about myself and what I was truly capable of. I met incredible people and made lifelong friends.

Q: What are some of the biggest challenges you've faced as a woman entrepreneur, and how have you overcome them?

A: Internal fear and worrying about what family and friends would think were significant challenges. I had to learn how to grow a thick skin and stop worrying about what others thought. Once you're on social media, you're open to all sorts of comments.

I read more books and learned how to remove these fears. I did a lot of self-reflection and spiritual healing as well. I had mostly worked with men all my life, but then I realized my audience was women. It was a different experience learning to build friendships with women outside of the typical employer-employee relationship. I came to understand that I'm a connector, helping people connect with each other.

I never thought about how I wanted to be remembered if I were to die, but that realization was pivotal. I understood that I was here to do something meaningful. Dealing with people who disliked me on social media wasn't personal—it was just part of the platform. Learning to block people became easier each day.

Q: How do you maintain a work-life balance while running your own business? What strategies have you found most effective for networking and building professional relationships as a female entrepreneur?

A: I had to set clear boundaries, just like in a regular job. Mondays are my fully online day and evening, and my calendar starts on Tuesday. Wednesdays are dedicated to business, starting with networking events with BNI, followed by calls or training with my business partners. I began with three days a week. I've always avoided working on weekends as that's my time with my husband. However, if he's working, I'll take a few calls. I wanted a fully automated online business so I could travel for weeks on end without needing to be online. I can generate posts a month in advance and have affiliate links where people can start the buying process without my involvement.

We drop customers into a self-paced social media training platform that's easy to follow. We also have a dedicated sales team that conducts a 45-minute call to get them started. I've stuck to this schedule and can be flexible, but our family is our first priority, especially as they are nearing the end of their lives. This business works around us, unlike most others where the business dictates the schedule. I wanted a time-and-location freedom business model that didn't require me to work and still generated an uncapped income, which it has.

Q: In your experience, what are some common misconceptions or stereotypes about women in business, and how do you challenge or overcome them?

1. Skepticism: Women often wonder if they can succeed or think they know everything. When we ask a few questions, it's easy to identify the gaps.

2. Closed-Mindedness: Some women, especially those who have been in the space for a long time, may have a closed-door approach. When we conduct a social media overview, we can pinpoint their issues and offer recommendations. Many think it's easier to pay someone else, but at the end of the day, it's their business. If they don't understand it properly, things can go wrong. Once we show them how easy it is to learn, they gain control of their business, which can then grow more effectively.

3. Running Ads: Running ads is a common conversation topic, as well as achieving organic growth. We can train women in a few weeks, and before they know it, they have better ads running with more conversions.

Q: How do you approach leadership and team-building within your company?

A: I hold calls two nights a week with my team to mentor them during the first three months of their business. There's a lot to navigate, as they need to learn about automation on social media and the water business. We have a replicable business model that works and converts. I hold everyone accountable, and each week they self-assess whether they would hire themselves based on their performance.

We focus on attraction marketing, so they learn how people connect and buy from others. We move them through training each week, mentoring them through issues, and helping them break old habits to form new ones. We offer a 12-month social media training course for those with no prior business experience, as well as for advanced entrepreneurs who need to polish their skills.

Daina Gardiner is a Certified Holistic Nutrition Consultant supporting women in preventing and reversing perimenopause symptoms by teaching them how to identify the root causes first and tune inwards for food, nutrient and wellness choices that align with their body's unique needs.

Q: What advice would you give to other women who are considering starting their own businesses?

A: Entrepreneurship is a significant decision, especially for women seeking an escape from the corporate world for the sake of their mental well-being. It's crucial to establish your business for the right reasons. Ensure that your business's mission and purpose align with your passion. Be prepared to tackle technological challenges, share your stories publicly, and embrace the initial time constraints that come with entrepreneurship.

A common mistake is not starting with a clear vision. Crafting a precise business plan along with sales and marketing strategies is essential. Learn from my experience – make sure to have a solid understanding of your business's direction and potential challenges.

Q: Can you tell us about your journey as an entrepreneur and what inspired you to start your own business?

A: My passion for nutrition coaching ignited over 15 years ago. Experiencing personal health improvements fueled my desire to help women take control of their health and well-being. My holistic nutrition protocols not only resolved my chronic health issues but inspired a mission to educate women on hormonal health and a seamless transition into menopause.

Q: What sets your business apart from competitors in the market?

A: I've personally overcome a few health challenges, particularly Chronic Fatigue Syndrome. I understand the struggles of exhaustion and offer practical, achievable nutrition plans. I emphasize simplicity, debunking the myth that a complicated diet is the solution. My unique perspective and personal triumphs distinguish me from competitors in the market. I've also personally been laser-focused on rebalancing and maintaining harmonious hormones in pursuit of transitioning into menopause with little to no symptoms; unlike many other perimenopause coaches, I proactively started this journey and deeply understand how hormonal needs change as a woman gets older.

Q: How do you prioritize tasks and manage time effectively as an entrepreneur?

A: : Effectively managing time and prioritizing tasks are crucial skills for entrepreneurs and, honestly, weren't easy for me at first. I've transitioned from the misconception that busyness equals success. Prioritizing income-generating tasks and audience growth is paramount. Focusing on essential strategies prevents falling into the trap of "shiny object syndrome." Repurposing content is a valuable tactic, allowing for consistency and creativity when you're drawing a blank!

Q: Have you found any specific advantages or opportunities in being a woman in your industry?

A: What started as a natural approach to clearing hormonal cystic acne led to effortless weight loss, putting my chronic fatigue into remission, and resolving 20+ years of health issues. As a woman, I know firsthand the physical and emotional toll of hormone imbalances. True balance goes beyond medications and supplements—it's about finding the root cause. I share my insights to help women not only improve their health but also release limiting patterns and guilt imposed by society. I break the rules when it means better health, well-being, and vibrancy.

Q: What problem or need does your business solve, and what motivated you to address it?

A: When I discovered a little-known strategy that crushed my chronic fatigue, cystic acne, weight gain, insomnia, and more within a few years—without needing constant resets—I knew I had to dive deeper into using food as medicine. I'd always been into healthy eating, but understanding how to reverse health issues through food fascinated me. Now, I'm excited to share this simple, delicious approach with women because no one should have to live with frustrating symptoms. I'm here to help them get rid of them for good.

Q: How do you stay innovative and adapt to changes in your industry?

A: Staying innovative in the dynamic health industry requires a discerning approach. Many health coaches echo popular trends without verifying their legitimacy and I'm not one to follow health fads without proper verification of legitimacy. I regularly research and validate health claims, diving into studies and research papers. This commitment to science-backed information ensures that my ideas and advice are credible and relevant.

The key lies in aligning your business with your passion, creating a clear plan, and staying adaptable in the ever-evolving business landscape. And be honest with yourself about when help is needed – hiring coaches and mentors has been truly game-changing for my own business and personal growth.

Q: Pink or red lipstick?

A: Oh, and lipstick color? Pink for me, please!

Laura Gindac, Elite Business Strategist / Visionary Entrepreneurial Mentor | Wellness Advocate. Owner & Founder of XQ-SLESS WELLNESS SUPPORT TRIBE & OMNI-RISE.

Q: Have you found any specific advantages or opportunities in being a woman in your industry?

A: Women who run businesses have far greater opportunities for growth, I believe. We have an innate nature to be more attentive to small details, provide extra comfort, and show compassion for what clients deep down want and need. So, as women, we possess a quality that is superior. We are also great multitaskers; we can arrange multiple tasks to get done, whether it be by ourselves or by delegating accordingly. We are creators by nature, so we can think of extraordinary things, and with patience and resilience, we produce the necessary outcomes.

Q: How do you maintain a work-life balance while running your own business?

A: A healthy structure of habits is essential for success in any area of life. Prioritizing my well-being through movement of the body, stillness of the mind, and a healthy diet are non-negotiable for me. When overwhelm hits due to excess workload or any stressful situation, I then know my mind and body can guide me through the turbulence.

Q: What advice would you give to other women who are considering starting their own businesses?

A: First, follow your passion! If you do not love what you do, it will become a chore, and no one puts effort towards something they do not love. Love, passion, and desire create miracles, so follow your heart and don't worry about the 'how'; just stay loyal to your dream.

Q: How do you stay motivated and resilient during tough times in your business?

A: It's probably fair to say we cannot stay motivated 100% of the time; however, we can remember it's okay to take a rest from workload or prospecting. Most people believe they must be full throttle all the time to succeed; although motivation comes when feeling energetic and clear-minded, taking time out without feeling guilty allows new ideas to emerge when relaxed. The mind cannot produce creativity when stressed; it looks for any way to escape, resulting in desperation and potentially worse results or harming your business and personal identity.

Q: What problem or need does your business solve, and what motivated you to address it?

A: I help people who struggle to find confidence within themselves and believe in themselves without waiting for external validation. If we wait to feel successful because we have clients and then believe in ourselves, this process may never happen; or if clients leave, so does our self-worth. Knowing who you are simply because you choose to be that person is true, authentic confidence; this self-made self-concept ensures no one can make or break you. You will always find a solution and rise above on your own once you have this self-constructed self-concept of yourself.

Q: Can you discuss a failure or setback your business encountered, and how did you bounce back from it?

A: I had many setbacks when starting my business: from minimal clients to not having my marketing look professional, and thinking I had to look like and speak like everyone else on social media if I wanted to perform like those successful business owners. After some time, I realized these were my biggest blessings in disguise. The setback after setback was only an opportunity for me to see what mistakes I had made, and therefore, I was forced to rethink my whole situation. It provided me with the space to be more honest with myself, open my awareness, and step into a grander place with newfound wisdom that I had discovered. I knew the solution! It was my own created self-image that had dropped to a low level of unworthiness. I had to immediately upgrade my mindset to raise my self-worth. I had to go within my imagination and recreate the version of myself mentally. The rearrangement of my mind was the only work I had to do; the rest took care of itself.

Q: What sets your business apart from competitors in the market?

I don't see others in my field as competitors, but rather as potential partners in a shared mission. I believe there's enough abundance in the world for everyone to thrive, and that true impact comes through collaboration, not competition. My business is driven by the desire to unite like-minded individuals and organizations, each offering their own unique wisdom and perspective, to serve the greater good.

Together, we aim to lift up those who may be struggling in different areas of their lives, while helping entrepreneurs expand their reach and visibility. By collaborating, we can combine our strengths, share knowledge, and offer support that benefits all.

At the core of my work is a commitment to providing solutions that are accessible and affordable for everyone. I believe that no one should be left behind in their journey to grow both personally and professionally. My role is simply to help facilitate that growth, and I am humbled to be a part of that process.

Q: What do you believe are the keys to building a strong brand identity and reputation?

A: Self-confidence and self-belief, nothing more, nothing less!

Photo credit: Dawid Kozlowski

Magdalena Gulda with a Master of Philosophy from the University of Warsaw, is a Certified Experienced Sound Healer and Trainer, Craative Manager for Spas, Energy Coach for Business and the CEO of The Sound Healing Institute. With 24 years of experience, she has dedicated herself to the realm of sound and healing, primarily working in Mexico and Europe. Along her journey, Magdalena has played a decisive role in redefining and reshaping the paradigms of music, performance, and therapy. Today, she offers a unique opportunity to share her wisdom and expertise to the world.

My name is Magdalena, and I was born in Poland. I would describe my path as " THE CONQUEROR OF OBSTACLES". Some people don't know what they want to do in life; they haven't found their purpose or passion. I DID. From the very beginning. I discovered my musical talent when I was 4 years old, yet my family didn't want me to pursue a career in music. Despite this, I remained close to music while pursuing my academic career.

I was in the midst of a postgraduate program focused on healing through art when my tutor invited a sound healing specialist. Believe it or not, everyone felt that I HAD to do a session with her. Although it was extremely expensive for me at the time, and I was searching for excuses, my colleagues were so persuasive, I decided to book the session. AND IT WAS A MINDBLOWING AND LIFE CHANGING EXPERIENCE! When I experienced the first sounds of those professional singing bowls on my body, I felt at home. It was as if all my dreams were coming true. This was it. I belonged here. So, I made the decision to study sound healing. However, as this was about 25 years ago and I was still living in a country that had recently transitioned from communism, where access to resources was limited, it took me some time to find a place where I could learn it.

What I'm sharing here is, if something is meant to be, it will happen, even if it seems impossible. When I began my journey, I couldn't even fully envision the path ahead, from being just a student of sound healing massage with singing bowls to becoming a leading trainer and coach in my own growing company, providing training and courses worldwide.

The beginning was challenging due to the mainstream paradigm still dominating many areas of life. Many people still do not operate as sovereign beings, preferring to delegate their own power to others. Consequently, it was difficult for many to understand how sound healing works and how it can help them. I received many critics, even humiliation ("are we preparing a salad in those bowls?"), yet I had a strong will and belief, THIS IS MY PATH, THE RIGHT PATH.

Just today, slowly but surely, we started to receive comprehensive scientific studies on frequencies, brain waves, and heart coherence. Nowadays, I possess many more tools to make my work more efficient. I still observe that the sound healing industry is predominantly male-dominated. Men often find it easier to secure contracts due to their access to other men working as managers or directors at venues. They are also more adept at negotiating and securing favorable contracts. However, I see a growing demand for a more feminine approach. Women like myself are opening doors for others to follow. Personally, I send my students to various events to provide them with safe and well-paid experiences. Many of them have gone on to establish their own companies in different countries. This approach undoubtedly sets my business apart from competitors in the market.

As a woman, I foster unity, integration, and collaboration. I nurture new leaders, uplift people, and help them realize their unique qualities. When I teach students, I not only impart knowledge but also boost their self-esteem, highlight opportunities, and encourage them to recognize their strengths. I now see this as the most effective strategy for networking and building my professional business. Moreover, it contributes to the development of a new generation of conscious and collaborative leaders and the creation of healthier societies. This new paradigm places me in a completely different position from ego-centered, competitive-oriented businesses.

The most important message I share from my experiences is NEVER GIVE UP. Never let other people make you doubt your reality, your dream, your vision. Find people who speak the same language, support you, endorse you. Cut loose the ones who only project their own misery and complexes. If you have strong values and trust, sooner or later, you will receive all the information and help you need. You will start to connect to adequate circles, you will contract the best people to create your dream team. You will outgrow your own shadows and forge them into your superpowers. Believe in yourself! Concentrate on the positive. Don't hesitate to ask questions. Never stop learning.

I'm a great example of the rule that if you choose yourself, life will choose you!

Blessings to you! See you!

Jaishri Hall is a Holistic Empowerment Coach and Mentor.

Q: Can you tell us about your journey as an entrepreneur and what inspired you to start your own business?

A: My journey as an entrepreneur has been a rollercoaster of challenges and victories, each twist and turn shaping me into a resilient leader, driven by a vision to make a meaningful impact in the world and in the lives of others. My inspiration to fully commit to my business came in 2021 when I decided to invest in my first high-ticket program. I had considered it before, but this time, I knew I needed support. I sought guidance from someone who had already walked the path, allowing me to save time and join a community of women on similar journeys, supporting each other along the way.

Q: What advice would you give to someone who is considering starting their own business?

A: My advice to anyone considering starting their own business is to begin by deeply trusting yourself and your unique gifts. The journey will undoubtedly challenge you in ways you never expected, but those challenges are opportunities for growth, resilience, and expansion. Align your business vision with your personal purpose—what truly lights you up from the inside. Don't be afraid to take up space, even when self-doubt creeps in. Surround yourself with mentors, peers, and a support system that not only believes in your vision but holds you accountable to it.

Remember, you are the creator of your reality. Your energy and mindset will shape the success of your business, so cultivate an abundance mentality and believe in your limitless potential. Setbacks and failures are simply part of the process, and with each one, you'll grow stronger and more aligned with your true path. Invest in yourself, your healing, and your learning—both in business and in life. When you embrace this, not only will you succeed, but you will also inspire countless others along the way.

94

Q: How do you balance work-life commitments as an entrepreneur?

A: Whether I'm working or engaging in personal activities, I find balance by connecting them with my values. Time with loved ones, sports, bellydancing, and going to the beach all align my energy, allowing me to act from inspired actions and continuously learn from the best. Everything I do is intentional, ensuring it's in harmony with my core beliefs. My relationships reflect this alignment, and I make space for what truly matters.

Balance comes from respecting all areas of life, allowing them to flow together in harmony. When I play padel tennis, whether in a match or a tournament, I train my mind to push beyond limits, creating intentional growth by stepping out of my comfort zone. Similarly, bellydancing allows me to become an instrument of energy, flowing and moving through me. It's true what they say: the way you do one thing is the way you do everything.

Q: Can you discuss a failure or setback your business encountered, and how you bounced back from it?

A: Setbacks are simply opportunities to gain clarity, which always leads to growth and empowerment. As long as you keep this in mind, you can navigate the rollercoaster of challenges that need to be overcome. I faced a difficult period when I fell into an abusive relationship that mirrored the way I was treating myself, neglecting my own well-being. But I took responsibility for my role in it and embarked on a journey of healing and transformation. Losing everything helped me rediscover the most important piece of the puzzle: my true self. I emerged stronger, determined to lead with purpose. As I applied these lessons, the universe aligned with my new path, and people and opportunities began to appear, turning every obstacle into a blessing.

Q: What do you believe are the keys to building a strong brand identity and reputation?

A: The foundation of a strong brand identity and reputation lies in staying true to your values in both life and business. Challenges will arise, but as you give yourself permission to evolve and embrace the new version of yourself, things start to fall into place. You begin to attract from a place of authenticity. It's important to walk the talk—set an example, let your dreams fuel your actions, and build consciously, knowing what you stand for and fully owning it. Stand firm in your words, commitments, and mission. Be creative, flexible, and open to new opportunities while learning from other inspiring professionals. Most importantly, stay authentic to your truth.

Q: Looking ahead, what are your goals and aspirations for the future of your business?

A: My goal is to support, uplift, inspire, and empower millions of women globally on their transformational journeys. Together, we're creating a nurturing space where women honor their soul's calling, embrace authenticity, and wholeheartedly pursue their dreams. Through soul-led Coaching, Bellydancing, Mentorship and Manifestation Principles, I guide them to fully embody their essence, unleashing their inner power to manifest their deepest desires. We cultivate resilience, courage, and unwavering self-belief. This creates a ripple effect, igniting the magic within, and nurturing a global community of women who live their truth and manifest lives of profound fulfillment.

Q: Pink or red lipstick?

A: My instinct led me to shift from light, unnoticeable lipstick to bold RED. It symbolized the leader within me embracing a new identity—going all in and becoming unstoppable. Red became synonymous with confidence, silencing external judgments, and igniting my inner energy and unlimited potential. It wasn't just a fashion choice; it was a conscious embrace of inner strength and leadership. Each swipe of red lipstick reflects my commitment to passion and determination, going far beyond makeup. For me, red represents empowerment and self-expression.

Amber Hill is a busy wife, a mother of two beautiful children, and works as a Behaviour Interventionist for children with autism.

AMBER *Hill*

Q: Can you tell us about your journey as an entrepreneur and what inspired you to start your own business?

A: I was working for the School District as an Applied Behaviour Analyst (working specifically alongside children who have autism spectrum disorder), and the District made some very concerning changes to my job description, so I was faced with having to decide if I should stay, or leave after 10 years. Ultimately, I chose to leave and I started my own business doing ABA work privately. This change was totally unexpected and not in my long term plan. I knew I wanted to continue working in the autism field, so after considering all of my options, I took a leap of faith and went out on my own. I had the full support of family and friends and I soon realized that it was an amazing opportunity to work the way I wanted to – without restrictions being placed on me by administrators, etc.

By starting my own business as a Senior Behaviour Interventionist, it has allowed me the freedom to work directly in the child's home with the parents, siblings and caregivers, giving them tools and strategies for success. It has also allowed me to choose my own hours and therefore have a much more balanced lifestyle.

Q: What problem or need does your business solve and what motivated you to address it?

A: Many of my friends were approaching me with questions about autism. Some had concerns regarding their own child, some were concerned about a niece or nephew, sometimes it was about a neighbour or a friend's child. I offered advice about qualified websites to visit, how to go about seeking testing and diagnosis and tips for ways to best use autism funding. These interactions motivated me to start a Behaviour Intervention Instagram page, where this information would be available to a wider audience.

There is always a need to bring more awareness and understanding to the public about people who have autism spectrum disorder. My hope is that my Behaviour Intervention Instagram page will help make a scary diagnosis a little less scary and a little more manageable by providing tools and strategies for coping and succeeding. I provide a safe space for parents to ask questions as well as find support. I want to educate others on how best to interact with a loved one with ASD and generate more inclusion for those living with ASD.

Q: How do you balance work-life commitments as an entrepreneur?

A: For me, balance is really about setting priorities and then having a schedule that helps me stay organized. When I left my School District job, I went from a typical 7 hour work day to being at home all of the time, working on my business 10 minutes here and there throughout the day. That was too chaotic and unproductive. Now, I schedule my work time so I can go to a quiet space and stay focused on my goals. This allows me to be present for my family and allows me time to grow my business. By being my own boss, I can work as much or as little as I want.

Q: What advice would you give to someone who is considering starting their own business?

A: Whether starting your own business comes unexpectedly, like mine did, or it's something you have been planning for a long time, make sure you are doing something you love. Seek advice, talk to friends and family, do your research and create a sustainable business plan. Once you take the leap, you want to be well prepared and not have any regrets.

As I said earlier, I did not expect to start my own business, so before I made this decision I took the time to think about my future and what my priorities are. I love being a Mom, I wanted the freedom to be there for my 2 children as well as contribute an income for my family. Starting my own business and going into it well prepared has set me up for success. No regrets!

Q: Can you share a story about a particularly memorable customer interaction or experience?

A: A very close friend of mine has a daughter who was diagnosed with ASD at the age of two. She became my first client under my new business. Given that this is such a close friend, I definitely felt the pressure to succeed. I am, however, confident in my abilities, and I was excited about having the opportunity to help.

The household was chaotic as the daughter struggled with meltdowns and communication. I took time to understand the family dynamics, took extensive notes on the child's behaviour and triggers and developed a plan for moving forward. It was a plan for the entire family, not just the daughter.

Within six months of working with this sweet girl and her family, her communication, emotional control and anxiety had greatly improved. The entire family dynamic was so much calmer and happier.

I have had many messages of gratitude from my friend and it has given me the confidence to continue to pursue and grow my business. I love my job and always find it rewarding, but to have my friend trust me with her daughter, and to see the successes they have had together, has truly been one of the greatest things I have been a part of.

Q: Looking ahead, what are your goals and aspirations for the future of your business?

A: I definitely want to continue to grow my Behaviour Instagram page. There is so much for parents to learn once their child has a diagnosis of ASD and this is a free and easy place for them to start. I want to focus my posts on providing resources about Applied Behaviour Analysis, positive reinforcement , government funding, transitioning into a school environment and so much more. This is a space that allows encouragement and support, it reminds families that they are not alone, and most importantly there are success stories and experiences.

As for my business, I plan to expand my client base once my children are in school. I get many requests and have a lengthy waiting list, so as I add clients, I may need to hire staff to take on the extra workload.

Q: Pink or red lipstick?

A: Pink...definitely pink!!

Lynda Honing is the Founder and Facilitator at The Urban Oasis, located in White Rock, BC, Canada. As a highly skilled Reiki Master and Massage Specialist, Lynda brings extensive expertise and a deep commitment to holistic wellness to her practice.

LYNDA
Honing

Q: What inspired you to start your own business?

A: I was inspired to start my own business because I wanted to make a difference to others with respect to healing from my own journey of healing.

I had multiple MVA's and massage and Reiki healing were the best addition to my recovery. I knew from my own experience of suffering that this is how I could really help others.

At the time I was a hairstylist and I felt like I was missing something in my career. I was working at home in our garage that we converted into a Hair salon called "The Eagles Nest". My tagline at that time was "I'll trim your split ends but I won't clip your wings, I may even teach you to fly" Now I actually teach others how to find their wings ☺ and soar in my Reiki classes and also while I heal through my massages. I just didn't know it then but I was close to my mission in life. It all began with me massaging hands and shoulders of my clients while they were processing their colour through our deep conversations they inspired me to pursue a career as a massage therapist and healer. The fact that I grew to the business I have today was purely a blessing and I'm grateful everyday.

Q: How do you maintain a work-life balance while running your own business?

A: Finding a life balance is easy for me for a couple of reasons. My wellness Center is located in my garden and my family are all Reiki Masters trained by myself. They completely understand the importance of healing others and want me to be successful. My family get to "see" each individual as they come and go and our connections to so many. It's a beautiful thing to witness the growth in others as they become more aware of themselves, their goals realized and aspirations fulfilled. Not only do I feel such gratitude in my heart but also my family blooms as we watch all those who come to see me also Bloom! My oldest son Makenzy has also become an RMT so he shares my healing space. Such a gift to have Makenzy work with me in the healing business. I also have a fantastic community of other professional women in health and wellness that we mutually refer patients. This is such a wonderful opportunity to be a part of the fabric of health within a small community.

Q: What problems does my business solve and how do you address it?

A: I feel that most people are living in a stressful environment and that causes symptoms of discomfort and disharmony within the body. My Reiki Massage treatments help in reducing stress which improves sleep by allowing the mind to relax. Reiki massages also boost the immune system and allow for more energy and vibrancy. Having the ability to listen and understand what my patients are feeling allows me to be a better healer thus helping find a more balanced life with solutions and guidance and direction. My massages are 1.5 hours followed by sound frequency to give each individual the time needed to really get to a place of calm and serenity. This is where true healing can occur. What has motivated me all through my career is the result I see after treatment. It's really beautiful to witness someone in bloom.

Q: What sets your business apart from competitors in the market?

A: My garden in a small house built specifically for my massages. It's a lovely space and healing just from the fact that it's not the normal location most are used to. It's quiet. Peaceful and lends itself to having my patients feel grounded, soulful and taken on a special journey. Everyone leaves feeling so relaxed that sometimes they need to sit in the garden to take a moment before driving home. This is beautiful to witness the calm and healing they experience after my Reiki Massage. Having individuals experience this kind of healing from myself really brings joy and gratitude for the work I've chosen to do. Come and see me to experience your own Reiki healing journey. If you'd like to learn more about Reiki I also teach classes in Reiki. www.theurbanoasis.info

Q: How do you keep your patients?

A: I make sure to follow up and have them know that I am truly there for their health and wellbeing. I also connect regularly to ensure they stick to the plan we talk about. I often hear that they feel grateful that I've continued to keep in touch and to keep them on track with their health goals. My personalized approach demonstrates to them that I value their unique needs and I'm committed to providing exceptional care.

Q: Can you share a story about a particularly memorable customer interaction or experience?

A: I've had many amazing experiences with patients over the years and some very well known in the film and music industry. It was very interesting and lovely to massage one of my favourite actors. ☺ But one that really stands out for me is a lady who had breast cancer and then a double mastectomy. She came to see me for a very long time very regularly. I saw her go through a very difficult time but with my Reiki healing massages she recovered and did very well. This was a number of years ago and she's still experiencing a vibrant life!

Q: What do you believe are the keys to building a strong brand identity and reputation?

A: Building a strong brand identity and reputation. I believe that being involved in a business group is key to building success. I belonged to "Java Lovers" for a few years and through our business group I became more successful. When you have others to keep you accountable and working on the growth of your business it's truly the recipe for success. The other key is to create a business built on integrity, compassion and respect and people will refer and continue to see you. We all like to be seen and heard and treated with respect and kindness. This is the key to your business growth. People will always remember how you make them feel!

Q: Pink or red lipstick? A: PINK

Alyson Jones is a professional therapist, speaker, writer, educator, business owner and the Clinical Director of Alyson Jones & Associates. "The greatest joy in life comes when you think of others and contribute to their lives in a meaningful way."

ALYSON
Jones

Q: Can you tell us about your journey as an entrepreneur and what inspired you to start your own business?

A: I am a Registered Clinical Counsellor and have been practicing as a professional therapist for almost 30 years. My work has always been meaningful and satisfying to me. Around 16 years ago I started my business Alyson Jones & Associates where I provide guidance and support to other counsellors in the practice while ensuring that we provide a high level of mental heath services to our clients.

Q: What problem or need does your business solve, and what motivated you to address it?

A: Mental heath has been stigmatized and minimized, but mental health is health! We need services that support good mental health, and Alyson Jones & Associates has been on the forefront of providing this. Although people may seek our services due to a conflict or problem in their life, we try to help people see the opportunities in the challenge.

Q: What are some of the biggest challenges you've faced as an entrepreneur, and how have you overcome them?

A: Talking about challenges, I have certainly experienced a few! My business has survived stigmatization, recessions, and a pandemic. In addition, I had to find a way to merge business principles with professional standards. This took a high level of accountability and planning, but I was able to build a business that has been profitable while never compromising on the heart of the matter – supporting mental health.

Q: What are some trends or developments in your industry that you're particularly excited about?

A: It has been an amazing journey to see how the conversations and interventions regarding mental heath have shifted through the years. There was a time when seeking therapy was seen as a sign of weakness. This narrow vision inhibited health and movement. It is truly heartwarming to see how people have gained an understanding that seeking support for your mental health is a show of courage and strength.

Q: How do you prioritize tasks and manage time effectively as an entrepreneur?

A: That has always been a challenge for me as I struggle to rest when there is work to be done – and when you are an entrepreneur there is always work to be done! I organize my task lists and appreciate the satisfaction that comes with accomplishing those tasks, but I have learned there are times to put away the task lists and just enjoy life in the moment.

Q: How do you stay motivated and resilient during tough times in your business?

A: I know that I can bounce back because I have bounced back so many times before. My work as a mental health professional has helped me understand that resiliency is earned through falling and getting back up again.

Q: How do you maintain a work-life balance while running your own business?

A: I do not ascribe to the philosophy that you "Go home or go you Go big" - rather I believe you can "Go home and Go Big". "Go home" is your anchor and your relationships while "Go Big" is your purpose and your passion. It is not a question of choosing your home life or your work, but rather it is about the choices we make with our time. Stay mindful of where you are at and show up in your work and your relationships.

Q: Pink or red lipstick?

A: Red…always red!

Lisa Huppée is the owner of six Just Like Family Home Care locations throughout the lower mainland and Vancouver Island, in BC, Canada.

LISA
Huppée

Q: Can you discuss the role of networking and partnerships in growing your business?

A: Networking and partnerships is a really important part of any business. Referrals by previous clients or family members is also super important to let people know first hand how great our services are and how we customize care to each client and their situation. Making connections in the community and working together with other business professionals and businesses locally to refer business to each other to our clients helps everyone get what they need!

Q: What do you believe are the keys to building a strong brand identity and reputation?

A: Consistency and providing a high quality service with great communication, so it can continue to be excellent as needs change and services need to transition. Sharing client testimonials and experiences is important too!

Q: Does owning a business get easier the longer you do it?

A: Each day brings new and different challenges. Some aspects of owning the business become routine once you learn it and or hire staff dedicated to specific roles. The accountability lies with them and doing their job duties properly. Other things are just new situations so being able to deal with people and events in a timely thoughtful manner are super important. Hoping someone or something will go away or resolve itself without you dealing with it is a business person not taking initiative to resolve in an efficient manner. The important thing is to take action and make decisions. Sometimes making decisions are hard even when you look at the whole situation. The best advice I can give is don't be afraid to make a decision. Everyone has a gut instinct and also look at the facts. Make a decision and take responsibility. That's what leaders do.

Q: Can you share a story about a particularly memorable customer interaction or experience?

A: I just did a video testimonial of one family and how we helped from companion care for their family friend that lived with them who had dementia and how our care over 31/2 years transitioned from companion care to finally palliative care and how having our service made such an incredible difference in that families' experience with helping their friend through the dementia process and his end of life at home. That is a powerful impact and we are there to help families give their loved ones the end of life experience they want. This is why I do what I do.

Q: What advice would you give to someone who is considering starting their own business?

A: Be prepared to work a lot. Being a business owner is not a 9-5 job that you clock in and out on time! Starting and building a business is like climbing a mountain, it's a lot of work getting to a point that you can see all that work pay off and take a breather. Being resilient and being able to take one step forward and 3 steps back without giving up is important. It can be stressful but overall it is so rewarding!

Q: How do you balance work-life commitments as an entrepreneur?

A: Well being committed to your business and work will lose you some friends that don't understand the drive and things you must do to grow and make your business productive. Most people think it is easy and that it is easy to hire people that can help you, so you can take time off and have a life. Unfortunately employees are not as committed to your business as you are and hiring the right people takes time and energy, sleepless nights as well as being let down along the way. Your true friends will make time for you, whether it is for an impromptu coffee or for a dinner planned a month in advance. Building a business has trade offs and work life balance is a trade off at least till you get the right team in place to take pressure off you.

Q: Why is having ongoing professional development opportunities for staff important at your company?

A: As an owner, we want each individual whether a part time or full-time caregiver, office staff or a Community Health Manager to learn and grow in their role/position. We want them to feel engaged and have added background knowledge for their job. We have 91 training modules as of this month! Being a lifelong learner is important, not just for a job but for your own personal growth intellectually and emotionally. Staff who are keen learners have more opportunity to advance and grow with the company.

Q: How do you build and maintain a strong team, and what qualities do you look for in potential hires?

A: Look for people with heart and drive to help others. Will they stay the extra 10-20 min to finish up a task so someone isn't left without care? Dedication and self direction to do the right thing, be the better person, do the better job. Be a leader in your role. Having a team that communicates positively and consistently and uses all the programs that enable work to get done in the most time efficient manner. Recognizing staff for going above and beyond, having bonuses and recognition in our staff newsletter as well as shout outs! Having tons of professional development opportunities so they can learn and grow in their roles and hopefully move into other advanced positions.

Q: Pink or red lipstick?

A: Pink lipstick of course, preferably with a little glitter!

Ellie Kamankesh works in financial industry and has helped numerous individuals, families, and businesses to protect their health and families. She is also an assistant project manager in construction, as well as an entrepreneur and the co-founder of Neshuny, a Persian Business Directory.

ELLIE
Kamankesh

Q: Have you found any specific advantages or opportunities in being a woman in your industry?

A: Absolutely. Women are often recognized for their strong communication skills, which can be invaluable in building relationships, especially in marketing businesses. Also, women entrepreneurs often demonstrate high levels of resilience and adaptability in the face of obstacles, which are essential qualities for success in the unpredictable world of business.

Q: What role do you think mentorship and support networks play for women in entrepreneurship?

A: Having a mentor who believes in their abilities and supports their goals can significantly boost a woman entrepreneur's confidence and self-esteem, empowering her to take on new challenges and pursue ambitious ventures. Also, mentorship provides women entrepreneurs with guidance and advice from experienced professionals who have navigated similar challenges. This can help them make informed decisions and avoid common pitfalls.

Furthermore, having a support network and seeing other successful women entrepreneurs, can serve as powerful role models for aspiring entrepreneurs, inspiring them to pursue their own entrepreneurial dreams.

Q: How do you stay motivated and resilient during tough times in your business?

A: Having clear objectives has always given me something to work towards and has kept me motivated. I use visualization techniques to envision my desired outcomes and success. Visualizing my goals helps reinforce my commitment and motivation to overcome obstacles and persevere through tough times. I remind myself why I started this business in the first place. This reconnects me with my passion and purpose. Also, it is important to maintain a positive mindset. I practice gratitude for the progress I've made, no matter how small, and look for silver linings in difficult situations. And do not forget about self-care. It's essential to prioritize self-care, especially during stressful times, whether it's exercise, meditation, spending time with loved ones, or pursuing hobbies. Always remember that tough times are temporary.

Q: How do you prioritize and manage your goals and tasks as an entrepreneur?

A: Prioritizing and managing goals and tasks efectively is crucial for success at any business. I start by defining the overarching business goals, both short-term and long-term. Goals are to be specific, measurable, and achievable. Then I break down each goal into smaller, actionable tasks or milestones to make them more manageable. Once I have a list of tasks, I prioritize them based on their importance and urgency using priority management techniques. I try to avoid multitasking and instead focus on completing one task at a time. This helps maintain productivity and ensures that each task receives full attention and efort, and therefore creates the best result.

Q: What problem or need does your business solve, and what motivated you to address it? And what sets your business apart from competitors in the market?

A: As an immigrant finding the services that I need has been challenging sometimes, especially in the beginning years of immigration when the language barrier can add to the challenges of the new and unknown environment. Also, I have seen the entrepreneurs and newly established Persian businesses in my community that were looking for ways of getting more exposure and being known and supported within their community. I was browsing in net and asking around each time and I could find some but not suficient information about Persian businesses on diferent platforms and advertisements. The lack of a central platform with eficient search tools was the need that motivated me to develop an idea for a new directory.

Neshuny Directory addresses the needs of the growing Persian community in Canada to find the services they need. Neshuny provides a centralized platform where the Persian community can access information about various businesses, including their contact details, location, services ofered, hours of operation, and other relevant information. This accessibility makes it easier for consumers to find the products or services they need in their areas.

They can discover new businesses or services that they may not have been aware of previously. They can browse through listings based on categories, keywords, or location, and this allows them to explore diferent options and make informed choices. Users can also browse through maps of the cities and neighborhoods.

Neshuny also serves as a platform for Persian businesses to gain visibility and support within the community. It serves as an additional marketing channel, helping businesses reach a wider audience and attract new customers who may be searching for products or services online. By providing this directory, I aim to facilitate connections, encourage entrepreneurship, and promote economic integration among Persian businesses and the wider society.

Neshuny ofers unique features or services not found in other similar directories. This includes innovative search functionalities with quick search capabilities that provide an advanced search experience that can narrow down the search result to the specific needs, a simple, intuitive, and user-friendly interface with easy navigation through maps in multiple layers of countries, cities, and even neighborhoods', rating, and mobile optimization. Neshuny also ofers value-added services such as advertising opportunities, and digital marketing on both web-based and Instagram platforms.

Q: What advice would you give to someone who is considering their own business?

A: Starting your own business is an exciting but challenging endeavor. Before diving into starting a business, thoroughly validate your business idea. Research your target market, identify your potential customers, understand their needs and pain points, and assess the demand for your product or service. Build your business around providing value to your customers. Create a Solid Business Plan that outlines your business goals, target market, competitive analysis, marketing strategy, operational plan, and financial projections. A well-thought-out business plan serves as a roadmap for your venture and helps attract investors or secure financing. Keep in mind that entrepreneurship requires dedication, resilience, and hard work. stay committed to your vision and keep pushing forward, even when faced with obstacles.

Believe in your vision and finally, believe in YOURSELF.

Q: Pink or red lipstick? A: Red

Becky Kehoe is the Founder and owner of Haven Ridge School of Hypnotherapy in Salmon Arm, BC, Canada and is a certified clinical hypnotherapist, who cares deeply about people, the planet and prides herself in facilitating healing growth. Becky is also the author of the book Perceptional Hypnotherapy.

Q: Can you tell me about your journey as an entrepreneur? What inspired you to start your own business?

A: My journey as an entrepreneur has been an incredible and transformative experience, deeply intertwined with my personal story. Becoming a hypnotherapist and spiritual counselor was born out of a profound personal loss: the passing of my son. This moment had me searching rapidly for answers, healing, and connection.

I also had to find a way to contribute meaningfully to society as, during my own challenges, I discovered a strong desire to connect and help others facing similar challenges, guiding them toward a path of healing and self-discovery.

Years later, a realization came to me while I was teaching my clients self-hypnosis and introducing them to creative techniques they could incorporate into their daily routines. This part of my job made me see how much I love teaching. I found that helping people one-on-one was great, but what I really wanted to do was teach others, share what I know, and give them tools to change their lives. Seeing my clients/students succeed is the most rewarding part for me.

Q: How do you maintain a work-life balance while running your business? What strategies have you found most effective for networking and building professional relationships as a female entrepreneur?

A: Maintaining a work-life balance while managing my business has always been a priority for me, and I've found a rhythm that suits my lifestyle perfectly. I dedicate two weeks each month exclusively to work, immersing myself fully in my business endeavors. The remaining two weeks are spent with my husband and son, and for play and rejuvenation—this is when I indulge in my passions for music, writing, painting, and hiking. This balanced approach not only keeps me motivated and energized but also ensures that I'm always at my best, both professionally and personally. When working on a project, I set a timer so that I can focus undisturbed for an hour at a time. This simple time management technique has helped me a great deal with keeping my projects moving forward.

When it comes to building professional relationships, I believe authenticity is key. My strategy revolves around being genuine and presenting my true self in all interactions. This means showing up not as who I think I should be but as I am—embracing my unique qualities and values. Finding people who are like-minded and want to share their authentic self's, is equally important connections are vital. In this electronic world, I still believe word of mouth and forging real relationships are crucial to business growth. We should take the time to create meaningful connections with colleagues, clients, and other professionals in our field.

Q: Can you share a particular memory, success story, or milestone from your entrepreneurial journey?

A: For me, writing the book Perceptional Hypnotherapy has been a massive achievement. Anyone who knows my background will understand what a significant personal leap this was. Being able to express my passion on paper and get it published was something I always dreamed of but was also scared to attempt. I had to overcome my own hurdles, like worries about grammar and feelings of imposter syndrome. I did some hypnotherapy to get past these fears and change my personal beliefs. With support from my family and colleagues, I managed to heal and move forward, turning the dream into a reality. Now, I've created something special: a book to share my passion with the world.

Q: What advice would you give to other women who are considering starting their own business?

A: It's crucial to ensure you have the time and dedication for what you're creating. Flexibility is key—be open to learning and embracing new ideas and perspectives. Acknowledge that challenges will arise but stay committed and have a support system in place. I know in my heart that if it weren't for the men in my life, I wouldn't have the foundation to create what I have. Make sure to choose mentors who have achieved something like what you're aiming for, even if their path or ideas slightly differ from yours. Take the time to talk with potential mentors to find someone who truly resonates with your vision. Remember, support can often come from places you least expect it.

It's also essential to put on your business hat and differentiate yourself from the competition. Ask yourself, what makes you unique? This requires a sharp focus: the ability to heal the belief systems that no longer serve you and manage the time needed for your goals, both personally and professionally. And you need to dedicate time to keep yourself healthy—mentally and physically—with meditation, hypnosis, yoga, or whatever practice you align with. Maintaining a balance between the masculine and feminine aspects of yourself is vital. Embracing both can help you stand out in your field, allowing you to create a unique and authentic brand, product, or image.

Being diverse doesn't mean you can't be inclusive. It's about being open to all possibilities and using them to craft a persona that's truly your own in the entrepreneurial world. This balance and diversity are what will define your journey and enable you to leave a distinct mark on the world.

Q: What sets your business apart from its competitors in the market?

A: What sets Haven Ridge School apart from its competitors is our unique approach to the curriculum, which emphasizes that both perception and practical application are as equally important as focusing on book or theory work. We believe that learning should go beyond the paperwork and be more about experiencing and understanding the real-world applications of hypnotherapy.

Additionally, the opportunity for one-on-one mentoring with our teachers, Heather Haslam, and myself, Becky Kehoe, enhances the support system for our students once they move into their new careers. This personal touch prepares them to enter a diverse world, equipped to address various elements, belief systems, and habits through hypnotherapy. Haven Ridge School of Hypnotherapy is a career-oriented program encouraging individual perception and growth. Our hypnotherapy school creates a community of certified clinical hypnotherapists who care about quality, people, and the Earth, and we prioritize an inclusive environment that celebrates diversity.

Q: Pink or red lipstick?

A: I prefer pink lipstick, especially the pink/brown blends that harmonize with nature's colors.
I find the pink shades offer a soft, fresh look that's easy to match with most outfits and occasions.

Ashleigh Kirsten, RN, BSN, is the CEO and founder of AK Consultants & Healthcare, LLC, a full-service growth management company for post-acute care healthcare businesses.

ASHLEIGH
Kirsten

Q: Can you tell me about your journey as an entrepreneur? What inspired you to start your own business?

A: I was born to entrepreneurial parents, both tennis professionals, yet I never imagined I'd one day start my own business. My path began in nursing and gradually shifted as I became an expert in turning clinical solutions into viable, salable realities. Seven years ago, I started my business, and my vision has evolved over time, driven by the needs of my clients, market trends, and my desire to create a platform where top healthcare consultants could channel their entrepreneurial talents through a growth management firm. The gig economy, the allure of the American Dream, the lack of job security in healthcare, and my passion for impacting multiple healthcare businesses inspired me to create a unique consulting and fractional services company tailored to the healthcare industry.

Q: What advice would you give to other women who are considering starting their own businesses?

A: If you feel called to become an entrepreneur, pursue a business that solves a problem you're passionate about. Be realistic about the time it will take to see a return, and fall in love with your vision. That vision doesn't have to be perfectly clear from the start—allow it to evolve over time. Flexibility is crucial on the entrepreneurial journey. You need to be adaptable and open to the unexpected, especially when chasing long-term goals.

Q: How do you balance work-life commitments as an entrepreneur?

A: I don't believe in work-life balance; I believe in work-life presence. Entrepreneurship requires an "all in" mindset—a combination of grit, resilience, and love for what you do. It demands time, our most precious and non-renewable resource. However, your personal life—family, friends, and pets—are just as much a part of who you are at work as they are at home. When you're with them, be present. It's in those little moments, whether at work or with loved ones, that the most meaningful and impactful memories are created. Being fully present in mind, body, and spirit is key to making a commitment both in work and in life.

Q: What do you believe are the keys to building a strong brand identity and reputation?

A: Lead with integrity. It may take longer to reach your goals, but maintaining integrity and a strong work ethic will build a reputation that clients, peers, employees, and the community will trust and respect. In the end, this trust is invaluable to long-term success.

Q: How do you approach leadership and team building within your company?

A: I believe in leading by example. I'm the first one up and the last one to bed. Growing and scaling a company requires doing what most people aren't willing to do—staying the course when others would likely give up. Leadership is about perseverance, determination, and being there for your team every step of the way.

Q: How do you measure the success and growth of your business?

A: While success and growth can be measured quantitatively, such as through financials or meeting KPIs, it's important not to "grow to go broke" or succeed at the expense of long-term sustainability. As your business grows, you need to continually re-evaluate your targets and ensure you are staying aligned with your original vision. Qualitative success, however, is felt in the small victories—when you reflect on the grit and determination it took to achieve something meaningful, such as positively impacting a client, an employee, or the direction of the business. These moments are often the most rewarding.

Q: Looking ahead, what are your goals and aspirations for the future of your business?

A: The future is incredibly bright. On August 1, 2024, AK Consultants & Healthcare merged with Griffin Resources, combining two powerhouse, self-made, women-owned businesses. This partnership allows us to offer the full spectrum of consulting and fractional services across the United States. In my new role as an Advisor, I will focus on growth initiatives, strategic planning, and provide executive guidance to the CEO, Michelle Griffin, Ph.D. Together, we'll scale the leadership team, establish benchmarks, and maintain profitability while responding to market demands with innovative approaches. As my company becomes part of a bigger vision, my entrepreneurial journey continues in an even more dynamic way than I could have ever imagined.

My parting advice to fellow entrepreneurs is to be willing to work hard every day and remain open to the evolution of your business. Your company may grow beyond your initial vision, leading to new milestones and infinite possibilities. Each achievement is a stepping stone toward greater success in the ongoing journey of entrepreneurship.

Q: Pink or red lipstick?

A: Gloss – Hey I am a disrupter, an entrepreneur!

Jen is a single mom, raising 2 teens currently 18 and 20. She is the lead singer of a country band.And she has been working in business for 35 years. Jen started her career as a Banker and worked her way through various sectors in the financial space from Insurance Agent to Mortgage Broker to being a Broker of Private Equity for 10 years. Currently Jen is self employed as a Business Consultant helping companies launch and bring them to the marketplace.

JEN
Krahn

Q: Can you tell me about your journey as an entrepreneur? What inspired you to start your own business?

A: I watched my Father, who had a Grade 3 education from a 3rd world country, become a well-known business man in a large city and I knew there were no excuses for me. It was exciting to watch the impact he had on countless lives around him, and I could not help but desire the same for myself.

At the age of 19, I was hired at a large bank from a pool of 100 applicants, most of which were much more qualified than I. I knew from a young age that I could create my own destiny even from a hard work perspective. As well, I knew that my attitude would get me where I needed to go.

My banking career turned into 30+ years of various aspects in the Money Management world. They say 'opportunity breeds opportunity' and without question this was true for me. Eventually, as I would sit on various boards, I was offered great opportunities. I became involved in my Community and ultimately, I became a Broker of Private Equity for 10 years which exposed me to countless connections across North America. This led me to realize I could broker deals on my own with my experience and my connections.

Watching my father become what he did inspired me to understand that I could certainly achieve great things, considering the level of education I had compared to what he had. It has been a beautiful journey in business.

Q: Can you share a particularly memorable success story or milestone from your entrepreneurial journey?

A: I have many memorable stories from business, but I always tell the very first one. I was 19 years old and hired for a job I was not qualified for, against many much more qualified applicants. On my first day of work, my new Manager called me into his office. He said, 'Do you know the first rule of banking?' I said no. He looked at me and said, 'CYA'… always cover your ass in banking. From that day forward, I always undersold and overdelivered in my career. Eric K gave me a chance, which I believe was the catalyst to my entire career. He gave me the confidence to believe in myself as a young woman.

Q: Can you discuss the role of networking and partnerships in growing your business?

A: My entire career has been built on networking and partnerships. I have met people on flights, on holidays, on the golf course, and in board rooms. You never know where you will meet your next connection. Some of these people have become great friends of mine and others have become partners in business. I have learned to have an open mind.

Q: Looking ahead, what are your goals and aspirations for the future of your business?

A: The goals and aspirations for the future of my business are really just to leave a mark. I believe that I have been able to connect people to others who have taken their business to great levels as a result. I hope people remember me for helping to bring excellent connections and concepts to expose and to grow their businesses.

Q: Looking back, what are some things you wish you had known or done, or not done in your career?

A: My biggest regret is not finding my confidence and my voice sooner. I had great opportunity to be a professional country singer in Nashville. If I knew then what I know now, I would have thrown caution to the wind and sang my heart out to see where it would go.

I knew I always loved business as well, so I took that route and developed my business skills. Though I come by business honestly with my family roots, I often wonder what would have happened had I followed my dreams. Business was and still is a passion of mine. I am grateful I had the opportunity to develop my skills over time with many wonderful people. I would tell my younger self to step into my natural giftings and strengths with a hope and a prayer. That I would in fact figure everything out along the way and that I would meet all the right people. I would tell myself to get out of my own way and to chase after my dreams. That if I change course along the way, it is all part of the journey. In the end, I am in full gratitude for the years of business I have experienced, and the incredible people I have met along the way. Just do it. Face the day. Day by day. And it will be as it is meant to be.

Q: Pink or red lipstick?

A: No lipstick for this girl. I have a Carmex addiction. In sweatpants, in a dress, in a gown, at all times I will have Carmex on me through the day and the night. That's as sexy as I get with my 'lipstick'.

Karen Kobel is a performer, instructor of dance, yoga and Pilates, and founder of Kahlena Movement Studio.

Q: Can you tell me about your journey as an entrepreneur? What inspired you to start your own business?

A: When I was a child, around 6 or 7 years old, when Bon Jovi came out with Slippery When Wet, my best friends and I decided to create a front lawn performance series. We would choose a song and create a dance, gymnastics, or roller-skating piece to perform for our parents and neighbors. This was the start of something big for Karen! I knew I wanted to create my own shows or studio. These shows continued and evolved into Swing Set showcases. I was already in dance classes and had yearly dance recitals, which eventually turned into competitive dance. Another best friend from dance class and I planned to open our own dance studio when we got older. This vision, dream, and goal sat in a file, waiting to be opened when the time was right.

Q: Can you share a particularly memorable success story or milestone from your entrepreneurial journey?

A: Throughout the last seven years of owning Kahlena Movement, it has been an honor to be named the favorite Pilates Studio in North Vancouver for more than half of that time. I was also honored and nominated for the YWCA Women of Distinction Awards in 2021 for our hard work, perseverance, resilience, and so much more throughout the pandemic. We created the Kahlena Curbside Crew, which traveled to seniors' homes, the Lions Gate Hospital ER entrance, seniors' patios for those in lockdown, and the sidewalks of North Vancouver, offering outdoor dance performances, exercise classes, and connection. I was also featured in IMPACT Magazine's Top 10 Fitness Instructors edition for 2021. In a time of uncertainty, I was fortunate to be recognized for my work and for fostering community connection when it was so desperately needed.

Q: What advice would you give to other women who are considering starting their own businesses?

A: Starting your own business comes with the understanding that you will have many clients who love you, support you, and are loyal. It also comes with some haters, and that is okay. Not everyone who comes into your business is there to stay; many come to teach us lessons and remind us of the things we need to implement, such as boundaries. As I said to my newer instructors this week after dealing with "my one unhappy client a year" moment: I knew what I was signing up for when I decided to open this studio and be the business owner. It is not for the faint of heart. Kill them with kindness, yes, but learn how to deliver the message to them in the kindest way that their unkindness is not okay when delivering their "feedback" and projecting onto us.

Starting my own business was always in the cards; it was just a matter of time. I was fortunate to have worked at many different studios over my years of teaching dance, fitness, Pilates, yoga, and more. This allowed me to observe each studio owner's approach to running their business and take notes. Taking the first step to offer your own classes, rent space, market, create, and make it all happen is a scary thing. But it comes somewhat naturally to me, so I ran with it. In 2011, I created Kahlena, starting with making posters to promote my own classes and googling what "Kahlena" meant. I saw this word/name various times while in Maui and loved its sound and flow. When I decided to use it as my business name, I googled its meaning and found that Kahlena is the Hawaiian name for Karen. There it was, right in my face: Kahlena Movement Studio = Karen. My logo was already in place because I had been using it with my name for a while, so I had it reworked into the Kahlena Movement Studio branding, and off we went.

Q: Can you tell us about your journey as an entrepreneur and what inspired you to start your own business?

A: The years flowed with me still teaching at other studios while offering Kahlena on the side. Then, in 2017, the time came when some people in my life believed in my vision. The old studio owner, for whom I had worked for years since moving to Vancouver, offered me the opportunity to take over the space. It was honestly an immediate YES! Private investors, including a client and my parents, stepped in to help get things started, and off we went!

Kahlena Movement Studio has always been about classes and wellness experiences deeply rooted in community and connection. We have a passion for creating opportunities for clients of all fitness levels to look within, focus, refocus, and facilitate transformation in a supportive environment.

Q: Can you discuss a failure or setback your business encountered, and how did you bounce back from it?

A: For every small business, the last four years have undoubtedly been the biggest setback we've faced. From complete lockdowns to restrictions, and the constant back and forth between these conditions, being a business that provided movement-based services during a time when social distancing was crucial presented major hurdles. Despite these challenges, we adapted and became very creative with our offerings and structure. We introduced private classes, semi-private classes, rehab classes, outdoor classes, family classes, and online classes. We pivoted, innovated, and made it work for our community, which recognized and supported our efforts. We also launched a GoFundMe campaign for family and friends who wanted to support our dream and help cover the rent. We provided a welcoming space for everyone in the community, with no judgment. The word "Yoga" means unity and community, which is what we've always strived for. Our morals, values, and ethics have consistently guided us. The biggest accomplishment throughout Kahlane's existence has been maintaining our authenticity.

Dana Kovacic is a certified coach dedicated to helping women in businesses to make more money, and live a life they love.

DANA
Kovacic

Q: Can you tell me about your journey as an entrepreneur? What inspired you to start your own business?

A:I grew up in a world where generational poverty was the norm, and nobody I knew owned a business. But when I read Richard Branson's "Like a Virgin," something clicked. With 95% of the world's wealth held by business owners and investors, I knew that stepping into entrepreneurship would not only offer financial opportunities but also the creative freedom I craved. At just 24, I dove in headfirst and bought my first shop, not knowing exactly how I'd make it work, but dead set on succeeding.

That leap of faith didn't just start my business journey; it launched my dream to empower women to have it all—without having to pick and choose between being a mom, a wife, or a business owner. We don't have to settle for just one aspect of life; we can indeed excel in all. It's my personal mission to live financially free and empower other women to achieve the same success through their businesses.

Q: How do you maintain a work-life balance while running your own business?

A: For me, keeping a work-life balance is all about remembering that my business isn't me—it's something I choose to do.

This perspective is essential to maintain high energy, frequency, and vibration, which not only boosts my productivity but also enhances the enjoyment of life's other passions. I actively set healthy boundaries, am not shy about saying 'no' when necessary, and delegate tasks to my VA. This approach frees up my time, allowing me to focus on both my business and personal life without sacrificing one for the other.

Q: How do you approach leadership and team building within your company?

A: As leaders, we're like the bus driver, and our business is the bus. It's our job to make sure that everyone knows where we're headed and that they're on board for the ride. With a clear mission and vision laid out, it's like setting the GPS for our journey—we know exactly where we want to go. Our core values and high standards are what keep us on the right road. When we communicate these clearly, every team member feels like they're part of a bigger picture. They're not just passengers; they're co-navigators, actively involved and invested in our shared journey. This approach helps us not just meet our goals but exceed them, making sure our business doesn't just move forward—it zooms ahead.

Q: What role do you think mentorship and support networks play for women in entrepreneurship?

A: Mentorship is crucial because it directly impacts our personal and business growth. Our business is a reflection of us, the leaders, and it can only evolve as much as we do. If something about our business isn't right, the good news is that we can change it. Mentors help us see the blind spots, challenging us to grow and adapt. This transformation under their guidance ensures that as we develop as leaders, our business advances alongside us. It's so important to have a support network. Our network is your net worth. Hang out with people who have the results you want and hold you to a higher standard. We never achieve our highest dreams, we always achieve our lowest standards. Align them both for true success.

Q: What problem or need does your business solve, and what motivated you to address it?

A: I understand that for women entrepreneurs, time is our biggest commodity—we can always make another dollar, but we can never make back another minute. A Lot of women I speak with think that working harder is the answer. And it's not. The answer is working 'ON' the business more and not 'IN' it. That's why my focus is on helping my clients systemize, prioritize, and monetize their businesses effectively. Through transformative coaching, we guide women to streamline their operations, highlight their most impactful tasks and help to create a clear path of next steps of what to focus on.

Q: Can you share a story about a particularly memorable customer interaction or experience?

A: One of my favorite success stories is about one of my VIP clients. She used to bring in around $60k a month, but after we introduced our 'Sales With Care SystemTM' and really focused on empowering her team, she skyrocketed to having a $103k one month—and that's with taking seven whole months off to enjoy life! Now, she's consistently making over $80k every month, and she's well on her way to hitting her big goal goal of her seven-figure year.

REBECCA
Bucci

Rebecca (Bec) Bucci is an American board-certified Sexologist, Clinical Sexuality Coach, Clinical Hypnotherapist, Global Speaker, and Relationships Sexpert.

Visionary and founder of the Ways of Wisdom Book series she has brought to life the Women of Wisdom Anthology Series and Warriors of Wisdom Anthology Series, 11 times International best sellers in 7 countries. Creator of G Spot Sex Therapy Down Under, her work educates couples and individuals in all areas of taboo, sexual dysfunction, and rehabilitation. Her passionate approach to inspiring women to embrace their complete sexual selves and express their deepest desires around pleasure has led her to be featured in international best-selling print magazines and international best-selling books as a featured coauthor.

Through online instruction and the Love Lab subscription app, Rebecca facilitates couples, women, and men's workshops and retreats globally. A Free subscription to the App is available via the website becbucci.com.au.

Rebecca states, "Becoming a sexologist was my calling, my life's work, to open the door to acceptance of the weird, of the taboo, of the kink, of the extra-ordinary expressions we can experience while living through this human experience. My purpose is to inspire all women to step fully into their femininity now, to embrace it, allow it to ignite by trusting it, and finally nurture it through its many stages of maturity. ALWAYS tend to the fire within. Don't wait to become...

An unapologetically, authentically raw, and real 100% woman.

As a Sexologist, founder of Rebel Wolf Media™, creator of the Women of Wisdom Book Series™, inventor of the Love Lab™ App and the visionary of our pleasure products "Pussior™" my journey to becoming an entrepreneur has been a thrilling adventure filled with challenges, triumphs, and many moments of self-discovery. It's a path that requires courage, resilience, and an unwavering commitment to turning your dreams into reality.

The journey must begin with a spark of inspiration—an idea that ignites a passion deep within you. It could be a solution to a problem you've encountered, a product you've envisioned, or a vision for making a positive impact on the world. This initial spark sets the wheels in motion and propels you forward on your entrepreneurial journey. Remember that dreams are free and that it doesn't matter how many times you fail only have many times you keep trying. Our launch product for Pussior™ was a small bullet vibrator in the shape of a pussy cat, 42 prototypes later we hit the mark on a product that reflected our brand image and value, so don't be afraid of perfection and sticking to your guns. Trust your gut and your instincts, after all this is your baby and should be treated as such.

As you embark on this journey, you quickly realize that entrepreneurship is not for the faint of heart. It requires determination, perseverance, and a willingness to embrace uncertainty and take risks. You will encounter obstacles and setbacks along the way, but you must refuse to let them deter you from pursuing your passion and purpose.

One of the first challenges you face is turning your idea into a viable business concept. Spend the time to conduct market research, validate your idea with potential customers, and refine your value proposition. You must create a business plan outlining your vision, goals, target market, and revenue model—you will need a roadmap to guide your journey and keep you focused on your objectives. Take the time to slowly build a team of talented individuals who share your vision and your level of passion. You must be prepared to wear many hats as an entrepreneur, especially in the startup phase, from CEO to janitor, as you work tirelessly to turn your vision into reality. I cannot emphasize enough, to build a passionate team that believes in the product or vision, they need to be Fuck Yes individuals.

As your business begins to take shape, you will face the challenge of building a brand and establishing a presence in the market. Along the way, you will encounter moments of doubt and uncertainty. You may question whether you have what it takes to succeed and whether your idea is truly worth pursuing. But you must practise drawing strength from your passion, your purpose, and your unwavering belief in yourself and your vision. When I decided to create a PORN alternative that focused on lovemaking and intimacy via film, I came under fire from family, colleagues and industry. However, I knew the importance of offering a porn alternative to young people that would educate them about respect, love and intimacy. Be ready to be brave, you will need courage on this incredible journey of personal and professional development. Never let the opinions of others get in the way of your success, you must have deep commitment to your conviction and the best way to do this is by creating positive change in the world.

Red or Pink Lipstick? Red all the way!

Stephanie Lehr is a Relationship Coach and Founder of Stephanie Lehr Coaching, Registered Rehabilitation Professional, Amazon #1 Best-Selling Co-Author, Self-Published Amazon Author, Podcast Guest and "Thought"Speaker from Vancouver, Canada.

Q: What inspired you to start your own business?

A: Let me start by sharing something very personal with you. I am the Founder of Stephanie Lehr Coaching. I'm a Relationship Coach who specializes in couples work because I've been there…I've walked in your shoes.

Several years ago, my world came crashing down when my ex-husband blind-sided me by telling me he wanted to end our marriage. There was no reason given and he didn't want counselling, coaching, or any help to save our relationship.

I was utterly shocked, lost, afraid, ashamed, and heartbroken…there were lots of tears, anger, name-calling~ you name it, I said it! I mean this was my best friend of 25 years! I thought I knew him and that he had my back. Things got so bad, that at one point, I even thought about ending my own life, believing that at 42 years of age, my life was over.

But here I am today, standing stronger than I have ever been. I am better- not bitter -because I did the work to heal and change my life. I emerged from that dark place, and I realized that I had a longing- a calling, a purpose – to help others and be a light for other couples who are navigating rough roads in their own relationships.

That's why I founded Stephanie Lehr Coaching. My journey taught me that there is hope, there is help, and there is a way to reconnect, find peace, and rediscover the joy that relationships can bring.

Q: What problem or need does your business solve, and what motivated you to address it?

A: Let me ask you: Are you happy?

Chances are you're not.

The sad reality is that 80% of couples are not satisfied in their relationships~ leaving ONLY 20% that are thriving in their partnerships.

I'm on a mission to provide hope and help to struggling couples who want a better connection.

If you're struggling, then I'm here for you.

Maybe you don't talk to each other anymore like you used to.

Maybe when you do talk, all you do is argue.

Maybe you are so tired in the relationship that you have given up and think that you are stuck in a loveless, roommate-kind-of-relationship.

Maybe you want out…

My intention is to help save you from experiencing the devastating pain that I experienced with divorce by sharing some tried and true, effective tools and techniques that you can learn and use right away in your own relationship to start improving connection, increasing intimacy, managing conflict and deepening shared meaning.

I wish I had had these tools much earlier in my own life. However, I use them in my current relationship because I now know better. If they've helped me, then I know they can help you. You don't have to stay stuck or face this journey alone.

I believe that when we focus on our relationship to be even 1% better, we have a world that can be 1% better… day-by-day. That's a world that I want to live in and leave behind.

Q: Looking ahead, what are your goals and aspirations for the future of your business?

A: I'm developing an online show where I will collaborate with other thought leaders in showcasing their personal stories and good works. There will be live coaching and lots of fun and prizes~ all in an effort to serve you to inspire you to take action in your own life.

Q: Final Question: Pink or red lipstick?

A: Pink!

DeeAnn Lensen is an Eight-time Best Selling Author, Award Winning, International - Advanced Esthetic Educator, Spa Consultant, and Spa Product Distributor. DeeAnn is also a Certified Coach and NLP Practitioner. Her proudest impact has come from lacing self-esteem and empowerment coaching into her vast wellness and skin care knowledge.

DEEANN
Lensen

Feeling stuck? You may very well have "Covid Hangover"! In business, many are still functioning as if they are still somewhat limited by Covid restrictions. There is no better growth potential than real connection and face to face interaction. Wow… this really applied to me. Why was I still holding back? And more importantly, overall, why was I still not living up to my full potential? Can you relate on either of these levels?

I recently realized just how stuck I was when I saw a photo of a chateau in France that used to have a mote around it. As I contemplated why people used to stay inside the mote to protect themselves, a fable came to mind:

"She was living a comfortable life in a castle surrounded by a mote. Beyond the mote was the land of full potential. She kept building a bridge to access the promised land, but it was left unfinished until it rotted. Why, for safety. It was said that there were self esteem trolls who would force her to look in the pool of reflection on the other side, where she would see all her faults and failures."

Is there a part of you stuck in the land of safety? Every woman I have coached or led in business experiences this at some level. Here's a power tool that you can put to work right now.

The biggest Dream Stealer in your life and business is likely YOU! Whether you realize it or not, the internal dialogue running through your mind every day plays a massive role in shaping your reality. What you tell yourself, consciously and unconsciously, during every waking hour becomes the foundation of what you believe you can or cannot achieve. Imagine Michael Jordan stepping up to take a game-winning shot and telling himself, "I doubt I can make this"? Never! His confidence came from relentless mental conditioning, habits that eliminated doubt and replaced it with unwavering belief in his abilities.

Now ask yourself: When you looked in the mirror this morning, with no makeup or fancy clothes to hide behind, did you truly appreciate the person staring back at you? Most women don't. In fact, the harsh inner voice many of us use to criticize ourselves would never be directed toward a child or a loved one. So why do we attack ourselves with destructive self-talk? Here's the kicker: YOU are still programmable. Even as an adult, your mind can be rewired, and it all starts with self-respect. Self-respect naturally leads to group respect, and that's the kind of energy that radiates out into your business, your relationships, and your entire life. There is no such thing as a bully with high self-esteem! People who love and respect themselves don't feel the need to tear others down.

Personal growth should be a lifelong activity. Imagine bringing that increased level of self-awareness into your business. Picture the transformation in the atmosphere when you and your team are operating from a place of confidence and mutual respect. The results are powerful, and the energy is infectious. It's that kind of environment where winning happens at work and at home.

Want to have deeper, more meaningful relationships? Want to increase your business revenue? Dream of becoming debt-free or having an abundance of energy? The first step lies in what you tell yourself right now in each of those areas. Often, the 'programming' we received as children—whether from parents, teachers, or society—doesn't serve us in adulthood. Some of it definitely didn't serve me! That's where coaching came to the rescue. A powerful coach can help you break free from those outdated, limiting beliefs and empower you to rewrite your internal script. So, I urge you: give yourself permission right now to take care of YOU, from the inside out!

There's a reason self-care is so powerful—it's scientifically proven that when we prioritize our own well-being, we become more capable of giving to others. And this positive ripple effect touches every relationship in our lives, both personal and professional.

No Regrets: Your WHY should make you cry! As someone who's passionate about consulting and coaching, my time spent with clients has always been deeply rewarding. But my true WHY is my family. I have seven grandkids, and if I'm being honest, I already regret not spending more time with them while they're still young. This realization led me to make a business pivot. I've added a new income stream (without inventory), one that's both leveraged and residual, giving me more freedom to spend precious time with my family. After 24 years of supporting spas and coaching women on skin C.A.R.E. (Cosmetics Applied Respectfully Enhance), I saw an opportunity help women and businesses find the Peace of Mind they tell me that they crave by offering a program that provides cutting-edge, affordable legal and ID protection at a very low membership price! The results? An augmented level of support for my clients, plus leveraged, residual income that not only supports my family but also gives me the flexibility to live a life with no regrets.

What is your WHY? Why do you wake up every morning and do what you do? Connection is at the core of our human experience. Neurobiologically, it's what we need and crave, even if we often get distracted by the noise of modern life. Put down your phone. Step away from your computer. Connect with the people who matter most and do it with focus and intention. You'll be amazed at how transformative these moments of genuine connection can be.

Get Unstuck. Become a Mote Jumper with me! Access my GET UNSTUCK guide, where you'll find coaching tips, proven wellness and beauty hacks, plus information about the family and business protection programs mentioned. Upgrade your self-care and you will unlock doors you didn't even know existed, and step into a future full of possibilities.

Photo credit: Todd Duncan Studios

Ashika Lessani is a Certified Leadership Coach, Speaker and Author. She resides in North Vancouver BC, Canada. She is a former registered holistic nutritionist, personal trainer specializing in personal mastery for women looking to improve their leadership skills, mental wellbeing, physical and emotional health to live a more fulfilled and abundant life!

Q: What advice would you give to other women who are considering starting their own businesses?

A: There are two critical things when it comes to starting your business whether it is services based or a physical product. Number one is your relationship with money, understanding that it is energy, and the growth of your business will depend on how you value your service or product. As a mentor for women, I often encounter clients that have difficulty with putting a respectable dollar amount on the value and transformation they bring to their clients. Number two, be prepared to play the long game if you want your business to make a difference in others lives and your own. As a leadership mentor, registered nutritionist and women's health educator for female entrepreneurs, taking care of your health is investing in your business. Burnout (chronic fatigue) is the most common reason female businesses fail in the first 2-5 years of business. Making sure you have a strategy in place to take care of your mental, physical, emotional and spiritual well-being is critical for the longevity and success of your business.

Q: What role do you think mentorship and support networks play for women in entrepreneurship?

A: Mentorship and support play a critical role for female entrepreneurs. There is a difference between growing your audience and growing your community of support. Your audience benefits from the solution your service or product provides. Your community and mentors provide you with tools, skill sets and support to show up for your business and grow your reach. And you also have the opportunity to do the same for them. There will be many days you will feel "run over," not worthy, unclear about your next step ect. Having a close network of support and mentors with a strong mindset provides strength, guidance and accountability. This is priceless.

Q: What problem or need does your business solve, and what motivated you to address it?

A: My business is deeply committed to challenges of self-doubt, mental and emotional burnout and societal pressures that women face when transforming their life and or business. Beyond addressing their health and belief systems, I aim to dismantle the self-imposed judgment and criticism that often throws them off track. By fostering a supportive narrative aligned with their values, I not only help them thrive in their businesses but also live a life of fulfillment while defining success on their own terms. Through this holistic approach, they become catalysts for positive change in their circle of influence. My motivation stems from my own journey as a registered holistic nutritionist and personal trainer turned entrepreneur. Prior to having my own business I had a great career as a dental hygienist but becoming a single parent in my mid 30's, I decided to go back to school and further my education in health and wellness, and start my own business which allowed me more time with my son. I experienced firsthand the toll neglecting my well-being took on my business, my family and relationships. During this time of a complete transformation in mylife, I acquired tools, skills and the mindset to support my health, which allowed me to show up for my son and my clients. I had to put my health as the number one priority. Since then I have been dedicated to helping others avoid similar pitfalls. With over a decade of experience, skills and framework, I provide accountability through group coaching, workshops, webinars and private 1:1 coaching. I aim to inspire women to prioritize their health, enabling them to thrive in both their personal and professional endeavors.

Q: What are some of the biggest challenges you've faced as a woman entrepreneur, and how have you overcome them?

A: As a woman entrepreneur, I've encountered challenges like the fear of being seen, imposter syndrome, and navigating the pressures of cancel-culture. These obstacles are all too common in our industry, where the pursuit of perfection can leave us feeling inadequate. I've learned that true empowerment comes from recognizing and embracing our unique journeys. Instead of comparing myself to others, I shifted my focus to my own growth and progress. Overcoming imposter syndrome meant shifting my perspective and surrounding myself with a supportive community that celebrates and encourages me to not give up on my purpose. This has also helped me give back to my community as well. Remember, you are more than enough, and with the right mindset and support system, you can overcome any challenge and fulfill your highest potential!

Q: How do you stay motivated and resilient during tough times in your business?

A: To maintain motivation and resilience in my business, I've found strength in seeking guidance from mentors and coaches who provide invaluable support and accountability with essential tools and skills. Prioritizing my health and well-being – mental, emotional, physical, and spiritual – through dedicated practices and rituals has also been critical. Embracing joy and laughter, and integrating fun into my life, has shown me that success and happiness go hand-in-hand. I view life and business as interconnected, and my motivation stems from being internally inspired and deeply connected to my purpose, recognizing the value I bring to my community and the transformative impact I facilitate. This sense of purpose fuels my resilience, driving me forward in my mission to serve others and make a meaningful difference as a mentor and mother to my son.

Q: How do you prioritize tasks and manage time effectively as an entrepreneur?

A: Juggling entrepreneurship, a parent and personal relationships involves planning, where I map out my days, weeks, and months in advance to align with my personal and professional goals. Utilizing productivity apps streamlines tasks, while delegating to my assistants frees up valuable time for focused work as a creator, coach and mother. Prioritization is key and an understanding of what truly matters in both short and long-term contexts. Nurturing my physical and mental well-being ensures sustained energy and productivity throughout the day. Intentional time off is also crucial, allowing for rejuvenation and fostering creativity. By establishing clear boundaries with myself and others, scheduling dedicated periods of working " on' my business and working "in" my business helps me optimize my time. The key thing to keep in mind, sometimes things won't go as planned no matter how well you've planned it, that's when you have to let go of self judgement, reassess and reset! And remember, multitasking is the fastest way to burnout.

Q: Pink or red lipstick?

A: I love wearing red lipstick! To me it represents confidence, power, vibrancy, and courage. It adds a bold statement to my look and uplifts my mood, empowering me to face the day with strength and determination!

Robin Lipnack is a highly accomplished professional in business development working with multiple industries. Robin has over 20 years of experience helping businesses grow and scale. Known for her strategic vision and ability to unlock new opportunities, Robin has successfully guided organizations through transformative growth.

ROBIN *Lipnack*

Q: What are some of the biggest challenges you've faced as a woman entrepreneur, and how have you overcome them?

A: I believe that some of the biggest challenges have been for me to be accepted, respected and included in meetings and strategies with male C suite executives. I have a business development company and have often been called "The Marketing Girl". "Networking Maven" and all kinds of other titles like that. And yes, that's even with a master's degree. After I have made an introduction, I often have had to ask to be included on emails and at meetings. I have learned that I have to assert myself and ask for what I want. You often have to teach people how you want to be treated. Always be kind and professional.

Q: How do you maintain a work-life balance while running your own business? What strategies have you found most effective for networking and building professional relationships as a female entrepreneur?

A: I try my best to maintain a work – life balance by making sure that I schedule in the gym, meditation, yoga, family and friends. I often can get caught up in emails, texts and social media in the evening and on weekends if Im not careful. Networking is essential for my business in order to make introductions for my clients. I have found that Linked in (yes, I do reach out a lot to people, Im not hesitant to ask them to speak in the hope of doing business together) Facebook and live events are the best way to meet new people and keep relationships moving forward. People do business with who they like and trust. The MOST important part is the follow up. If you don't hear back, then try again in a week or 2. Persistence is not a bad thing if timed properly.

Q: Can you tell us about your journey as an entrepreneur and what inspired you to start your own business?

A: I was working as the head of business development for an MRI company. The company was sold, and a new company took over. They took away a lot of my salary, accrued vacation, my title and even my office. I was very unhappy. I had gone into a coffee shop as I was visiting doctors one day and someone that I knew was sitting there. He mentioned that I looked very unhappy and stressed (gee thanks so much) but he ended up knowing of another medical company hiring and I ended up with that job but it was only part time. It was then I decided to start my own business development company. I hosted some amazing events for myself and met a former NFL player. I began to see myself going into other industries besides healthcare and so I did! (I even got him an audition with Dancing with the Stars) I also was given the opportunity to be in the live audience and still am in close contact with one of the music producers and working on a project) You never know where life's chance meetings will take you.....Have an open mind when meeting new contacts, there can be MAGIC in that!

Q: What sets your business apart from competitors in the market?

A: I don't have a lot of competition because there are not a lot of business development companies. Most are digital marketing now. I also have worked in many industries: real estate, technology, professional sports, finance, healthcare, legal, entertainment and maybe a few more. A lot of people have advised me to stay within 1 or 2 industries, I decided to pave my own path. It makes me more well-rounded and interesting as a person. I also work very hard, always get back to people, have integrity on what I say I will do and I follow up!

Q: Can you share a story about a particularly memorable customer interaction or experience?

A: I was working with a former NFL player with the New York Giants, and he called me one day to ask me to get him an audition for Dancing the Stars. I had no idea where to begin. I started by calling ABC in NY and in 15 min I was speaking with the casting director. My client was flown out to LA and auditioned but he wasn't picked. I was also working with a Global Licensing company at the time and wanted to get a very well-known artist to perform so I was connected to a music producer at DWTS. He and I became fast friends, and I was invited to be in the live audience. It was one of the best experiences I ever had, and he and I are still in touch and working on a project in casting together with one of my movie producer/director contacts. Talk about a memorable experience, WOW!!

Maria Lyons is an entrepreneur with roots in the USA and the Philippines.

MARIA *Lyons*

Q: What inspired you to become an entrepreneur?

A: I grew up with my mom owning a business, and I loved the thought of being in business. I was surrounded by my parents' friends, who all had a great lifestyle that I admired. I said, "One day, I too will be an entrepreneur." I was 13 years old at that time.

Q: What are some of the biggest challenges you've faced as a woman entrepreneur, and how have you overcome them?

A: Because I was a woman entrepreneur in my country, the Philippines, it was mainly a man's world in business. I saw my mom not being taken seriously, and she had to prove herself to stand out among men, which she did successfully. My entrepreneurial spirit kicked in for me at age 28. I was married with five children, and it was a challenge to balance my work life and family life while raising kids. Thank goodness I had a very supportive husband. I networked and marketed my business, mostly around men who looked at me as a wife with a hobby. That did not sit well with me, so I invested in personal development courses, workshops, and leadership development. These made me look at my business on a whole new level, and my confidence soared. When that happened, my income grew, and the men started asking me how I did it. As my income increased, I gained a lot more respect in the world of women entrepreneurship.

Q: What strategies have you found most effective for networking and building professional relationships as a female entrepreneur?

A: When I network at business events, I don't feel the need to go all over the room handing out my business cards. Instead, I look around the room to see who reciprocates a smile. I introduce myself and listen to them—about their life, work, family, hobbies, etc. Then I ask if we can meet for coffee to get to know each other more. It's at this time that they get to know more about me, my purpose, my business, and my products.

Q: Have you found any specific advantages or opportunities in being a woman in your industry?

A: Yes, as a woman, more women are attracted to successful women and look up to you. They see a woman entrepreneur as a mentor and someone to follow. Men also started introducing me to their wives who have a business mindset.

Q: Can you share a particularly memorable success story or milestone from your entrepreneurial journey?

A: Yes! When a team member rises to become a leader and they, in turn, mentor and inspire their own team, it's a very proud moment. Seeing all of them up on stage, with tears of joy, is an unforgettable experience. Because I have walked their journey, and now it's theirs.

Q: In your experience, what are some common misconceptions or stereotypes about women in business, and how do you challenge or overcome them?

A: Most men see women as just having a home hobby to stay busy. The more mentoring I do, the more money I help these women make. Eventually, the men stop talking and let us be.

Q: What advice would you give to other women who are considering starting their own businesses?

A: Know your "why" for wanting to start a business or join a network marketing company. Attend all the self-development workshops they offer, go to leadership camps, and write your goals. Put them up on a wall where you see them often. Write down your progress in a notebook to chart your journey, and be honest about what you did to get closer to your goals.

Q: How do you approach leadership and team-building within your company?

A: When our company puts out leadership team-building events, even though I have attended several, I will do all I can to get everyone on the team to qualify and attend. I share my experience and how it has shaped me to be where I am today.

Q: What role do you think mentorship and support networks play for women in entrepreneurship?

A: Mentorship is crucial for women who are just starting out. We carry so many responsibilities in life and can easily be distracted, so mentorship helps keep them on track, seeing the finish line, and bringing someone new along with them to triumph together.

Q: How do you stay motivated and resilient during tough times in your business?

A: We all need to "gas up" when we take road trips. In the network marketing industry, you have a team, yes, but you are also an independent business owner, and we can run out of gas. For motivation, I meet new people to talk to, read leadership books that inspire and motivate, revisit my goals, and pick a new person in the business—someone I don't know—to get to know and mentor. I also ask myself, "What is my 'why' that keeps me going?" Our "whys" change, as mine did when my husband of 41 years passed away a year and a half ago. He was my business partner, and we worked together, strategizing and rolling up our sleeves. I miss all that, so I keep it alive by meeting someone new and helping them identify their "why."

With a fearless spirit and unstoppable determination, Cindy leads the charge in helping conscious business owners discover and embody their unique rhythm in business so they can transcend the status quo and shatter their glass ceiling. She is a Numerologist and Success Coach for Conscious Business Owners, Best Selling Author, International Film Festival Award winner, Host of the Life at Full Blast Podcast, and passionate advocate for the Central Okanagan Food Bank.

CINDY
Van Arnam

Q: What are some of the biggest challenges you've faced as an entrepreneur and how have you overcome them?

A: One of the biggest challenges I've faced as an entrepreneur would be what some refer to as the 'sister wound.' Having started a business without any experience or background, I hired several coaches and mentors in the beginning so I could learn quickly.

Why reinvent the wheel right?

One of these mentors turned out to be one of my greatest abusers - manipulating me into believing I should work for her for free, publicly humiliating me on social media, and displaying classic narcissistic behaviour.

I finally saw what was happening and decided to take my power back. It required me to leave a community, a deep friendship, and a business partnership so that I could stand on my own two feet. This was one of the hardest things I've ever had to do - and yet it was the best decision I could have ever made.

In choosing me, and my own greatest experience, I am now free from abuse. Within a year of leaving that mentorship, I became a first-time homeowner, started my own business again, got engaged, produced and acted in a short film about my life, and got featured in a major documentary.

Q: How do you maintain a work-life balance while running your own business, and how do you prioritize and manage your time?

A: I don't believe that 'balance' actually exists. I believe there is a rhythm to our lives, and sometimes we're more busy in our business and sometimes it's slower.

Learning to tap into this rhythm and accept it is the hard part. As an overachiever, I love to work, and I often forget to take care of the other parts of my life.

However, knowing my values, and including them in all aspects of my life has helped me to maintain focus on what's most important. So, when business is busy, I can give myself permission to let up on other areas, and when business is slow, I don't beat myself up for taking some down time.

Q: How do you stay motivated and resilient during tough times in your business?

A: Motivation and resilience during the tough times in business comes from having a clear vision, one that has been painted in my imagination in high definition, and then knowing on a deep level why that vision is so important.

This why runs so deeply through every aspect of my life that it drives me forward no matter what obstacle I come up against. I know who I am, I know what I want, and this why helps me to find solutions when it seems I've run out of options.

Being an entrepreneur guarantees one thing - that you will become a solution finder. This deep burning why guides me to those solutions, and keeps me moving forward no matter what.

Q: What problem or need does your business solve, and what motivated you to address it?

A: I help conscious business owners discover and embody their rhythm in business so they can transcend the status quo and break their glass ceiling through the nuance of numbers and Universal law.

When I first started my business I had a serious lack of self-worth and confidence due to my past filled with abuse and cocaine addiction. I didn't have a lot going for me other than my determination to succeed.

In not only overcoming my challenges but also learning to thrive and create wildly wealthy experiences for myself, I started to witness a phenomenon in the business world - one where so many business owners are trying to fit themselves into the box of another's making.

In learning to make big bold moves for me, and now being part of an award-winning film project, a major documentary, and becoming a 10X best-selling author, all while living life at full blast without burning out - I know the missing piece that most business owners need to understand.

It's all about learning to dance to the beat of your own drum.

Q: What advice would you give to someone who is considering starting their own business?

A: Learn who you are at the core of your being and have a clear, high-definition vision of what you want to experience. Ask for help and get advice, but always stay true to the core of your truth because that will guide you forward, even if people give you shady advice.

Q: What do you believe are the keys to building a strong brand identity and reputation?

A: Authenticity. Consistency. Commitment.

Q: Pink or red lipstick?

A: Neither - but I think I have a red lipstick somewhere in a drawer.

Worldwide Title, CEO and Founder Marcie Gregorio is a new generation expert specializing in luxury residential and commercial real estate closings and investment opportunities in the State of Florida.

MARCIE
Gregorio

Q: Can you tell us about your journey as an entrepreneur and what inspired you to start your own business?

A: My journey as an entrepreneur began in 2017, during a very challenging time in my life. I was going through a difficult divorce, raising my three-year-old daughter, and had no financial resources to start with. However, I was driven by a deep-seated desire to create something of my own, something that would allow me to provide for my daughter and build a future for us. The real estate industry had always been a part of my life, having grown up in a family business centered around real estate. This background, combined with my passion for helping people achieve their dreams of homeownership, inspired me to start Worldwide Title.

The decision to start my own business was also motivated by a desire to break free from the limitations that were holding me back. I wanted to create a company that not only set a new standard in the title and escrow industry but also empowered me to overcome my personal challenges. My grit and determination to succeed were indescribable, and I was determined to build a company that would stand out in an extremely competitive industry.

Q: What were some of the biggest challenges you faced when starting your business, and how did you overcome them?

A: Starting my business came with its fair share of challenges. One of the most significant hurdles was obscurity. In a

130

competitive industry like real estate, it's not enough to be good at what you do—people need to know you exist. In the early days, I had to work tirelessly to get my name and my company's name out there. I participated in seminars, networking events, panels, and even appeared on TV and in magazines. I knew that to overcome obscurity, I had to be everywhere, showcasing the unique value my company brought to the table.

Another major challenge was establishing credibility in an industry that often frowns upon newcomers, especially when they are women. I had to deliver 150% in every transaction, ensuring that our clients and partners experienced seamless, trusting care from the start of the transaction until closing day. Building these relationships was key to overcoming skepticism and earning the trust of the real estate community.

I also had to balance my role as a mother with the demands of building a business from scratch. It wasn't easy, but my daughter was and still is my greatest motivation. Her presence in my life gave me the strength to push through the toughest days, and she continues to inspire me to strive for greater heights.

Q: Can you share a significant milestone or achievement your business has reached, and what did you learn from it?

A: One of the most significant milestones for Worldwide Title was reaching a point where we began receiving multiple offers from Fortune 500 companies looking to buy us out. This was a clear indication that we had not only established ourselves as a major player in the industry but had also created a brand that was highly valuable. However, despite these offers, I decided not to sell. This decision was rooted in my belief that we still have more to achieve, particularly in elevating the standards of the title and escrow industry.

This experience taught me the importance of staying true to my vision and values. While the offers were tempting, I realized that my ultimate goal was not just financial success but also making a lasting impact on the industry and the clients we serve. I learned that success isn't just about reaching the top; it's about maintaining the standards and relationships that got you there.

Q: How do you stay innovative and adapt to changes in your industry?

A: Staying innovative in the real estate industry requires a deep understanding of both the market and the needs of our clients and partners. At Worldwide Title, we continuously strive to set the bar higher by embracing advanced technologies, such as proprietary software for managing deal flow and virtual closings. These tools allow us to offer a seamless, efficient experience for our clients, which is crucial in today's fast-paced world.

Additionally, I believe that staying innovative means being proactive in seeking out opportunities to learn and grow. Whether it's attending industry conferences, engaging with thought leaders, or simply listening to the feedback from our clients and partners, I'm always looking for ways to improve our services and stay ahead of industry trends.

Innovation also comes from a place of giving back and supporting others. By mentoring and encouraging other women to step out of their comfort zones and pursue their dreams, I've found that I, too, grow and learn in the process. The more I give, the more I receive, and this cycle of generosity and growth keeps me and my company at the forefront of the industry.

Lindsay Maheu is a dedicated mom and the owner of Vigor Advantage Fitness Studio, where she empowers people to reclaim their confidence through personalized fitness and wellness plans. With her expertise and passion for integrating physical and mental health, Lindsay helps clients achieve their goals while maintaining balance in their busy lives.

LINDSAY *Maheu*

Q: Have you found any specific advantages or opportunities in being a woman in your industry?

A: Many women who have stopped working with male personal trainers often share that they felt misunderstood regarding their fitness levels, were pushed too hard, or were uncomfortable discussing sensitive topics like menstrual cycles or pregnancy factors. When training women, I take into account where they are in life and adjust the intensity of their workouts accordingly, ensuring they feel comfortable. This approach has helped me build lasting relationships with my clients. They aren't just names on a roster; they're individuals whose thoughts and feelings I truly care about.

Q: What problem or need does your business solve, and what motivated you to address it?

A: I help women who no longer feel confident in their bodies due to reduced mobility, weight gain, postpartum changes, or injury. I guide them toward regaining confidence by pairing physical health with mental health and stress reduction as the foundation of our fitness plans. My motivation stems from my own experience in wrestling during high school and university, where I competed for Team Canada. I had to stop due to an injury, but the pressure of weight classes and constant stepping on the scale affected even the most confident athletes. After my injury, I gained weight and lost mobility, and it impacted my self-esteem. Although I was studying Kinesiology, focusing solely on my physical recovery did nothing for my mental and emotional well-being. That's when my mission was born:

To demonstrate a sustainable way to incorporate fitness into life without adding stress, to boost confidence in one's abilities by prioritizing both mental and physical health, and to motivate with genuine care, positivity, and focus in every interaction.

Q: What advice would you give to someone who is considering starting their own business?

A: Get as much experience as possible. Before opening my own studio at 25, I had already gained 10 years of experience in the industry. This allowed me to not only run my business efficiently but also truly understand who I could help the most.

Q: How do you prioritize tasks and manage time effectively as an entrepreneur?

A: Being both a mom to a toddler and a business owner can feel overwhelming, with constant demands pulling you in multiple directions. I avoid this by being strict with my schedule and using time-blocking. For example, my client hours are set and planned, but so is my family time. Keeping my "why"—my family—at the forefront of my business is always a top priority.

Q: How do you measure the success and growth of your business?

A: Get as much experience as possible. Before opening my own studio at 25, I had already gained 10 years of experience in the industry. This allowed me to not only run my business efficiently but also truly understand who I could help the most. Even when the experience is not the exact same thing, it will likely help in some way. I was able to increase my ability to speak in crowds by teaching group fitness classes. As well as strive to learn all you can within your field from a trusted mentor. Group training was never something I felt I wanted to lay all my cards in, however by obtaining over 20 fitness related certifications I was able to take valuable knowgale away from these instructors not just about fitness but also about how they ran a successful business. How they interacted and how they talked about fitness with new individuals is still some of the most important things I use today during onboarding for personal training, Get your experience from those who you look up to both in learning level and values.

Q: Can you share a particularly memorable success story or milestone from your entrepreneurial journey?

A: My biggest success came during the time when most were going through a lot of pivoting within their businesses. During covid and the shut down. It was during this year that I won my first award for best personal training, and was fully independent from my previous full time job. Achieving this award was my green flag that I was truly ready to swap out working the standard 9-5 to working on my dream job instead. Fast forward 4 years later and I get to enjoy the freedom of setting my own hours and have also continued to win that same award every year moving forward.

Q: What role do you think mentorship and support networks play for women in entrepreneurship?

A: When working for a self made business, at times it can be lonely. There is often no one working down the hall to stop in and chat with and no one planning holiday parties. When you take the time to network with others this loneliness within your business can be easily solved. There are many events and summits for helping bounce ideas off like minded people, or just to celebrate the goals you have hit that family would not as easily understand.

Q: Pink or red lipstick?

A: Red.

Lynda Moffatt is a multi-faceted artist living in South-Western Ontario, Canada. She creates representational paintings with oils and acrylics, from small en plein air paintings, to life size large scale paintings. Enjoying all this variety and subject matter keeps her creative energy flowing.

LYNDA
Moffatt

Q: Can you tell me about your journey as an entrepreneur? What inspired you to start your own business?

A: I have always thought like an entrepreneur. Nothing else seemed to fit. Growing up with my family living in a border city, it became natural for me to learn about the dynamics of different countries, money, and the diversities that united us along the lakes. My creativity was always at the forefront of my mind, and it always found a way to surface, no matter what else I was trying to do.

Eventually, people started knowing me as the artist, without knowing about my formal education for that "real" job.

There is no road map for artists like there is for other businesses. However, there are certain avenues one might find to travel on and discover what works best for them. I believe this is truly why they call it a "Life Study of the Arts."

Q: What are some of the biggest challenges you've faced as a woman entrepreneur, and how have you overcome them?

A: Some of the biggest challenges I've faced as a woman entrepreneur include learning that it's okay if people don't like you. It's also okay if they don't like your artwork. You toughen up a bit, yet stay true to yourself. Enjoy the life you wish to live. Learn to be okay with the outcomes. Always have a plan A, B, C, and maybe even D and E.

Q: How do you maintain a work-life balance while running your own business?

A: Very carefully! I have several calendars linked, and it really helps on Sunday evening to reflect on the past week and set new goals for the upcoming week. I always take half a day to regroup, refresh, and rejoice in my accomplishments.

Q: What strategies have you found most effective for networking and building professional relationships as a female entrepreneur?

A: Over the years, I've belonged to several networking communities in different areas. These relationships have now lasted for more than 20 years. Keeping in touch via social media, email, and in-person get-togethers is by far the most effective.

Q: In your experience, what are some common misconceptions or stereotypes about women in business, and how do you challenge or overcome them?

A: When I first studied Art Business while working for a major art gallery in the States, it was evident that galleries could and would take advantage of women artists, often stereotyping them as air-headed, scattered, and lacking organizational skills. Each woman artist that came into our gallery received one-on-one training from me on how NOT to get ripped off by galleries and how to get organized.

Q: What advice would you give to other women who are considering starting their own businesses?

A: I would advise them, as I was once advised, to be true to themselves, listen to their own hearts, and stay real. I would also add, nowadays, never use themselves as a pawn to move forward. Sex sells, but to whom? Stay classy!

Q: What role do you think mentorship and support networks play for women in entrepreneurship?

A: Mentorship plays a huge role, and it's important to both give and receive it. We should strive to learn, grow, and share. If we do it right, those who come after us will be better than us. Networking with each other is also very important. You may be the connector in your network, which seems to come naturally to me.

Q: What are some trends or developments in your industry that you're particularly excited about?

A: I am very excited to see art movements happening all over the world. Being part of one personally is not only motivating for me, but it is also a force that is growing and moving forward collectively!

Pink or Red lipstick? Warm Pink.

Kim Mowatt passionately loves horses and dedicates herself to raising awareness about mental health. With her background as a horsewoman from the Cariboo and her role as the founder of Wise Women on Horseback, she blends her love for horses with her expertise in mental health, as she holds credentials as a Registered Psychiatric Nurse and Certified Professional Counsellor. She excels as an author and an educator, specifically teaching individuals how to transition from stress to happiness.

KIM
Mowatt

Kim has co-authored a book called "Emotional Intelligence Mental Health Matters" and is currently working on her upcoming book, "The Wild Horse Within; Seven Essential Skills to Reset From Stress to Happiness." This book aims to guide readers on taking control of their emotional responses to stress, achieving a state of well-being and make happiness their new normal.

"Happiness can be found, even in the darkest of times, if one only remembers to turn on the light." J. K. Rowling

Natalia embarked upon a voyage that morning, traversing countless miles in pursuit of a compassionate listener and refuge. Her journey, originating from the bustling streets of Vancouver, led her to the serene expanse of our lakeside Chrome Heart Ranch. When she arrived in her jeep, a torrent of her words released, trembling on the brink of articulation that depicted her spouse in stark, venomous hues. The revelation of her husband's infidelity, coupled with the realization that her children had forged paths of their own, left her confronting a reality where her once vibrant world lay in fragments.

The intensity of Natalia's emotions was palpable, mirrored in the intensity of her speech, and her gestures were a vivid portrayal of the turmoil raging within. Upon her arrival, her slender frame quivered, with fury simmering beneath her composed exterior. I became an empathic witness to her rage, sorrow, confusion, and human vulnerability. Her quest for solace found a temporary haven in our shared connection, her tears carving rivers of mascara down her cheeks, yet in those moments of shared silence, she found a fleeting peace.

Our encounter unfolded against the backdrop of the ranch's tranquil beauty. As the day gave way to dusk, the melancholic cry of a loon pierced the air, its lament echoing Natalia's own. Clad not in the armour of her professional attire but in the casual grace of denim, leather chaps and red heart patchwork pointed toe cowgirl boots, she presented a stark contrast to what she wore in the urban jungle of Vancouver. In our connection, simple acts came alive. We savoured a hearty meal, and watched the graceful flight of sand-hill cranes, their wings slicing through the air, while their calls filled our ears with a symphony of nature. As we went horseback riding, the rhythmic hoofbeats resonated through the earth. In those moments, her anguish unraveled, revealing glimpses of her resilient spirit, like a fragile flower pushing through concrete.

She tenderly bonded with Karma, our loyal Maremma guard dog, and lightly climbed onto Fantastico, our serene Peruvian Paso, and the vibrant fields of wildflowers stretched out in front of her, filling the air with a sweet floral scent. The kaleidoscope of colours danced in the sunlight, while the sweet scent of blossoms filled the air. While she began her journey towards healing, a gentle breeze brushed against her skin, bringing about a deep sense of tranquillity and the promise of renewal. These encounters created a bridge that connected her to a world where she could renew trust and connection. Guided by the soothing rhythm of Fantastico's Peruvian horse gait and surrounded by the healing power of nature, Natalia embarked on a path of self-reflection and personal growth.

The Heartmath Quick Coherence Technique became a pivotal tool in her journey, offering a tangible means to calm the storm within. Witnessing the transformation of her heart's rhythm from chaos to coherence was a testament to the power of heart intelligence, a concept championed by the Heartmath Institute. This method, grounded in the principle that positive emotions can harmonize the heart, brain, and nervous system, provided Natalia with a sanctuary from the cyclone of her emotions.

As a Registered Psychiatric Nurse, counsellor, and riding instructor, I've observed the deep-seated anxieties and stresses that plague many. The adoption of the Heartmath Biofeedback tool at Chrome Heart Ranch, integrated with our equine therapy programs, represented a confluence of science and nature. Through this holistic approach, Natalia, like many before her, found the means to navigate her emotional landscape, journey from the depths of despair to the shores of self-discovery and transforming her pain into a source of strength and resilience.

Lipstick is coconut and pear Burts Bees moisturizing lip balm combined with a soft pink Shiseido.

Saireen Neilsen is a Vancouver-based entrepreneur and coach who developed a course called Loving Menopausitivity™ designed to help perimenopausal and menopausal women prepare for and manage their menopausal symptoms and be healthy, strong, sexy, confident and thriving. In 2021, Saireen received a Global WIIN award for outstanding achievement for her course.

SAIREEN *Neilsen*

Q: What problem or need does your business solve and what inspired you to start your own business?

A: I help perimenopausal and menopausal women prepare for and manage their menopausal symptoms in a natural way without hormone replacement and side effects. Menopause is a beautiful transition and doesn't have to mean the decline of health and beauty that people often think it does. By utilizing my system, The Loving Menopausitivity™ Way, women can minimize or eliminate symptoms naturally, without medication or prescription HRT. My Loving Menopausitivity™ program helps women during their menopausal journey to be strong, healthy, sexy and thriving and be more alive and vibrant than ever before.

When Dean Graziosi put me in the hot seat during his inner circle he asked me what I was passionate about and since I suffered from severe menopausal symptoms for over ten years and had researched and interviewed women who had gone through it and were going through it, I was passionate about sharing my knowledge, experience, and awareness.

It inspired me to design my Loving Menopausitivity™ program about perimenopause and menopause.

Q: How do you stay motivated and resilient during tough times in your business?

A: There were times where I felt unmotivated but knowing that there are so many women out there who don't know what to do about their menopausal symptoms motivates me. Everytime I slow down, I hear stories about women who are being misdiagnosed and treated with disrespect. That motivates me to learn other modalities to help women. In the past few years

I've become a Quantum Release Practitioner; a Certified Hypnotist; and a Certified Usui Reiki Practitioner – Level I & II. Even Oprah couldn't get her doctors to take her menopausal symptoms seriously. Recently Halle Berry's menopausal symptoms were misdiagnosed. I was one of these women and I have so much depth of knowledge, experience, and awareness that I can share to guide them through their uncertain times during their perimenopausal and menopausal journeys and give them hope and natural ways to deal with their symptoms so that they don't have to suffer like I did. That is motivating to me.

Q: Can you share a story about a particularly memorable customer interaction or experience?

A: I feel blessed to have helped several women bring awareness to what they are going through and let them know how they can deal with it differently and naturally. They learn that what they are going through is normal and that they can do something about it. They are better equipped to ask questions of their doctors. They can design their own menopausal journey.

Q: What role do you think mentorship and support networks play for women in entrepreneurship?

A: I think it is healthy to have mentors who can guide you through a process. You don't know what you don't know until you've gone through it and you don't need to know everything until you get there and are ready. When you get stuck it is valuable to get unstuck by having mentors and support networks to help you with your next steps. When you are able to articulate where you are at with your business and don't know how to move forward, it is great to have an opportunity to learn from someone who has gone through it and can meet you where you are at. We brainstorm on how best to move forward and determine what resources we need to launch or to move forward with our programs.

Q: Can you discuss the role of networking and partnerships in growing your business?

A: It is important to network and collaborate with other women because menopause is about dealing with changes from head to toe. When you collaborate with someone, they may have different insights and experiences in a particular area. They become your go to and they become your inner circle and support group. It allows you to be inspired by and to grow with other like-minded women.

Q: Can you share a particularly memorable success story or milestone from your entrepreneurial journey?

A: In 2021 I received an award from the Global Women Inventors & Innovators Network, (Global WIIN), a global organization that focuses on innovations that benefit individuals in the workplace and business environment. My Loving Menopausitivity™ Program was recognized for outstanding achievements, tenacity, and commitment capable of impacting lives.

I flew to London, UK and met with Dr. Bola Olabisi, the founder and CEO of Global WIIN who presented me with the award.

It was such a privilege and an honour to be a recipient of this award from an organization that shines the spotlight on the creativity of hundreds of women in North America, Europe, Asia, Africa and the Middle East.

Q: Pink or red lipstick?

A: Pink!

Lise Parton is a late-blooming writer, poet and author. Her interest in storytelling, journaling and writing bits and pieces all her life, has grown into becoming a fully published writer and author of several multi-genre eBooks. Lisa lives in the Okanagan, BC, Canada.

LISE
Parton

Q: Can you share a particularly memorable success story or milestone from your entrepreneurial journey?

A: Writers and creatives are generous about defining milestones. Each project, each creative endeavour feels like the birth of a unique baby and is most certainly considered an important milestone, especially if it has taken months or even years to bring to life. Let me share some of my significant milestones with you.

I suppose, like a first kiss, or your first car, my first published eBook was a special milestone. Toys On Guard, a seasonal Christmas children's story, was a milestone and a legacy story for my two boys, and delightfully published with my youngest son's illustrations drawn when he was about 7 years old, (he is now in his mid 30's). It also had an audio clip of a bedtime song I often sang to my young children before bed. *Toys on Guard* is the only eBook I published on iTunes iBooks platform to date, as I now use Amazon.

Another impactful milestone was *The Magic Stick,* a youth fantasy story with magical forest creatures, a treasure hunt, and practical information about all the wildlife in and around our remote off-grid cabin. It was a story created to teach my boys to respect and love the lake and forests in a way that was sprinkled with adventure and magic. For this book, I taught myself to digitally draw in order to illustrate the book the way I wanted. That was a huge milestone for me. *The Magic Stick* is available as an eBook on Amazon in Kindle format.

I could not leave out the milestone of realizing my life-long dream of writing and publishing a romance novel. This project was 30 years in the making. I wrote it in the 90's when I was a busy mom, wife and worked full-time, with a home and a summer cabin. It took COVID and a focus at a later time in my life to get back to completing it, with the editing and finally publishing. *Act One Willow Beach* is a lovely adult romance, available as an eBook on Amazon.

Other milestones include, *Your Power To Heal Is Real,* a book with healing affirmations and poems and prose for those needing support during a healing crisis. This book has helped others (and myself) when we are faced with an accident or injury along life's journey. It is a private cheerleading companion of proactive self-help for you. Even the accompanying photos in this book are a visual delight in healing. (Also available on Amazon as an eBook).

Even though I have had multiple milestones in my writing career, I think of each one as special and unique and I am very grateful for each one. Stories or poems I have written by request for others, *The Boot Under The Bush & Could It Be? Is That The Boot I see?*, two rhyming, short children's books written for a grandmother to share with her grandchildren about an incident involving a lost boot; or *Love, Magic & Mermaids,* a story I wrote for two young neighbours of mine who were little mermaid souls. Even my other poetry books like the one written about my love and passion for the card game of Texas Hold'em, *The Rhythm of Poker,* or my love of food and food memories, *Tasty Treasure & Edible Pleasures*, are all unique milestones for me as a creative. Naturally, I have to mention my last exciting milestone, *Tropical Transformation,* an adult fantasy romance I released on Amazon last August. This was my first adult fantasy romance, and I loved creating it! It is a great 'beach read' for you, ladies. (Find all my book links on my home website: liseparton.com on my Bookshelf Page.)

What I would love to share with you is that each step you take in creating a business milestone can be exhilarating and rewarding! However, there is always room to create more and build in your career. This is what makes your journey worthwhile, your goals, with achievement of those goals, and continuing each day with hope, desire, focus and determination to continue to keep achieving in business. *Just remember to celebrate the little wins every day and acknowledge them, and not just focus solely on the big wins.*

Q: What role do you think mentorship and support networks play for women in entrepreneurship?

Honestly, mentorship and support networks are critical for both women and men. The invaluable support, knowledge, expertise and guidance I have always received through my writing communities and mentorships have played a huge role in my writing experiences. I highly recommend joining peer groups and attending networking events in your individual fields. Every business, every career, every field is related to so many others. Your success is always linked to others. Just consider, if someone is not interested in what you have to offer, someone they may know might be, keep on connecting.

Q: How do you prioritize and manage your goals and tasks as an entrepreneur?

As a creative, I tend to flow where the wind blows, as I have several projects on the go and tend to work on what inspires me at the time. Having said that, my field is a little more forgiving in that aspect, yours may not be. However, I am committed every single day to work on my writing, and I start every morning in a creative headspace. After my personal affirmations, with coffee in hand, I sit down to write. For several hours every morning my focus is on my writing work, and my regular day's activities start after that. Focus and set routines are a valuable entrepreneurial asset. Stick to it.

Q: What role do you believe technology plays in the success of your business?

As a publisher of eBooks, I am completely relying on technology in so many aspects of my writing career. I publish digitally, draw digitally, use digital photos and rely on digital software to produce my digital social media for much of my networking. I also create my stories and poems on a device now, having discarded pen and paper as well. It has been my evolution, though I do not fault anyone who chooses to use different means of operating their own businesses. However, it is obvious that we are in a digital age and must utilize it where possible. Recognize and use any technology that can assist you.

Q: What advice would you give to someone who is considering starting their own business?

Get your ducks in a row. Research, create a plan, ask for help and then jump! Everything doesn't have to be figured out immediately, life, including business is always a learning curve. However, just remember that if you have to look back on your life, consider Lucille Ball's quote,

"I'd rather regret the things I've done than regret the things I haven't done."

Q: Pink or red lipstick? A: A *strong pink* lipstick!

Billie Aadmi the Founder of Go Mindspire Inc. She is a Board Designated Trainer of NLP, Time Line Therapy, Hypnotherapy, and Master Results Coach. She is committed to helping others get out of their own way and get on the path to their MagnifESSENCE. She is a single mom to two beautiful children and fur baby.

Q: What challenges have you faced as a woman entrepreneur, and how have you overcome them?

A: Growing up in a traditional East Indian family, I was often told I couldn't achieve certain things simply because I was a girl. Instead of accepting this, it fueled my determination to prove that not only could I accomplish anything, that being a woman WAS my superpower. Over time, I realized it was because I am a woman that I could excel in ways others doubted, including spending nearly two decades as a Police Officer. What was once labeled a weakness became my greatest strength, teaching me resilience and igniting my inner drive to succeed.

Q: Have you found any specific advantages or opportunities in being a woman in your industry?

A: After 20 years as a Police Officer, where I often faced trauma head-on, I've gained a deep understanding of the emotional pain people carry. My natural compassion and empathy—once seen as "too nice" for the role—allowed me to connect on a profound level. Now, in my journey as a healer and teacher, those traits have become invaluable assets. As a woman, I can hold space for others, guiding them from their pain and darkness toward their healing and light. My ability to "see through" people's pain gives me the unique advantage to facilitate their transformation in an authentic and nurturing way.

Q: What role do mentorship and support networks play for women in entrepreneurship?

A: Mentorship and support networks are essential to thriving as an entrepreneur. They elevate your energy and mindset, keeping you on the path to success. For women, sisterhood has never been more important. Growing up with two brothers and lacking strong female support, I often felt isolated. However now, surrounded by a community of like-minded practitioners, trainers, and students who share my values and goals, the journey toward growth and uplifting humanity is more fulfilling and successful.

I believe in continuous learning and having a "one hand up, one hand down" philosophy—always learning from those ahead of us and sharing that wisdom with others. A good mentor will challenge you to expand your perspective and inspire you to reach new heights. If you want to keep evolving, having a mentor or coach is non-negotiable in unlocking your full potential.

A: I don't have a "NO" number. Every "no, not right now" is just one step closer to the person who needs my light to be shone to brighten theirs. When you find your purpose, it becomes bigger than you, and the drive to fulfill it overcomes any obstacle. My mission is to help others release unnecessary suffering, just as I've done for myself. I'm no longer running toward emergencies with lights and sirens; instead, I offer people something more transformative—lasting change. Teaching Time Line Therapy and the world's most powerful mind-body tools that help people resolve deep emotional pain without reliving it is both gentle and powerful, especially for First Responders like myself. Knowing this keeps me moving forward, no matter how tough things get. When your purpose is to uplift humanity and raise the consciousness of the planet, there is no time to procrastinate.

After I went through my full personal breakthrough in 2023 using these tools I now teach since we always start with self, I've made extraordinary strides in my real estate investing career. This journey of self-discovery has empowered me to replace my living expenses with passive income, being awarded the Freedom Fighter Award, and enabling me to retire from my role as a Police Officer and dedicate myself fully to this Great Work from a place of service and purpose. My experience stands as a testament to the incredible power of getting out of your own way and allowing the Universe to align resources that help fulfill your destiny. As life flows effortlessly, I am filled with gratitude and blessed to embrace the remarkable life I live each day.

Q: Can you share a memorable customer interaction or experience?

A: There have been so many life-changing moments with my clients—some earn more money, others experience physical pain disappearing, and all of them walk away happier. One stands out: a woman I met randomly at a home show later took my Practitioner course and told me it had changed her life forever. After years of practicing meditation, she had never reached the level of peace she found through Time Line Therapy. The "quiet" in her mind was so profound, she said it felt like a true awakening. Moments like that remind me of the power of this work.

In two decades of policing, I never heard anyone say I had changed their life. Yet, in just eight months of pursuing this new path, I've been blessed to hear several people share how profoundly their lives have been transformed. The joy and fulfillment that come from guiding others towards their true MagnifESSENCE are beyond measure.

Q: What advice would you give to other women considering starting their own businesses?

A: Heal yourself first. Uncover your inner gifts and live your purpose. When you align with your mission, it's no longer "business"—it becomes service. From that place, you're not just building a business; you're fulfilling a calling and living your destiny.

Q: How do you maintain a work-life balance while running your business?

A: As a single mother of two beautiful children, balance means being fully present in the moment. When I'm with my children, they are my focus. When they're with their father, I focus on my mission. By showing my children that I can be a powerful and successful businesswoman, I'm also teaching them that once you find your passion, nothing can stop you from living life to the fullest.

Q: What strategies have been most effective for networking and building professional relationships as a female entrepreneur?

A: I approach networking from a place of service, not selling. I focus on the powerful skills I offer others to help them grow, evolve, and heal. I put myself in their shoes and think, "If someone could help me like this, I'd want to know about it." This mindset of sharing knowledge has allowed me to form deep, meaningful relationships, rather than transactional ones. My job is to hold up the light for others to come towards when their journey calls for an uplevel.

Q: Looking ahead, what are your goals and aspirations for your business?

A: My ultimate goal is to share Time Line Therapy and these transformative mind-body tools with the entire world. I envision myself on large stages, inspiring others to find their light and embrace their MagnifESSENCE. This work has the potential to change countless lives, and I'm committed to making Time Line Therapy a household name and ultimately end needless suffering by uplifting humanity, increasing the frequency of the planet and raising consciousness.

Bonus question—Red or pink lipstick? Definitely RED! The colour of LOVE

Erica Paynter is the founder and CEO of My Virtual Bookkeeper, a bookkeeping practice dedicated to helping cleaning business owners improve efficiency and foster growth. She was born and raised on the coast of Virginia and has spent her entire adult life as an entrepreneur in multiple service-based industries. Erica has a deep love for helping people, which is reflected in her commitment to supporting business owners focus on what they love most.

ERICA *Paynter*

Q: Can you tell me about your journey as an entrepreneur? What inspired you to start your own business?

A: As a teen mom, I made the quick decision to become a cosmetologist to be able to support our young family, but it wasn't my dream. My dream was to become an accountant, but that wasn't feasible at the time as I was 19, pregnant, and needed income fast.

Sixteen years later, as many will never forget, March of 2020 brought a lot of change – to the world as a whole, but specifically to how the workplace operates. A cosmetologist and salon owner at the time, I was struggling with the idea of having to sit at home during all the shutdowns. It wasn't being at home that was such a struggle; it was the inability to work to feed my family.

I knew this was my chance – my mulligan – my second chance at my dream. So I put myself back through school with the intention of starting my own bookkeeping practice. One year later, in March of 2021, I opened My Virtual Bookkeeper – and every moment since then has been like living a dream.

Q: What problem or need does your business solve, and what motivated you to address it?

A: Business owners go into business because they have a passion to help others. Rarely do they go into business saying, "I can't wait to do my own bookkeeping!" It's a part of business that many ignore because they just don't enjoy it. But it's not only necessary, it gives the business owners the data they need to make decisions such as when to spend, when to save, when to hire, when to scale, and when and how to grow their business.

This is the part of owning a business that I'm truly passionate about. So why not fuel my passion, help others with the part of business they don't love, and make money all at the same time?

It's where my passion, purpose, and paycheck meet!

Q: How did you come up with the idea for your business, and what was the process like from concept to execution?

A: Oh man it was totally a God-thing. As I said before, COVID shut down salons across the country and I was left at home - bored to tears. I started conversing with my husband about creating a home-based business, something we had talked about for years but didn't have the time to really launch anything. I started searching the internet for home based businesses and one of the first things that popped up was something that aligned with my forever-ago dream.

I knew God was using this awful COVID experience to allow me to pursue the career that I had once given up to be able to raise my family. Had I pursued accounting years before, I probably would have ended up in a corporate setting which didn't align with my passion of being present with my kids. Everything lined up just as it should. In God's perfect timing, not mine.

Q: What role do you believe technology plays in the success of your business?

A: My virtual-based business would not be possible without technology and the constant innovation that occurs. Laptop and internet are two obvious technological components of operating a virtual-based business, but there is so much more that ensures seamless operations. For instance, cloud-accounting software makes it possible for me and my clients to access up to date financial information from anywhere in the world, automation tools reduce the burden of repetitious tasks, and secure data sharing and storage platforms protect sensitive information and allow my team to access the same things I access without having to give them passwords across an unsecure email or text. Client portals give a centralized location for communication between my team and my clients.

Technology plays a role in the scalability of my business, as well, with tools like time tracking software, task management software, and so many other softwares that help with communication and collaboration. I think it's safe to say that my business wouldn't be without technology.

Q: How do you measure the success and growth of your business?

A: I feel like success is relative. For instance, at what point does one consider they "made it"? Does having a bad day, week, month or year erase all the progress made before that and prevent future progress?

Success is consistently learning.

Success is making the best of the situation you're in.

Success is letting God take the reins and trusting He's leading you in the right direction (even if it's not the preferred direction).

Success is working smarter but sometimes still harder.

Success includes being content in the valleys because you know it's a matter of time before you'll be back on top of the mountain.

I'm not a millionaire. I can't go on a Kim K shopping spree. I'm not where I want to be, but I'm better than I was before. I have the encouragement of family (especially my extremely supportive husband and kids), friends and clients. And because of God's grace, mercies and favor, I feel kind of successful.

Q: Pink or red lipstick? Pink!

Kerri Anne Kedziora is a woman on a mission to empower cleaning business owners to overcome obstacles and claim success.

KERRI ANNE
Kedziora

Q: How did you come up with the idea for your business, and what was the process like from concept to execution?

A: When COVID hit my cleaning business was approximately 98% residential cleaning and when the government announced service providers were not allowed to enter homes we lost 98% of our business and became homeless. We spent 3 months in a decrepit fifth wheel trailer with no plumbing or water. At this time we took every opportunity that came available to stay in vacation rental properties just yo have a sense of home....and a hot shower now fnd then! What we found was that there was not one single property that was clean to my standards and I realized that there are no industry standards for vacation rental cleaning so I set out to create an employee training system and coach cleaning business owners how to attract, retain and train amazing employees!

Interestingly enough; I called my highly priced mentor and asked his opinion of my idea. I was excited and looking for advice to get started. He told me to forget it, that it was a total waste of my time. I immediately ended the arrangement with him as my coach and set out to find a new one!

I joined Russel Brunsons "One Funnel Away" challenge and started building my business. I always feel a sense of pride at the woman I was in that time. Proud of myself to not let anyone talk me out of the idea I knew would change my life!

Q: What were some of the biggest challenges you faced when starting your business, and how did you overcome them?

A: When I began, I had no idea how to use social media and other digital marketing products. I didn't want to post and was shy about "strutting my stuff." I had been raised to believe that women should remain quiet and reserved. We should be clean and pretty but never speak above a whisper. Putting myself "out there" on social media, proclaiming my expertise, was scary.

I sought out a new mentor who would help me learn the strategies to create this business, and I learned social media strategies. Most importantly, I forced myself to ignore the voices in my head that told me I was not enough.

A: I am a hands-on mentor who takes time to spend with my clients, helping them overcome imposter syndrome and the limiting beliefs that creep up with each level of growth. Typically, my clients need help letting go of the belief that the business can't possibly run without them. I help get them out of working IN the business and empower them to work ON their business.

A: Moving from teaching business owners how to run their business to facilitating teams to run those owners' entire administration was a huge undertaking that took immense courage. It has been almost a year since we launched the freedom program, and I am continually amazed at the massive strides we have made. Even though we still have a ways to go, it is absolutely awesome!

The biggest realization has been that, many times, the thing that stands in our clients' way when it comes to growth and success is actually the client themselves!

A: Constant learning, pivoting at will, and always seeking higher education are the things I feel are most important. Seeking relationships of proximity and being open-minded are key in this fast-paced environment.

A: One Christmas, we had a huge setback as we had put all of our financial efforts into marketing and growth. Sales dropped before Christmas, and we lost a huge monthly client. On top of that, a client from almost 6 months earlier disputed their payment, causing money to be taken from my bank account. I was short on payroll, and so broke I couldn't afford my monthly prescription! At a time when I had been promising employees a Christmas bonus, we couldn't even make payroll.

I had no choice but to be honest with the staff and explain that we didn't have enough money to cover payroll. I split the money we had left equally among the staff and created a promo that brought in new clients at an extremely reduced rate to raise money to catch up on payroll. My husband and I did not celebrate Christmas traditionally that year. There were no gifts, and we were too broke to have a nice meal. In fact, we put together a meal of remnants from the fridge: veggie sandwiches and lemonade! As always, we were grateful to have each other and celebrated that our employees were kind and thoughtful about the payroll issue.

A: I have had the pleasure of working with clients who have overcome massive obstacles to find their success. So many come to mind, but one of my favorite stories is about my client Erin (a co-author in Brains and Beauty), who started in my program at a reduced rate on payments due to her limitations as a single mom just starting out. I could see that she was a woman who deserved more from life, and she had the strength to excel! Throughout our first year working together, she grew her business slowly and methodically until the new year of 2024 when she took over our cleaning business, which we wanted to exit as we headed out on our mission to become digital nomads and experience traveling the world.

This opportunity increased her annual business revenue from around $30k per year to $50k per month! She is right up there with our top growth success clients.

A: I am looking forward to strengthening our admin team and providing services to 100 owners per month. My husband and I are on a mission to buy a 1 Euro home in Italy and, over the next couple of years, renovate a home while running our program from abroad. We plan to implement an exit plan within 5 years and pursue real estate in the future.

Pink!

Shelly Smee, Personal Real Estate Corporation, Associate Broker, Oakwyn Realty Ltd. Founder of Integrity Real Estate Group.

SHELLY
Smee

Q: Can you tell me about your journey as an entrepreneur? What inspired you to start your own business?

A: When I was 25 I was studio manager for an Architectural Glass Artist. One of our clients was a builder, his wife was a Realtor and the general contractor for their business. She came to the studio often, was very smart, organized and wise. She encouraged me to take the Real Estate Exam and become a Realtor, as it was a great career for a woman, with no glass ceiling and no unpredictable artists to manage. I was very interested in architecture, construction, interior design and I loved the opportunity to grow my own business.

Q: Have you found any specific advantages or opportunities in being a woman in your industry?

A: My personal experience has been one of being able to build trust quickly and have a deep empathy for what my clients are embarking upon. There have been many times where I have made connections with people because of my smile and attitude. Early in my career I took the time to really explain everything well, and became known for my firm and friendly negotiating style and patience. I learned quickly that creating Win-Win situations, while being a strong negotiator helped bring deals together. I believe women are great with the soft skills, such as being able to multi-task and reading a room and adjusting course quickly. One has to be prepared to do all the roles in a business until you figure out what is more cost effective to outsource.

Q: What role do you think mentorship and support networks play for women in entrepreneurship?

A: In the past 10-15 years I have noticed a huge shift in the number of women-led organizations that offer mentorship opportunities for female entrepreneurs.

YMCA, Dress For Success and The Forum, are known for their programs for women in various stages of their journey. One also needs to understand it's ok to ask for help. The idea of mental health and work life balance is a healthier mindset that is more acceptable and encouraged presently. Being an entrepreneur requires grit and determination so sometimes the idea of balance is nice but not possible. Every industry has an established pecking order, and as women have garnered more senior positions in tech, finance, real estate and higher education, the number of women able to mentor other women has also grown. I would like to say I had mentors or role models early in my career, but it just was not the culture of Real Estate 30 years ago. This was one of the reasons I became a Managing Broker in 2013. I am so proud of the many women who I have mentored over the past 10 years. It is rewarding to watch these women rising to the top of our industry and forging their own path. I believe in life-long learning, and in giving back. Being a mentor is important. It helps perpetuate a culture of excellence, passing on best practices and helpful tips to the next generation of women.

Q: How do you stay innovative and adapt to changes in your industry?

A: We are "blessed" with mandatory PDP courses to maintain our licenses, and for most top level agents, being a total nerd about learning new ways to innovate service and work smarter, not harder. This has meant we are often early adopter's of new technology. I have also learned that it is better to delegate things I am required to do, but I don't love, such as accounting and graphic design. We are one of the most regulated industries, so it helps to be adaptable to the constant legislative changes and understand a broad range of topics from finance, construction, legal, immigration, taxes and marketing.

Q: Can you discuss the role of networking and partnerships in growing your business?

A: I have always loved being a "Joiner". LOL..this is my 4th project with Pursuit 365! I have been a member of many different organizations from the Vancouver Board or Trade, Forum for Women Entrepreneurs, Managing Brokers of BC, as well as writing PDP courses for the Greater Vancouver Realtors and being a member of the Professional Conduct Committee. I also Volunteer on the Board of Directors of the Terminal City Glass Cooperative and spent many years as President of BC.

Diving, a Provincial Sport Organization. Through all of these interactions with a diverse range of people, I have developed a reputation for being a reliable and responsible person who will do whatever it takes to get the job done, while not losing my sense of humor. Ethics are a dominant core value for me, so naming my team The Integrity Real Estate Group seemed obvious. I am proud of the large network of people I interact with and as most of my business now comes from referrals, it is my main source of new business. Helping like minded people find home and make the next transition in life is very rewarding.

Q: Looking ahead, what are your goals and aspirations for the future of your business?

A: I am really excited about 2024. In September 2023 I made the tough decision to step away from my Managing Broker role and focus 100% on Integrity Real Estate Group. This transition through the next chapter of life. I also value my volunteer roles, traveling and making art, so it is important to carefully craft the succession plan for my role in the team and know that the next 10 years are going to look very different from the last 10. I am pursuing an additional designation, that of Certified Executor Advisor. I already specialize in Estate Sales, so having the CEA designation will further solidify my expertise in this area. With AI, Blockchain and many other technologies, what remains certain to me is the value of human connection and the satisfaction I feel from helping others.

Q: Pink or red lipstick? Pink!

Jessica Bouchard is the Creator and Owner of Crystal Therapy Intentional where she creates luxurious spa like products, organic herbal and caffeinated teas and coaches women through Crystal Therapy The Intentional Woman. She is an artist, a writer, a wife to a talented man, and mom to an extraordinary little girl.

Crystal Therapy was created in 2019 after asking my coach what I should do for a business. She asked me what I love and I jokingly replied wine and crystals.

Six months later I opened Crystal Therapy selling crystals and aromatherapy sprays. I held crystal classes and meditations with crystals.

January of 2020 I opened a meditation studio. It was very successful with community support. We had months of pre-booked classes, but sadly closed our doors when the world shut down.

I could have given up completely. In fact, for a brief moment I did.

Riddled with fear, I listened to guided meditations by Joe Dispenza.

One day, I came out of a meditation, went to my kitchen apothecary, and began blending teas. Recipes came to me from the ether. I had always blended healing teas, but these were different.

I added crystals infused with intention just like my sprays, and thus Crystal Therapy Intentional was born.

I started coaching women on self-love; how to move past the hard self-talk, and find their worth. I teach them how to pamper themselves with luxurious organic products, and how, through self-nurturing, they could expand out of their current situation into something more beautiful and satisfying.

I realized my mission had profound purpose as I helped women become who they longed to be, finding their true beauty within, and feeling free from self-doubt and outside ridicule. Healing through Self-love.

Healing often begins with ritual and reflection: drinking tea, having a salted bath, lighting a candle while journaling, and hiring a coach for accountability and guidance.

In helping others I've learned how to love myself more and have become inspired to share this love and intention with the world, one tea at a time.

I am inspired by powerful, influential, and loving women. Women who encourage others to expand who they are. I wanted to help others on a deeper level, and so, the tea and crystal shop was born.

Thank you, Earlene Vining. I'm eternally grateful to you for your nudge to stop making excuses and make it happen.

Women supporting women is an important part of success. As others help us, we must also take initiative and be there to support and help our sisters.

I like to believe that my business, which includes the help of my eight-year-old daughter and my husband, incorporates love and connection which is needed so much more now than ever before. This sets us apart from others. There is so much disconnect in the world today that we must counteract with love and intention. Open the heart, connect, and love.

I am quickly learning that there is no such thing as work-life balance. I must then include my daughter and husband in the process and make an effort to connect with my friends and family in between. Life is fleeting. Relationships are valuable.

I'm not where I ultimately desire to be yet, but I make goals, plan for the future, and get clear about what I want, so I can make it happen and know who I want to bring with me.

I have the most magical experiences in my shop. Experiences that show me that I'm living my purpose.

A woman I coached had longed for a better life. She came in broken, but within a few sessions, she sat in my chair crying because her level of gratitude ran so deep. She couldn't believe that the simple things in her life were starting to change because she took the action steps I shared with her.

A young man told me that the beautiful soap I make didn't give him a reaction. This was the first time he has used soap in 10 years.

People drink my tea. They love how good it tastes and how it makes them feel. They love the essential oil blends, bath salts, and beautiful candles.

I get to make a difference- one small action, one coaching session, one healing session, one product at a time. This is how I measure my success. It's by how many lives I can touch every single day. It's by the genuine hug and look in someone's eyes. The "'thank you" I receive because I helped to make a difference in their life. It's seeing people leave in a better state than when they walked in.

My next step is to learn how to scale a successful wholesale business, for my products to become international best-selling products so they can heal the world from the inside, out.

Red or Pink Lipstick? Red

Barbara Morandi is a passionate wellness expert and the founder of NutrYoga, blending the principles of nutrition and yoga for holistic well-being, with a special focus on women over 40. As a certified Flowcoach and Yoga Instructor, Barbara helps women navigate pre-menopause, menopause, and self-care with mindful movement. She is also dedicated to supporting individuals with neurological diseases like Parkinson's through her specialized CoShiatsu practice, providing relief and emotional support. Her approach to health and beauty prioritizes the connection between body and mind, inspiring women to embrace their inner and outer beauty and lead healthier, more balanced lives.

BARBARA *Morandi*

Q: Can you tell us about your journey as an entrepreneur? What inspired you to start your own business?

A: Freedom and independence fueled my entrepreneurial journey. I wanted to be my own boss and never imagine my future or livelihood dictated by someone else's decisions. Additionally, I craved a life that allowed me the time and space to build a family and be present with my children.

Q: Have you found any specific advantages or opportunities in being a woman in your industry?

A: When I first started as a yoga instructor, flow coach, and shiatsu therapist, these professions were often seen as mystical or even misunderstood. I leaned into this perception, embracing the connection between women and magic, drawing inspiration from the rich traditions of the women in the mountains and the deep-rooted beliefs of small-town life. While younger generations viewed me with skepticism, it was the elders who recognized the value of my work. Their word-of-mouth support played a pivotal role in growing my business.

Q: What advice would you give to other women who are considering starting their own businesses?

A: My advice is simple: Be yourself, unapologetically. Embrace both your shadows and your light. Be genuine, and most importantly, consistent in everything you do.

Q: How do you balance work-life commitments as an entrepreneur?

A: I developed a routine that allows me to maintain balance. I divide my day into dedicated time slots for teaching, learning, socializing, and caring for my well-being. I also learned the art of setting boundaries, saying "yes" to the right things and "no" when necessary. Every day, I remind myself to follow my mantra: *Breathe, Laugh, Move,* and I begin my day with gratitude over a mid-morning café latte.

Q: Can you share a story about a particularly memorable customer interaction or experience?

A: One story that stands out to me happened in June 2020, during the lockdown. I was teaching yoga and self-shiatsu online to people with Parkinson's and their caregivers. At that time, my lessons focused on providing tools to manage symptoms like anxiety, digestion issues, and headaches. One day, I received a message from the wife of a Parkinson's patient, who was his caregiver. She shared how, after the passing of her mother, she felt too overwhelmed to drive to be with her in her final moments. In that moment, she remembered one of the shiatsu techniques I taught for managing shock and anxiety—tapping between the lip and nose. She took a deep breath, used the technique, and was able to gather the strength to be with her mother when she passed. Knowing that my work made such a profound impact on someone during such a pivotal time was deeply moving.

Q: Can you discuss the role of networking and partnerships in growing your business?

A: Networking and partnerships are essential, especially in the wellness industry. They allow me to support clients holistically. Over the years, I've had the privilege of collaborating with naturopaths, nutritionists, and doctors, which not only yielded better results for my clients but also enriched my own professional growth. These partnerships have led to the creation of new programs, including a yoga and nutrition course with a naturopath and a special program for women co-created with a psychotherapist and nutritionist.

Q: Pink or red lipstick?

A: Pink lipstick.

Marika Wessels is the founder of 'Let's Go CORE: Reclaiming Your Crown - From Trauma to Triumph'.

Q: What role do you think mentorship and support networks play for women in entrepreneurship?

A: Mentorship and support networks serve as critical lifelines for women in entrepreneurship, offering guidance, resources, and the invaluable benefit of experience. They act as a compass, helping navigate the often-tumultuous business-building journey. For women who may face unique challenges in the entrepreneurial landscape, these networks provide professional guidance and emotional support, helping break down barriers and fostering a sense of belonging and community. By sharing wisdom and insights, mentors empower women entrepreneurs to make informed decisions, avoid common pitfalls, and harness opportunities for growth and innovation.

Q: Can you tell us about your journey as an entrepreneur and what inspired you to start your own business?

A: My journey as an entrepreneur began from a deep desire to create meaningful change and provide support for women who've experienced abuse or trauma. Having navigated my own path of healing and self-discovery, I was inspired to establish a platform that addresses the external aspects of personal growth and professional development and delves deep into emotional healing. The inspiration came from my own life chapters—from navigating the challenges of an unstable childhood to breaking cycles of abuse and finding my voice. This transformative experience ignited a passion to empower other women to do the same, leading me to launch a business focused on holistic healing, personal development, and creating a supportive community.

Q: What problem or need does your business solve, and what motivated you to address it?

A: My business is designed to address the deep-seated need for a holistic approach to healing from abuse and trauma. Recognising the gap in support for women who are on a journey to break cycles of pain and fear, I was motivated to create a safe, empowering space that offers more than traditional therapy or counselling. Our programs incorporate mindfulness, journaling, affirmations, EFT tapping, and more to equip women with tools for emotional resilience, self-discovery, and empowerment. The drive to offer this comprehensive support comes from my own experiences and the understanding that healing is multifaceted, requiring attention to both the mind and the spirit.

Q: What sets your business apart from competitors in the market?

A: Our CORE philosophy—Courage, Overcome, Responsibility, Enjoy—distinguishes our business, which underpins all our programs and services. We don't just focus on the symptoms of trauma but aim to empower our clients to take charge of their healing journey, fostering a sense of responsibility and self-efficacy. Our approach is profoundly empathetic and personalised, acknowledging the individual stories and strengths of each woman we work with. Additionally, our community is a vital component, providing a network of support that reinforces the message that no one is alone in their journey. This holistic, community-driven approach sets us apart in a market that often focuses on quick fixes rather than sustainable personal growth.

Q: What do you believe are the keys to building a solid brand identity and reputation?

A: Building a solid brand identity and reputation hinges on authenticity, consistency, and engagement. Authenticity means staying true to your core values and mission, letting them guide all your actions and communications. This genuineness resonates with your audience, building trust and loyalty. Consistency in your message and quality of service reinforces your brand's reliability, making it easier for customers to understand and embrace your value proposition. Finally, engagement with your community through active listening, feedback, and participation creates a dynamic relationship that fosters brand advocacy and growth. By embodying these principles, a brand can establish a strong, positive identity and reputation in the market.

Q: How do you stay motivated and resilient during challenging times in your business?

A: During tough times in my business, I stay motivated and resilient by deeply connecting with my purpose and the women I aim to serve. My motivation comes from creating a safe and empowering space where women can heal, grow, and break free from past traumas. I remind myself that every challenge I face is an opportunity to develop new strengths, just as I encourage others to do.

When obstacles arise, I lean on my CORE framework: Courage, Overcome, Responsibility, and Enjoy. I cultivate courage by facing challenges head-on, seeing them as gateways to growth. I focus on overcoming by reframing setbacks as lessons, knowing that each step forward contributes to a larger impact, no matter how small. I take responsibility for my well-being by setting healthy boundaries and practising self-care, ensuring I can show up fully for my community. Lastly, I find joy and fulfilment in the little victories and witnessing the transformation of those I support.

I also draw strength from my community. Knowing that I am not alone and that other warrior queens are on this journey with me fuels my determination. It's a shared mission; together, we rise above the setbacks, creating positive change.

Q: What role do you think mentorship and support networks play for women in entrepreneurship?

A: Mentorship and support networks are essential for women in entrepreneurship. They provide guidance, wisdom, and a sense of community and belonging that can be transformative. In a world where women often face unique challenges, from self-doubt to systemic barriers, having a mentor who has walked a similar path can be a game-changer. It's about having someone who believes in you, who sees your potential even when you can't, and who can offer the kind of advice and encouragement that comes from experience.

Support networks, on the other hand, create a collective power. Women lift each other profoundly When they come together to share their stories, resources, and support. These networks offer a safe space to celebrate wins, learn from setbacks, and brainstorm solutions without fear of judgment. They remind us that we are not alone in our journey and that our challenges are not insurmountable.

Mentorship and support networks have been lifelines for me. They've helped me navigate the highs and lows of entrepreneurship, giving me the strength and resilience to keep going. They are places where ideas are nurtured, confidence is built, and dreams are encouraged. In short, they are vital for any woman looking to survive and thrive in her entrepreneurial journey.

Katrina Thompson is a talented photographer passionate about capturing the beauty and majesty of remote wilderness areas. As a wife and mother, she also values the importance of family and cherishes the moments she spends with her loved ones. Her love for nature shines through her interpretive photographs, which skillfully weave stories and evoke emotions in the viewer.

KATRINA
Thompson

Q: What are some of the biggest challenges you've faced as a woman entrepreneur, and how have you overcome them?

A: As a female landscape and wildlife photographer, the most perplexing challenge I've encountered has been the physical demands of the job, which is often considered more suitable for men. This includes carrying heavy equipment through rugged terrains and enduring long hours in remote areas. However, I've overcome this challenge by prioritizing physical fitness and consistently delivering exceptional work, proving my dedication and capability.

Networking within this male-dominated field has also been challenging. Nevertheless, I've successfully navigated through both online and offline photography communities, sharing my perspective and expertise. I've sought mentors who value diversity and established a supportive network that empowers women photographers.

My success is largely due to resilience in the face of skepticism regarding my technical proficiency and concerns about safety. Yet, I've remained steadfast in my work, consistently demonstrating a deep understanding of the environment. As a result, I've achieved significant accomplishments in my field.

Q: Have you found any specific advantages or opportunities in being a woman in your industry?

A: As a female photographer specializing in landscape and wildlife photography, I have a unique opportunity to capture the natural world from a fresh perspective, highlighting details and stories that might otherwise go unnoticed. My sensitivity enables me to craft powerful narratives that resonate deeply with audiences and clients seeking new ways of seeing the world. This storytelling approach has allowed me to connect with a broader audience, including women and families who are increasingly interested in nature and conservation. These connections have opened doors for collaborations with brands and organizations focused on sustainability and environmental education.

Additionally, being a woman in this field gives me the chance to mentor aspiring female photographers, fostering a more inclusive and supportive community. I am passionate about advocating for diversity in photography and highlighting the importance of incorporating varied perspectives to accurately capture our world.

Q: In your experience, what are some common misconceptions or stereotypes about women in business, and how do you challenge or overcome them?

A: As a female photographer, I often face two stereotypes. The first is the assumption that I'm unable to handle the physical demands of wildlife and landscape photography, as well as the risks involved in remote locations. The second is the perception that my male counterparts possess superior technical knowledge. I've worked hard to debunk these stereotypes by showcasing my skills and dedication through various publications and a strong social media presence.

Another misconception is that pursuing a photography career requires compromising personal life. I believe that integrating my passion for photography into my personal life has brought me a sense of fulfillment. I aim to inspire photographers, both male and female, to reimagine the role women play in the field. By participating in discussions about gender in photography and mentoring upcoming female photographers, I hope to shift these outdated perceptions.

Q: What advice would you give to other women who are considering starting their own businesses?

A: If you're a woman looking to pursue photography as a business, the first step is immersing yourself fully in the craft. Your passion for nature and photography will be the foundation of your business. Start with a clear vision and a well-thought-out business plan that reflects your unique perspective and style. Networking with fellow photographers, conservationists, and enthusiasts is essential—this community will be your support system, offering advice, collaboration, and opportunities.

Be prepared to face challenges, as they will fuel your growth and learning. Use social media to showcase your work, as your distinctive take on nature will likely resonate with a specific audience.

Remember, resilience is key. The path may not always be smooth, but remaining adaptable and open to change will ensure your success. Your journey can inspire others—pursue it with determination and passion.

Q: How do you stay motivated and resilient during challenging times in your business?

A: The impact of photography on nature conservation and fostering a connection with the environment serves as a source of courage and inspiration during tough times. Reflecting on past successes reminds me of the power of my work, whether it's through a conversation about conservation or an image that deeply resonates with someone. Celebrating small victories helps me stay focused on the larger impact of my work. Setting achievable goals, such as mastering new techniques or organizing exhibitions, keeps me moving forward.

Engaging in self-care and reconnecting with nature renews my spirit and creativity. I view every negative experience as a learning opportunity and an avenue for improvement. One key principle I live by is to remain open, adaptable, and willing to pivot when necessary, while embracing novelty and trying new things.

Q: Looking ahead, what are your goals and aspirations for the future of your business?

A: Looking ahead, my primary goal for my landscape and wildlife photography business is to expand the reach of my work globally, connecting with a broader audience. I plan to broaden my portfolio to cover ecosystems and species that are less documented on the continent, raising awareness of their beauty and the challenges they face. I believe that advances in photography technology will help me achieve this, allowing viewers to experience the wonders of nature as if they were there in person.

Sustainability is another key focus for the future. I aim to adopt sustainable practices in all aspects of my business, from fieldwork to operations, promoting conservation through photography.

Diversity and inclusion are also important to me. I want to create an inclusive narrative in nature photography, showcasing the diverse beauty of the world and making my work accessible to people from all walks of life.

By establishing partnerships with conservation organizations, educational institutions, and eco-tourism entities, I aim to create a legacy that not only celebrates photography as an art form but also advocates for urgent environmental stewardship.

Q: Pink or red lipstick? Pink—equal parts sweet, pretty, and sexy.

Vicky Theunissen is a Holistic Psychologist and the founder of Let's Make Miracles True, a practice dedicated to transformative healing and personal growth.

Q: What problem or need does your business solve, and what motivated you to address it?

A: I help people to regain their identity. I'm doing this by helping them bring their body, mind, and soul back into balance. What motivated me to do this is that I have learned through my own life experiences and through study that an imbalance in our body, mind, and soul is the cause of how mental and physical problems arise.

Q: How did you come up with the idea for your business, and what was the process like from concept to execution?

A: This idea arose after losing my mother to Alzheimer's disease at a young age and after escaping death myself. I was wondering how it is possible that doctors who we put all our trust in can only diagnose a disease when it is already advanced and why they can't tell us how these diseases arise and why they have no solution for it but all they can do is giving us medication to suppress the problem.

This made me decide to do research by myself. I started to study life deeply and that's how I discovered that every mental and physical problem is a result of suppressing our emotions. Emotions are meant to flow and to feel but if we don't allow them to do where they are meant for it's going to our head which makes us overthink and that gives stress and this feeling goes to our body and get stuck in there and when we ignore these feelings for a matter of time we develop physical symptoms what can turn out in the worst diseases. So it's very simple how diseases arises actually and that's why it's also very simple how to solve it but there is no "normal" doctor who is telling us this because they simply don't have this knowledge.

The idea to start this business arose after I escaped death myself and the doctors told me that the chance of survival was very low and that if I should come out I would be bedridden for the rest of my life. Luckily I experienced already how little knowledge they had and I'm someone who is always listening to my own voice, so I told them that this is not going to happen and that's how I fight myself literally out of the dead. From that moment people started to reach out to me to ask me if they could talk with me because they felt inspired by me and the doctors and therapist I saw told me that I needed to do something with this because they said that it's a miracle how I fought myself out of this and I can help a lot of people with my story. I didn't understand why they reacted in this way to me because I did nothing special in my opinion.

That was the moment that I started to get to know myself and found out that It looked like a have a special gift. Because for me it's normal to think and act in this way. Because it's all about mindset and discipline. However, I started to realize that it's not that easy for everyone to think positively. I have the luck that I'm just a very optimistic person and I'm very well connected with myself which gives me the possibility to listen to myself and see through a lot of things but not many people are connected with themselves and that's why they don't have self-love and self-esteem what results in not knowing who they are and that's why they listen what others are telling them.

So, the biggest advice I give to people is to listen to your inner voice, always. And if you don't know how to find that voice. Please contact me because I would love to help you find that voice from within yourself. Because I don't have a special superpower. We all have it, but you need to be willing to find it. This isn't an easy journey at all but it's worthy I can tell you, because after you can create heaven on earth for yourself and we all deserve this. So this is what motivated me to do this work.

Q: What were some of the biggest challenges you faced when starting your business, and how did you overcome them?

A: My biggest challenge was to ask for money. I helped a lot of people for free for a long time and I did volunteer work in hospitals and nursing homes because I sincerely help people from my heart and I couldn't think about start doing this in a business way and asking money for this because it's about our health. But this is why I decided to do a few studies to develop myself as a Coach and in Holistic Psychology and since I got my diploma and certifications I dare to call myself a professional and I started my own business.

Q: What do you believe are the keys to building a strong brand identity and reputation?

A: First of all, do all the healing work by yourself to make sure you are in the right place with yourself. Especially when you want to start in Health care. But also outside of the Healthcare, this is important. Because you are your brand, and you attract people based on who you are not for your services. Because it's all about energy, when you are aligned with yourself you attract everything naturally towards you. Because you can make decisions based on who you are instead of out of emotions and then you can make all of your dreams come true. Because when the foundation is good, the rest is just about decorating.

Q: How do you stay innovative and adapt to changes in your industry?

A: To simply keep developing myself every single day, to make sure that I'm staying in the right place with myself and keep myself updated on the new knowledge and techniques around the work that I'm doing

Q: Looking ahead, what are your goals and aspirations for the future of your business?

A: My goal is to also start finally with speaking on events, I want to do a combination of Coaching, Energy work and Speaking around the world and I also want to start with organize retreats in the future.

Q: Pink or red lipstick?

A: Red lipstick!

Jasmine Tella, widely recognized as the Face Yoga Expert, is also a renowned author with a strong online presence. Her engaging videos and programs are designed to reduce wrinkles and tone facial muscles, empowering individuals to rejuvenate their appearance naturally. In addition to her online success, Jasmine is the proud owner of Jasmine Tella Skincare, a brand that complements her holistic approach to beauty and wellness.

Photo credit: Lewis Patrick

My entrepreneurial journey began with a passion for holistic wellness and a desire to help others look and feel their best. A midlife realisation that I wanted more than just going through the motions spurred me into action. With a background in marketing and a love for beauty and wellness, I saw an opportunity to combine these passions into something meaningful. I developed my expertise in face yoga, which led to the creation of my own business, allowing me to share these benefits with others. This journey even took me to a new country, where I've met inspiring people and embraced new experiences.

Overcoming Challenges as a Woman Entrepreneur

One of the biggest challenges I've faced as a woman entrepreneur has been balancing societal expectations and business demands. There are often preconceived notions about our capabilities and roles. To overcome these, I've focused on building a strong personal brand and continuously honing my skills. Networking with other women entrepreneurs and seeking mentorship has been crucial in navigating these challenges and finding the support needed to thrive.

Maintaining Work-Life Balance

Maintaining a work-life balance is essential for long-term success and personal well-being. I prioritise my time by setting clear boundaries and schedules, dedicating time for work, family, and self-care. Regular face yoga practice helps me stay grounded and reminds me of the importance of taking care of oneself. Delegation and having a supportive team are key strategies in managing my responsibilities effectively. I also enjoy walks in the English countryside with my dog and petting my cat for a good dose of happy hormones and rebalancing.

Advice for Aspiring Women Entrepreneurs

Just go for it! Why hold on to your dreams when you can live them? It's not going to be easy; some days you'll wake up doubting your choices, hearing sceptical voices saying, "Don't do it!" or "You are mad to leave your well-paid job!" My advice to other women considering starting their own businesses is to believe in your vision and stay persistent. Surround yourself with a supportive network, seek mentorship, and don't be afraid to ask for help. Focus on your strengths and continuously work on improving your skills. Being adaptable and open to feedback will help you grow and navigate challenges more effectively.

Staying Motivated and Resilient

Staying motivated and resilient during tough times involves a combination of passion, purpose, and self-care. Meditation and gratitude practices are crucial for maintaining my focus and reminding myself of the opportunity I've given myself. My passion for face yoga and helping others drives me forward, even when challenges arise. I remind myself of the positive impact my work has on my clients' lives, which fuels my motivation. I am seeking the right investors to help take my business to the next level, and I'm confident it will happen. I believe in manifestation, and in many ways, the vision is already becoming reality as I continue to bring it to life.

Through these practices, I maintain a clear vision and remain committed to my goals, ensuring continuous growth as an entrepreneur. Being my own boss has shown me that giving yourself a chance, even through tough times, truly pays off. You don't have to dive in all at once; it's possible to start part-time, as a side hustle, while balancing other commitments. We all have bills to pay, and I've had to make compromises too.

Yet, staying true to my vision has led to incredible milestones—like being featured in The Times as a Face Yoga Expert, gaining the support of some of my favourite actresses, and living a life full of exciting opportunities and connections.

Start by smiling at yourself in the mirror, and affirm that you deserve the chance to be unapologetically you and shine.

Embrace the journey with confidence, knowing that giving yourself permission to step into your true potential is the first step towards achieving your dreams. Everything else will follow.

Krystal Stephens is the founder of The WorkSource, a platform dedicated to the Health, Wellness, and Fitness industries where they not only connect businesses with industry-experienced freelancers but also empower owners with the tools and knowledge to outsource successfully. Krystal resides in Brisbane City, Queensland, Australia.

KRYSTAL *Stephens*

Q: Can you tell me about your journey as an entrepreneur? What inspired you to start your own business?

A: My entrepreneurial journey began with a very personal struggle. A few years back, I faced the overwhelming challenge of finding the right freelancer for a family business. The endless search cost me time and money, which left me frustrated. It was that experience that inspired me to create The WorkSource—a platform dedicated to helping Health, Wellness, and Fitness business owners find the right freelancers, without the stress or risk.

But beyond just providing access to freelancers, I wanted to go further. I realised that successful outsourcing isn't just about hiring someone; it's about learning how to outsource effectively, and creating the right network. That's why I also focus on providing education around outsourcing, helping business owners make informed decisions, and offering networking opportunities through our community. The goal is not only to connect businesses with freelancers, but to empower them with the tools and knowledge they need to succeed.

Q: How do you maintain a work-life balance while running your own business?

A: Maintaining balance is definitely a challenge, but I make it a priority. I use time-blocking to allocate specific periods for work and personal life, so that everything gets the attention it deserves (well, most of the time!). I've also learned to delegate tasks by outsourcing to freelancers—whether it's marketing, admin, or anything that takes too much of my time. This frees me up to focus on the bigger picture and actually enjoy some personal time without feeling like I need to be everywhere at once. It's not always perfect, but it's essential for my health and happiness.

Q: What advice would you give to other women who are considering starting their own businesses?

A: My advice to aspiring women entrepreneurs comes down to four key points: Believe in your vision, Stay consistent, Step out of your comfort zone, and Don't be afraid to try and fail.

Believing in your vision gives you the drive to push forward, even when things get tough. Staying consistent is what keeps the momentum going—showing up, day after day, no matter the setbacks. Stepping out of your comfort zone is where the real growth happens; the things that scare you are often the things that help you evolve the most. And finally, don't be afraid to try and fail. Every failure is a stepping stone toward success, and each one brings you closer to your goals.

Q: How do you stay motivated and resilient during tough times in your business?

A: I stay motivated by revisiting the "why" behind my business. Knowing that The WorkSource helps Health, Wellness, and Fitness business owners find the support they need keeps me passionate. When things get tough, I remind myself of the positive impact we're making by reading through testimonials or thank-you notes from clients. I also lean on my incredible network of businesswomen for support and advice—sometimes a fresh perspective is all it takes to find a solution.

Q: What sets your business apart from competitors in the market?

A: The WorkSource stands out for our commitment to personalised, community-driven support. Unlike larger, impersonal platforms, we focus on connecting Australian Health, Wellness, and Fitness business owners with vetted freelancers who truly understand their industry. Our platform also goes beyond just matching freelancers with businesses—we offer education on how to outsource effectively and provide a supportive community where members can network and grow together. This focus on quality, education, and relationship-building helps both businesses and freelancers thrive.

Q: Can you share a significant milestone or achievement your business has reached, and what did you learn from it?

A: One of the most significant milestones for me was being selected for a female founder scholarship, which gave me the opportunity to connect with an incredible group of talented women entrepreneurs. This experience was transformative—it wasn't just about gaining knowledge and resources, but about the power of community and support. Being surrounded by women who were navigating their own entrepreneurial journeys helped me see the importance of building a network of like-minded individuals. It reinforced my belief in the need for connection and collaboration, which is something we also encourage through The WorkSource.

The relationships I formed and the insights I gained from this experience have been invaluable, both personally and professionally. It taught me the importance of surrounding yourself with people who challenge and inspire you, and that success is not only about what you know but also who you have in your corner.

Q: How do you approach leadership and team-building within your company?

A: My approach to leadership is built on collaboration, trust, and empowerment. At The WorkSource, I believe that building a strong team means hiring people who are smarter than you in their areas of expertise. I've always believed that you don't hire freelancers to simply tell them what to do—you hire them to bring their own ideas, insights, and solutions to the table.

For me, team-building starts with finding freelancers who are not only skilled but also share the values and passion that drive our work in the health, wellness, and fitness industries. Clear communication and mutual respect are essential. I want everyone involved in The WorkSource to feel like they are part of something bigger—a mission to help businesses thrive.

Tanya Steele is a former EMR turned entrepreneur. She is now a Podcast host, Speaker, MC, Safety Trainer & Consultant. Utilizing her 28yrs of experience she speaks to business owners, supervisors and managers on how to train their workers effectively.

TANYA
Steele

Q: Is that true that being successful is 20% education and 80% personality?

A: I did not amount to much in either "Beauty and Brains" categories. In school, I was a very average student. For me, this meant relying on my personality to get through life. Throughout my teen years, I worked hard to craft my approach with different people. Imagine my surprise and horror when one teacher said to me, "Tanya, you're never going to make it in the world just on your personality." If only they could see me now!

As a consultant in the safety industry, I must show up with personality if I'm going to be successful. I need to be warm and welcoming, with layers of depth and empathy. The same is true when I'm a speaker on the stage. It's not enough for me to share information. I have to be innovative and entertaining. And don't get me started about my role as a safety trainer who teaches people provincial legislation. Most people would rather poke their eye out with a fork than sit in an 8-hour course educating them about legislation.

I am also a co-host of the Safety Debris podcast, where we interview safety leaders from all over the world with all different personalities, beliefs, and dreams. Do all of these need an approachable adaptable personality? You betchya!

I guess you could say that I have spent a lifetime developing my "personality". Which means that, for me, the answer is yes—your success depends 20% on your knowledge or education and 80% on your ability to connect with people.

Q: Do you have any advice you would give to other women who are considering starting their own business?

A: When I was young, I constantly questioned myself. "What is my purpose?" I'd wonder. "What is the call on my life?" People often wrestle with these questions, trying to figure out who they're supposed to be in this world. In my early 20's, a mentor blessed me with a simple statement: "Tanya, the need is the call." I instinctively paused as soon as I heard those words. That was it! Instead of trying to find my "calling," I simply needed to look for needs and learn how to fill them. That is truly what business is about, finding your clients' needs and meeting them. My ability to see a need and then take action to serve my clients has been the driving force behind my success.

Q: What role do you think mentorship plays for women in business?

A: Not only do I serve my clients, but I brought that same principle to my business —specifically for my staff. I believed that if I served my staff, to encourage them and help them grow, they would step into their strength and have the freedom to excel in whatever they wanted.

So, I would daily ask, "How can I help you today? What can I do to make your life a bit easier?" I would do what I could. I wanted to make sure they felt supported. More than that, I wanted them to know that I believed in them and in their abilities. Today, while I serve on different boards and associations, I make myself available for anyone to call me and get support and mentorship. My family asked me once, "Why don't you charge for your mentoring service?" For me, the answer was easy: it is more valuable to see women standing on the shoulders of previous generations. I am honored to help propel them into the future so they can do greater things than we did.

I also believe that when you give, you receive hundredfold. There are people I mentored years ago that now hold executive positions. I am blessed that they think of me when they think of joint health & safety committee or supervisor safety training. Now, they are my clients! And not just clients but raving fans. Isn't that what we all want?

Q: What sets me apart from competitors?

A: This question echoes in my brain constantly. For me, it's not just about being the best: it's about loving what I do and passionately embracing the ever-evolving landscape of innovation and technology.

Once, I asked a client, "Why do you keep bringing me back every year?" His answer: "We hire you because you're always creative, innovative, and ahead of the curve." Those words resonated deeply. They capture my motivation to continually seek new business streams, push boundaries, and stay one step ahead. I embrace change. I do not mind trying something and failing because I know that I will always learn something.

I believe in excellence—not perfection, but the pursuit of doing my best in everything I do. It's about consistency, showing up day after day with a commitment to surpass my clients' expectations. I don't just want to blend in and do what everyone else is doing. I want to be memorable.

A perfect example was when we all found ourselves facing the seismic upheaval of the COVID era. Many of my competitors waited, complained, and refused to grow. Some even retired early. However, I saw opportunity. In the face of canceled courses and conferences, I didn't retreat. I adapted. I dedicated hundreds of hours to mastering Zoom, transforming my offerings into online courses, and setting up a studio in my home. My business found new and better ways to bring in income. As the landscape of business seems to shift regularly, I remain steadfast in my resolve—to innovate, to evolve, and to remain forever ahead of the curve.

Q: What were some of your significant milestones or achievements?

A: I remember when I hit my first six-figure income in my early 30's. Me and my parents were shocked! Then a few years later my company hit one million dollars in sales. What?!

As I was a pretty average student, I did not plan to attend college or university. Yet, my administrative skills were pretty strong, and I loved the work. So, that's what I planned to do with my life. Neither I nor my family ever dreamed that I would eventually become a multi-business owner with 30+ full and part-time staff!

It all started when a friend recommended that I take a first aid course. Not only did I love this class—I excelled at it and was one of the top students. My world opened to new possibilities.

By my mid-30's, I had decided to take some safety courses and received my first provincial professional designation: Construction Safety Officer Registered (CSO(R)). Then I earned a national designation: Certified Health & Safety Consultant (CHSC). I began to think that maybe I did have brains. Maybe I actually enjoyed learning and could even excel if it was something I loved.

My most recent achievements were in 2024, when I received "Top Women in Safety" and "Top Safety Trainer" in Canada. I also received my Certified Speaking Professional (CSP) designation. It took me 10 years to achieve this recognition. At the time of writing this book, there are only 62 in Canada and just under 800 in the world. That's all to say: maybe you are reading this so I can remind you, "Yes, you can!"

Q: Pink or red lipstick?

A: Red lipstick for sure! It is bold and powerful. (And besides, "pink" does not look good on me.)

Ralitza Spassova is a Transformation Partner, Life Alchemist, and Mastery Method Coach who champions progressive health solutions with efficiency and depth. Drawing on her diverse expertise as an instructor, administrator, physician, personal coach, and entrepreneur, and backed by her Doctor of Medicine degree, she empowers individuals to unlock their full potential and achieve lasting transformation.

RALITZA
Spassova

Q: Have you found any specific advantages or opportunities in being a woman in your industry?

A: I absolutely love being a woman in my professional career and entrepreneurial endeavors. By fully embracing my authenticity, I've tapped into a unique advantage—balancing divine feminine traits like intuition, creativity, trust in the unknown, and being in flow, with divine masculine traits like planning, strategy, and taking aligned action. This powerful synergy fuels passionate, purpose-driven work, eliminating exhaustion and burnout.

Through my journey, I've realized that being a woman brings much-needed softness, compassion, and understanding, particularly in corporate environments where masculine energy often dominates. When women align their feminine and masculine energies, we become healers, visionaries, and peace-bringers, regardless of our role. It's our responsibility to harness these gifts to create harmony in our lives and those around us, beginning with ourselves.

My "Sexy Successful Sisterhood" Masterminds and Facebook Group provide a space for women to find this balance, fostering a safe, supportive community that encourages vulnerability and deep transformation.

Q: Can you tell us about your journey as an entrepreneur and what inspired you to start your own business?

A: At a low point in my life, I barely recognized the woman staring back at me in the mirror. I felt utterly lost. My initial goal was to pursue a Naturopathic Doctor degree to complement my Medical Degree, but I soon realized that business skills were crucial in the holistic health space. This realization led me on a path of deep soul-searching, which ultimately brought me to coaching—a decision that transformed my life.

Three years later, I feel immense gratitude for the journey that led me here. I've embraced my inner beauty and purpose wholeheartedly, and it's this path—what I call the "Authenticity Calling" journey—that drives my mission. I'm dedicated to helping 1.1 million people find their flow-state and live purpose-driven lives. I've even created "Authenticity Calling," a self-paced online course, to support anyone ready to embrace their calling. I also share my journey in the bestselling Amazon book, Beyond Coincidence: Visionaries Unlock the Mysteries of Synchronicities and Success.

Q: What were some of the biggest challenges you faced when starting your business, and how did you overcome them?

A: Some of the greatest challenges I faced were tied to self-doubt, seeking external validation, and a fear of judgment—what is often called "imposter syndrome," though I prefer to think of it as a "growth-edge activation energy deficit." We all need reminders of our greatness, but often lack the unconditional love and support required for that.

Not pursuing a medical license felt like a failure to my community, and my parents were devastated when I left medicine for coaching. However, in 2020, my gifts became undeniable, and I fully committed to coaching as my life's work while maintaining my professional career.

From my journey, I developed my Signature P3 Alchemy Mastery Method, which helps clients embrace their passions, live their purpose, and unlock their potential. As they say: "Life happens for you, not to you." Sometimes, we just need perspective and loving guidance to see it and use it to propel us into our most authentic selves!

Q: How do you approach risk management and decision-making in your business?

A: I trust my intuition and the natural flow of life, discerning between decisions that are divinely inspired and those that are misaligned. Early in my business, I used decision-making tools from the Institute for Coaching Mastery, taught by my mentor Alyssa Nobriga, which helped me hone my intuitive skills and align my choices with my higher purpose.

I also teach my clients a simple method: Take a few deep breaths, step into each decision option, and feel the energy in your body. Light, expansive sensations signal alignment, while contracted, tense feelings suggest misalignment. This practice sharpens intuition and helps clients make decisions with greater ease and confidence.

Q: Can you share a story about a particularly memorable customer interaction or experience?

A: A friend referred her sister to me, confident I could help her. What I always remind my clients is that coaches don't change lives; we simply mirror your greatness so you can take responsibility for your own transformation. Within just 72 hours of our session, this client experienced profound changes. She had been drinking nightly, stressed, and unable to conceive. After implementing the tools I provided, she stopped drinking, reconnected with her partner, and even ovulated for the first time in months.

During my medical training, I also witnessed recoveries that defied science. These experiences strengthened my belief in personal transformation and alignment, which ultimately led me to shift my career focus to coaching.

Q: Looking ahead, what are your goals and aspirations for the future of your business?

A: My vision is crystal clear: to impact 1.1 million people through coaching and education. I am already contributing to healthcare transformation in my professional role and plan to develop a certification course that makes wellness more accessible for both patients and providers.

I also feel a strong calling to contribute to educational reform, starting with children. I envision a system that teaches mind-body-spirit alignment, nutrition, healthy habits, and community service—all delivered through smart devices, available year-round, and designed to keep students connected to their health, nature, and intuition.

Driven by this vision, I refuse to let doubt, shame, or blame slow me down. I'm all in.

Q: Pink or red lipstick? A: Red

Susan Sheehan an inspiring speaker, and known for her mental strength, resilience, and ability to connect emotionally with her audience, her powerful insights inspire audiences worldwide, making a lasting impact.

Q: What are some of the biggest challenges you've faced as a woman entrepreneur, and how have you overcome them?

A: The biggest challenge I faced as an entrepreneur was overcoming the trauma from being raped multiple times as a young woman, which severely affected my confidence around men. Working for a company, I once had to present to eight male investors but was overwhelmed and fled the room. Recognizing my problem, I dedicated three years to studying and working with coaches. Eventually, I presented to 9 male Angel Investors with a combined worth of $100 million. During the presentation, I realized they were just "mere males with more money." This breakthrough gave me newfound personal power and taught me I can do anything.

Q: Can you share a particularly memorable success story or milestone from your entrepreneurial journey?

A: One particularly memorable milestone in my entrepreneurial journey was realizing the power of manifestation. While browsing in a bookshop, I discovered "The Secret." As I flipped through it, I chose John Assaraf, thinking, "He's handsome; I'll choose him." The next day, a CD from my Internet Marketing coach arrived, featuring an interview with John Assaraf. I registered for his newsletters and declared out loud, "I am going to work with you one day." Four years later, I attended one of John's webinars and applied to work with him. Out of 1800 applicants, he chose 17, and I was one of them. Three months later, I travelled from Australia to San Diego to work with John, truly understanding the power of owning my desires, believing in possibilities, and letting go of conscious hoping.

Q: How do you stay motivated and resilient during tough times in your business?

A: Staying motivated and resilient during tough times in business hinges on what I call the 7 S's to mental strength and resilience. First, the Story: if your life's story doesn't serve you, rewrite it. Next, Self-awareness: know who you are and who you want to be, embracing your authentic self. The third S is Stress management, which involves a healthy lifestyle plan—love, nutrition, supplementation, exercise, meditation, fun, sex, community, family, and friends. Fourth, a Sense of Purpose: create a vision of what you want and let it guide your journey. Fifth, be Smart: keep learning and let go of what doesn't work. Sixth, be Strong: practice gratitude, forgiveness, and do what it takes. Lastly, Seek help if needed. These principles have kept me resilient and driven, no matter the challenges I face.

Q: What advice would you give to someone who is considering starting their own business?

A: As a coach for 30 years, my key advice is: fall in love with numbers. Through interviewing celebrities, being coached and my experiences, I've learned that understanding your business's financials is essential. This knowledge is crucial for thriving as an entrepreneur.

Q: What do you believe are the keys to building a strong brand identity and reputation?

A: Viewing the person as the core value and the business as the result is crucial. Authenticity is your most powerful asset, while limiting beliefs are your number one enemy. Establishing a deep connection with yourself and achieving unconscious competence is essential for brand power. Additionally, knowing your brand personality and identifying the one thing that makes you unique are vital steps in creating a memorable and impactful brand.

Q: How do you prioritise your goals and tasks as an entrepreneur?

A: As an entrepreneur, prioritizing and managing goals effectively is essential to maintain momentum and achieve high-level results. I start each day with a structured morning ritual that primes my brain for peak performance, including breathwork, exercise, and sometimes dance to energize my mind and body. This routine helps me maintain focus, especially with an ADHD brain, and ensures I approach tasks with clarity and purpose. I believe in finishing everything I start to completion, and always at a professional standard—what I call the 'Pro level.' Each morning, I review sales and marketing numbers to stay informed and adjust my strategy as needed. Having the right people around me is also key, as building a team aligned with my vision and strengths helps in effectively delegating tasks and ensuring continued progress toward my goals.

Q: What sets you apart from others in the industry?

A: What sets our business apart is our unique blend of coaching and consulting expertise. We combine the visionary, creative mindset of an entrepreneur with the structured, detail-oriented approach of corporate experience. Our philosophy is 'people first, then business'—focusing on brain training, mental and physical wellbeing, and the development of both personal and professional identity. This holistic approach, paired with our global presence and access to unlimited funding, allows us to provide unparalleled support to our clients, ensuring they achieve sustainable success.

Jai Harvey-Yin is a Soul Sister CEO, Reiki Master Healer, and MindSet & Business Coach, helping others elevate their energy and business success.

JAI
Harvey-Yin

Q: Can you tell me about your journey as an entrepreneur? What inspired you to start your own business?

A: "Avon calling!" I've been in business since I was 12 years old (registered under my mum's name) for my very own Avon territory! For me, I have always wanted to be in control of my own future, having come from a strict upbringing full of love but lots of expectation. We were working class, and having money was something we had to earn, so if I wanted the things, I needed to earn! Very quickly though, I realised that I wasn't so much driven by money but a need to help people. I have a curious and creative mind, and a desire to make things simpler for others, through sharing my own experience and learnings. I love to pinpoint a problem to find a creative solution to it. It is my hope to inspire others through laughter, education and creating self-belief in those I works with.

With a strong business background, my experience includes successful entrepreneurial ventures such as successful salon owner, leading manufacturer education teams, maintaining an award-winning wholesale distribution, an international nail judge, and CEO to an RTO delivering all aspects of beauty therapy, an NDIS registered provider teaching people with a disability social and communication skills and more recently sharing her knowledge as a mentor, coach and business witch.

At a time when my life took a huge pivot, I discovered and then deepened my connection to the metaphysical and spiritual worlds – is a Reiki Master Healer, Master NLP & TimeLine Therapy Practitioner and facilitates the Priestess Program with High Priestess Australia, and speaking and teaching at "Witch School".

These days my passion is helping women 40+ who want to own their FABULOSITY by falling, and staying in love with themselves. I am a mindset & transformational coach for personal and business who uses tools such as Reiki, NLP & TimeLine Therapy to get the breakthroughs needed to step fully into a life & biz they love.

A: As a female in business, sadly the odds for success are against us, and I have to say sometimes that is with the fault of the woman herself. Controversial perhaps, but I take ownership of that opinion, and I did say "sometimes" (because beating those odds is very delicious indeed). We often try to wear too many hats, and I certainly have, some hats through necessity, and some hats through choice or expectation. Being superwoman is tiring, and can lead to crashes – so one of the biggest things I have learnt over the years is to :

1. Listen to my body (this took some years of practice … reminds me of that quote 'If you don't make time for your wellness, you will be forced to make time for your illness' I'm not sure who to credit, but it rings true.

2. Remember "No." is a complete sentence. Challenging those two little letters can be. You don't actually have to justify why, though we are conditioned to explain our reasoning. By removing the automatic "yes" response, taking a pause, and simply saying "no" can really change your life.

3. Embrace three of my favourite words : "action", "grit" and "consistency"- sure they aren't all as sexy as "overnight success" but we know that this is really living in a dream world. Consistent action mixed with grit moves you closer to your goals, always. Even if you make a wrong move, it is all data, it all helps you along your way. Small steps in business are usually much more sustainable than massive leaps.

A: Firstly I would ask the motivation. There are so many misconceptions about owning your own business, that many people believe it would be easier, and that is probably why so many give up even before they have a chance to break through.

So really dig in deep, ask yourself Why? Then again, Why? And again, Why? And again, Why? Keep going until you get to the absolute heart of the matter. This requires brutal honesty. If it is because you want to make a million dollars – easier said than done, why do you want to make a million? And what will that mean for you? And how will that impact the lives of yourself, your family, your community, even globally? And how realistic are you being with this ambition?

On deep reflection, you may find that it is because you are good at a thing, and someone said you should start a business – so was it ego? Or genuine desire to own a business and share your knowledge? You know what? both points are equally valid – maybe you want to feel the satisfaction that comes with accomplishing a goal and and being admired by those around you. Or maybe you remember the impact a mentor had on your and it has always been your ambition to pass that feeling on in your own unique way, but hadn't realised your own worth yet.

Whichever, start honest with yourself. Stay honest with yourself.

When you really connect with your deepest motivation, those long hours and rejections won't even phase you – rather they may energise you.

Find a mentor or coach and a community of like-minds. Being an entrepreneur can be lonely, and these two things are invaluable. They will become your new tribe, and reassure you that you are on the right path.

Oh and finally, remember to have fun – business is juicy, fun, expansive, stressful, a rollercoaster and the type of freedom you could hope for.

Jessica Rae is a creative entrepreneur who merges her passion for empowerment with business through collaborative partnerships, continuing to inspire and uplift others through art and community.

JESSICA
Rae

A Journey of Creativity, Resilience, and Empowerment

My entrepreneurial journey has always been rooted in creativity. For over 15 years, I built a successful business as an intimate portrait photographer in the Greater Vancouver area, empowering people by capturing their most vulnerable and authentic selves. As a solopreneur, I understood that being in business wasn't just about the art—it was about building trust, creating connections, and challenging traditional notions of beauty. I learned to merge creativity with entrepreneurship in a way that not only set me apart but also enabled me to carve my own path.

However, the road wasn't always smooth. After more than a decade of working alone, I experienced burnout. I needed to reassess both my professional and personal direction. This reflection led me to a pivotal moment of reinvention when I decided to move to the Shuswap. The shift was challenging, requiring me to pause and rethink how I could continue my mission of empowering others through a new lens—one that would give me space to grow while staying true to my core values.

Overcoming Challenges and Embracing Growth

Entrepreneurship is filled with unexpected challenges, and burnout was a significant one for me. Running a one-woman show meant I carried the full emotional, creative, and business burdens. Eventually, the weight of it became too much. But what I learned from that experience was invaluable: resilience doesn't mean pushing through every hardship—it means knowing when to pivot. It means understanding when to ask for help and realigning your goals with your well-being.

Burnout, while painful, gave me the clarity to shift my focus and create new opportunities for growth. Through collaboration, I discovered that entrepreneurship doesn't have to be a solitary pursuit. This is where my partnership with MisMacK Clean Cosmetics comes in. Working with a fellow female entrepreneur like Missy MacKintosh allowed me to combine my creative skills with a brand that shares my values of authenticity and empowerment. This collaboration underscored for me that business is not just about individual success—it's about building connections and fostering mutual support.

Empowerment Through Creativity and Beauty

At the core of all my work is empowerment through creativity. As a photographer, I saw my work as a way to help clients see themselves in a new, confident light. Today, I continue that mission by leading MisMacK's photography campaigns, where I not only tell stories that build the brand but also create space for individuals to embrace their true beauty. MisMacK's ethos of clean, cruelty-free beauty perfectly aligns with my belief in cathartic, authentic expression.

The intersection of photography and beauty has allowed me to stay connected to my entrepreneurial roots while evolving into a leader who can empower others both in front of the camera and through business strategy. Creativity remains my compass, but collaboration has become the foundation for my growth.

Community and Support Networks

Throughout my journey, the importance of community and support networks has been undeniable. My entrepreneurial success is not something I achieved in isolation; it has always been a collaborative effort. From partnerships like the one I share with MisMacK to the wider network of fellow entrepreneurs and mentors, the connections I've fostered have been instrumental to my growth.

Working alongside a visionary like Missy MacKintosh, whose leadership at MisMacK is a constant source of inspiration, has taught me that the most successful businesses are those built on shared passion and mutual support. Whether through formal mentorships, collaborative projects, or simply exchanging experiences, these relationships have enriched my entrepreneurial path.

Advice for Aspiring Female Entrepreneurs

To women considering starting their own business, my advice is this: don't be afraid to evolve. Entrepreneurship is not a linear path, and it's okay to pivot when something no longer serves your well-being or purpose. Creativity is one of your greatest assets—use it not just to create products or services, but to solve problems and forge meaningful connections.

Seek out collaborations and mentorships, because entrepreneurship thrives on relationships. Surround yourself with people who believe in your vision and can offer guidance. Most importantly, stay true to your values. Your authenticity will set you apart, and the challenges you face will help you grow in ways you never imagined.

Looking Forward

As I continue to evolve, I'm excited to explore the ongoing blend of art and business. My work with MisMacK has allowed me to align my creative vision with brand development, and through our photography campaigns, I'm able to empower individuals in new, profound ways. While I remain deeply connected to my roots as a portrait photographer, I'm also committed to expanding the impact I can have through business collaborations and creative partnerships.

Ultimately, I see my entrepreneurial journey as one that is ever-evolving, grounded in creativity, and strengthened by collaboration. As I move forward, I remain committed to empowering others—through my art, my business, and the communities I'm a part of.

As you reflect on your own journey, how might collaboration and creative partnerships play a role in taking your work to the next level?

Lipstick? Pink

Clarke Cornwell is a passionate Health and Wellness Entrepreneur and the founder of Fountain of Youth, a brand that emerged from her personal quest for better health. Frustrated by the lack of products that were both natural and effective, Clarke saw an opportunity to bridge that gap and create a line that promotes well-being while staying true to a natural lifestyle.

CLARKE *Cornwell*

Q: Can you tell us about your journey as an entrepreneur? What inspired you to start your own business?

A: Starting my own business has been one of the most challenging yet rewarding experiences of my life. The struggles of building a startup from the ground up are so real, they feel almost tangible. There were moments when the difficulties seemed overwhelming, and I questioned whether I could keep going. But my passion for health, education, and investment has always driven me forward. I believe that health is one of the most important investments we can make as individuals and as a society. My mission is to help people live longer, more vibrant lives with a sense of purpose, and that's why my products are designed to deliver. This passion is what keeps me going when the road gets tough.

Q: Can you share a particularly memorable success story or milestone from your entrepreneurial journey?

A: There have been several moments throughout my journey that stand out, but one in particular remains close to my heart. A client who had been suffering from chronic bronchitis for years started using my product, the I AM Amazing Organic

Barley powdered drink. After about 10 months of consistent use, she experienced a significant recovery. Hearing how my product improved her health and quality of life reaffirmed my belief in what I do. Moments like these are the true rewards of entrepreneurship, and they motivate me to continue helping others on their health journeys.

Q: What advice would you give to someone who is considering starting their own business?

A: One of the key elements to starting your own business is identifying what truly drives you. What are you passionate about? What is your "why"? Why do you wake up every morning, and what motivates you to keep going, especially when things get tough? There will always be distractions, challenges, and even moments of self-doubt, but the important thing is to push harder than you ever thought possible. As you progress, you'll discover that not only are you navigating those challenges—you're thriving through them. Passion, purpose, and perseverance are the foundation of success.

Q: How do you stay motivated and resilient during tough times in your business?

A: Staying motivated during tough times comes down to grounding myself in faith and belief. Every day, I meditate on God's words and promises. I hold onto the belief that we are meant to achieve great things if we take care of our health in the way that nature intended. There will always be challenges, but remaining focused and driven by my goals helps me stay resilient. In addition to this spiritual foundation, I belong to a supportive network where I can find mentorship and guidance. This combination of faith and community keeps me motivated to push through even the most difficult times.

Q: Looking ahead, what are your goals and aspirations for the future of your business?

A: My goal is to continue educating people about the importance of health investment. We all have the power and energy to live purposeful, fulfilling lives, and it begins with understanding our health. Health education is the foundation, and it's essential that people know how to nourish their bodies inside and out. By spreading this knowledge, I hope to help others live with vitality and intent. I truly believe that the more we invest in our health, the more we can live the lives we are meant to lead.

Q: Looking ahead, what are your goals and aspirations for the future of your business?

A: My goals and aspirations for the future is to share to people about health education and investment. We have the power and energy to live a life that is purposeful. And it will all start with health education and investment. Only with knowing what to put in your body inside and out is a gift in itself. By the time that we acquire the knowledge to do it, living life with vitality is something we are all in need of.

Q: Pink or red lipstick?

A: My favorite color has always been red, ever since I was a child. So, without a doubt, it's red lipstick for me. Red symbolizes power, passion, and purpose—three qualities that I strive to embody every day.

Rani is a compassionate spiritual life coach, 500 RYT yoga teacher, yoga therapist, breathwork and meditation facilitator, and psychedelic integration coach with over a decade of experience, guiding clients toward holistic spiritual growth.

RANI
Sanghera

Q: How do you stay motivated and resilient during tough times in your business?

A: Staying motivated during tough times is rooted in my deep commitment to holistic healing. I remind myself of my purpose: bridging gaps in healthcare through yoga therapy. Practicing yoga and meditation helps me stay centered and manage stress effectively. This personal discipline allows me to lead by example, showing clients the importance of self-care. I also lean on my community of wellness professionals for support and inspiration. Engaging with like-minded individuals who understand the challenges of entrepreneurship helps me stay focused on the long-term vision. Celebrating small victories and client transformations keeps my spirits high, reinforcing the impact of our work. By viewing obstacles as opportunities for growth and learning, I cultivate resilience. Ultimately, my passion for helping others heal and thrive serves as a powerful motivator, reminding me that every challenge is a step toward creating a more fulfilling life for myself and my clients.

Q: Can you tell us about your journey as an entrepreneur and what inspired you to start your own business?

A: My entrepreneurial journey began while working in pharmacy, where I witnessed the limitations of conventional healthcare focused primarily on medication. I noticed many patients lacked holistic support for their emotional and mental well-being. This sparked my desire to explore alternative healing methods, leading me to deepen my yoga practice and pursue yoga therapy training. I envisioned creating a space where individuals could address their physical, emotional, and spiritual needs in an integrated manner. I wanted to offer a personalized approach to healing that combines yoga, breathwork, and mindfulness. Opening my own yoga therapy clinic was a natural progression, allowing me to bridge the gap between Western medicine and holistic practices. With over a decade of experience, I am committed to guiding clients on their journeys toward self-discovery and empowerment, helping them find balance and fulfillment in their lives through a comprehensive, whole-body approach.

Q: What sets your business apart from competitors in the market?

A: What sets my yoga therapy apart is the comprehensive, integrative approach to wellness. While many clinics focus solely on physical healing, we emphasize the connection between mind, body, and spirit. By incorporating diverse modalities such as breathwork, meditation, and psychedelic integration, we offer a holistic experience that addresses the root causes of distress rather than just symptoms. Our personalized treatment plans are tailored to each client's unique needs, ensuring they receive the support necessary for genuine transformation. This individualized approach fosters deeper connections and empowers clients to take an active role in their healing. Additionally, my background as a pharmacy technician allows me to blend conventional healthcare insights with holistic practices, creating a bridge that resonates with a broader audience. Ultimately, our commitment to fostering emotional, mental, and spiritual well-being distinguishes us from competitors, enabling us to create lasting, positive change in our clients' lives.

Q: What do you believe are the keys to building a strong brand identity and reputation?

A: Building a strong brand identity and reputation involves authenticity, consistency, and client-centered care. Authenticity is crucial; clients are drawn to brands that genuinely reflect their values and mission. My commitment to holistic healing and client empowerment fosters trust and loyalty. Consistency in messaging, quality of services, and client interactions reinforces the brand's identity. Whether through social media, workshops, or in-person sessions, maintaining a cohesive message helps establish credibility. Additionally, prioritizing client needs and personalizing care enhances the overall experience, encouraging positive word-of-mouth referrals. Engaging with the community through workshops, collaborations, and outreach initiatives strengthens the brand's presence and fosters connections. Expertise in holistic practices, alongside a commitment to continuous learning, further enhances our reputation. Lastly, forming emotional connections with clients allows for deeper engagement, turning them into advocates for the brand. This holistic approach ensures that our brand remains strong, relatable, and impactful.

Q: Can you share a story about a particularly memorable customer interaction or experience?

A: One of my most memorable client experiences involved a woman struggling with severe depression and suicidal ideation. When she first came to me, she felt lost and disconnected from life. After an initial assessment, I proposed a personalized treatment plan that focused on breathwork as a starting point. We aimed to release her deeply rooted negative beliefs. After just two sessions, she reported significant changes; her suicidal thoughts had diminished, and she began to feel a renewed sense of hope and purpose. Over the following weeks, we continued incorporating yoga therapy and mindfulness practices, and I witnessed her transformation firsthand. She gradually reconnected with joy, laughter, and life, finding meaning again. Today, she leads a fulfilling life, often sharing her journey with others. This experience reaffirms the profound impact of yoga therapy and the importance of holistic healing, inspiring me to continue my work with passion.

Q: How do you measure the success and growth of your business?

A: Measuring the success and growth of my yoga therapy clinic involves several key metrics. First and foremost, client transformations are paramount. Witnessing clients overcome physical pain, manage mental health issues, and experience personal growth provides a tangible measure of our impact. Next, client retention and referrals serve as indicators of trust and satisfaction. A strong referral base indicates that clients value their experiences and feel empowered to recommend our services. Financial growth is another critical metric; monitoring revenue trends and expenses ensures the business remains sustainable. Additionally, I assess community engagement through workshop attendance and online interactions, which reflect the clinic's presence and relevance. Finally, I focus on my personal fulfillment; when I feel inspired and passionate about the work we do, I know we're on the right path. By combining these qualitative and quantitative measures, I can ensure that our clinic continues to grow meaningfully.

RED OR PINK LIPSTICK? A: RED/ORANGE blend

Dorela Iepan is an energy healer Certified in Emotion Code, Body Code, and Belief Code. She is also a Certified EFT & Matrix Reimprinting Practitioner, Magnetism Practitioner, and Guided Meditation Facilitator. As a Life and Holistic Nutrition Coach, Vegan Chef, and Aromatherapy Consultant, Dorela combines various healing modalities to support others in achieving holistic well-being.

DORELA
Iepan

Q: Can you tell me about your journey as an entrepreneur? What inspired you to start your own business?

A: My entrepreneurial journey began with inspiration from my father, who ventured into entrepreneurship right after the Romanian revolution. Witnessing my parents' experiences as both employees and entrepreneurs broadened my horizons and made me realize the vast possibilities available. One of my key motivations was the desire to work from anywhere in the world—not just to have endless vacations, but to have the freedom to blend work and travel without being restricted to a fixed location or a limited number of vacation days.

A pivotal moment came when I was working at a bank. I felt as though my entire life had already been mapped out, leaving no room for growth or new experiences. I could see myself old and unfulfilled, and it was clear to me that this couldn't be my life's story—there had to be more.

It took several years for me to transition into entrepreneurship and even more time to find my true calling. Eventually, all my skills and experiences came together, allowing me to help others in a meaningful way. I realized I wanted to be a guide for people, showing them how beautiful and fulfilling life can be when you break free from limitations.

Today, I'm here to inspire, support, and uplift those who are seeking to transform their lives, just as I did.

Q: What are some of the biggest challenges you've faced as a woman entrepreneur, and how have you overcome them?

A: I wasn't born with the ideal entrepreneurial mindset, but I was fortunate to have a mother who constantly reminded me that anything is possible for me. This belief became a core part of my identity. Whenever I think of something, I immediately tell myself, "I can do it," and this mindset has shaped my approach to challenges.

One of the biggest challenges has been overcoming self-doubt and societal expectations about what women can achieve in business. Instead of seeing obstacles as setbacks, I've always viewed them as opportunities for growth and learning. I believe that every challenge is an invitation to expand beyond our current limits and discover new strengths within ourselves.

By adopting a mindset that embraces possibility and perseverance, I've been able to navigate difficulties with resilience and confidence. This mindset has allowed me to turn obstacles into stepping stones, fueling my journey and helping me inspire others to do the same.

Q: Can you share a particularly memorable success story or milestone from your entrepreneurial journey?"

A: I'm thrilled to share one of my recent accomplishments. In the spring of 2024, I envisioned organizing the first-ever EFT Summit in Romania. What started as a mere idea soon gained momentum, and by August, we had successfully hosted the event. It exceeded all expectations and was a huge success, bringing together practitioners and participants in an empowering and transformative experience.

This milestone was a powerful reminder of how intention and aligned action can turn dreams into reality. It reinforced my belief that when we dare to pursue our visions with determination and heart, the universe conspires to make it happen. This success was not just a professional achievement but also a testament to the incredible possibilities that open up when we choose to act on our aspirations.

Q: What advice would you give to other women who are considering starting their own businesses?"

A: My advice is to deeply connect with yourself and gain clarity on what you truly want to achieve in life. It's difficult to navigate your journey if you don't first ask yourself who you genuinely aspire to become. Allow yourself to dream big and embrace the process of becoming the best version of yourself. When you are aligned with your true desires, life will naturally guide you towards the right path, and opportunities will unfold before you. Believe in your potential and take bold steps forward—your journey will reflect your courage and authenticity.

Q: What role do you think mentorship and support networks play for women in entrepreneurship?"

A: Mentorship and support networks are invaluable at every stage of the entrepreneurial journey. Wherever you are on your path, there is always a mentor who can guide you through that particular milestone. Doubting whether the right mentor exists can hold you back from taking the necessary steps forward. Being surrounded by a supportive group of like-minded individuals can turn the seemingly impossible into reality. When enough people believe in your dreams, the possibilities become limitless.

Q: "How do you stay motivated and resilient during tough times in your business?"

A: Staying motivated during challenging times comes from keeping a clear vision of my desired outcomes and taking at least one actionable step toward them every day. Even small progress fuels my resilience. A simple smile in the mirror can be one of the most powerful motivators, reminding me to stay positive and focused on the bigger picture.

Ann Lindholm is a mother and a nona. She is a Global Security and International Relations Specialist with emphasis on humanitarian crisis response and Facilitator of Holistic and Cultural Wellness, CEO/Founder of two businesses and one non-profit.

As the youngest of four, I grew up watching my mom balance small businesses like Mary Kay and real estate development while prioritizing family. When I became a mother of four, I embraced a similar entrepreneurial spirit, running a cottage food business, raising livestock, and even working as a personal trainer—all while maintaining flexibility for my family.

After the fall of Afghanistan, I was invited to join rescue teams, which brought me back into full-time work. That experience led us to create our own global security firm and humanitarian crisis response nonprofit. My goal was not just to help those in need but also to provide my team the flexibility to balance work and life.

Our team serves to engage, equip, and empower vulnerable and persecuted communities to become resilient Global Agents of Change and force multipliers, fostering positive local transformation while promoting global security, stability, and peace through education, training, certification, small business start-up, community development, and when necessary, relocation to safer communities.

Witnessing the persecution in Afghanistan, we felt compelled to act. Many had risked everything alongside Coalition Forces, only to be abandoned when the forces withdrew. Many suffer persecution due to their faith, ethnicity or sexual identity.

Birthplace is not a choice, and our duty is to support those who cannot protect themselves.

One of my most memorable milestones was rescuing a mother and her young daughter from the Taliban. Our ground team acted to rescue within two hours, securing them in one of our safe houses. Their gratitude was a moment I will never forget, reinforcing the significance of our work.

Leadership for me means empowering others to lead. Every decision I make is shaped by the feedback and expertise of my team, whose diverse skills and perspectives drive our mission. Diversity not only enhances our creativity but also reflects the strength of collaboration, enabling us to find solutions and foster innovation in ways that wouldn't be possible without it.

Our work isn't just about helping individuals; it's about creating a ripple effect of change, turning communities into agents of peace, security, stability, and resilience.

Building networks and fostering partnerships are essential to the success of any organization. Every introduction or person you meet holds potential, as one connection can often lead to new opportunities or collaborations. However, networking should not be approached with the mindset of "what can I get from this person," but rather, "how can I add value to them." Strong partnerships are founded on mutual benefit, where both parties strive to give and receive in equal measure. When relationships are built on genuine respect and a desire to support one another, both individuals and organizations thrive. On the contrary, exploiting connections for personal gain will eventually harm your reputation and diminish your credibility. True success lies in valuing people as friends and partners, not as stepping-stones.

Innovation and adaptability are crucial in industries like global security and humanitarian crisis response, where unexpected challenges arise frequently. The key is to stay prepared, flexible, and forward-thinking.

One important strategy I've learned from a former boss is to "never operate in crisis mode until it's absolutely necessary". By planning ahead, having contingency plans, and trusting in your team's skill set, you're better equipped to face challenges with confidence.

In fast-moving environments, being adaptable also means staying open to unexpected opportunities. Changes and challenges, while disruptive, often lead to breakthroughs that wouldn't be possible without them. Teams should embrace a mindset where fluidity and resilience are as important as preparation and structure. This helps foster a culture of innovation, turning obstacles into potential for growth.

Understanding local cultures, international laws, and technological advancements is another critical component of staying ahead in global security and humanitarian work. When working across borders, the ability to navigate legal frameworks and respect cultural expectations ensures smoother operations and greater success in unpredictable situations.

Ultimately, innovation requires flexibility and preparedness, but also a deep trust in your team, your experience, and your capacity to adapt on the fly. That balance is what enables us to respond effectively to global challenges, using the tools at hand while staying open to what the future may hold.

Paige Freeman is the Founder and Educator at The Business Vault, dedicated to supporting start-up owners and encouraging dreamers. A passionate advocate for change, she embraces her role as a future world changer. Known for her bold approach to life, Paige is also a "Runner with the Bulls," embodying the spirit of adventure in all she does.

PAIGE
Freeman

Q: Can you tell me about your journey as an entrepreneur? What inspired you to start your own business?

A: Throughout my employee life, I received countless remarks and insinuations about my appearance from male colleagues as if that was the only value I had. When I was scouted as the BDM for a mining company; I thought I'd finally be valued for my expertise. I learned the CEO didn't value what I could do for the business, his ambition was purely how I looked to potential new customers after being told by him, "Paige, remember, sex sells…" Despite handling these remarks for years across different industries, I always knew that what I could bring to the table was far greater than the misogynistic minds of those I worked with. I've always felt that I wasn't put on this earth to play small, so I wanted to start my own business to make the most of what I know I'm capable of bringing to the world, and eventually create a workplace where my employees feel incredibly supported and have a healthy working environment. Since becoming an entrepreneur I've received more respect and opportunities than ever before.

Q: What advice would you give to other women who are considering starting their own businesses?

A: YOU CAN DO IT. There will be days when your dreams may seem insurmountable, life or money can get in the way, and you may doubt yourself around every corner. The trick is to believe in yourself and become resilient. Planning and Strategising is also essential! Lower your self-expectations, don't rely on your friends and family to build your business for you and above all, be your own cheerleader and celebrate small victories.

Q: How do you maintain a work-life balance while running your own business?

A: With multiple businesses, starting a charity, and being a mum to my incredible daughter and 3 step-children life is a juggling act. I focus on 'harmony' in every area of work and life, giving attention to the areas that need it most. Working in

1.5-hour blocks helps me stay focused. My 5am work time is a lifesaver, allowing me to get more done before everyone wakes up. When I'm in hyper-work mode I try my best not to break it so I get the most out of my brain power and drive.

Q: What problem or need does your business solve, and what motivated you to address it?

A: I discovered early that starting a business from scratch requires A LOT of googling, understanding jargon, and misleading information. I learnt a lot over the years through success but most importantly failures and I wanted to harness every bit of information I learnt along the way and teach it. The Business Vault is a business school providing step-by-step courses, resources, and mentoring. I believe that no one should go through business alone and I'm dedicated to guiding entrepreneurs through their journey, providing support and expertise to help them succeed.

Q: Can you discuss a failure or setback your business encountered, and how did you bounce back from it?

A: The biggest challenge in starting The Business Vault was managing the emotional toll of my divorce. The legal battle left me mentally drained, affecting my focus. I had incredibly high expectations to launch quickly and start teaching. Whilst juggling my graphic design business, writing the curriculum, attending to my clients, the legal fight and trying to be an attentive mum stress and burnout hit me hard and I thought I had failed before I even began. Realising I was burdening myself with unrealistic expectations, I learned to listen to my body and mind, granting myself permission to take my time and be kind to myself.

Q: What sets your business apart from competitors in the market?

A: There's no denying that there are an incredible number of business coaches and mentors worldwide, and they're all needed. What sets me and The Business Vault apart is that I guide and teach holistically. I always say that business is personal. The first three years of starting a business can be tough if you don't know which way to turn. This uncertainty can affect your business, personal life, finances, and mental and physical well-being, and that's where we address and strategise in the areas that need to be altered. One of the greatest traits I've instilled in all of our courses is my Australian, down-to-earth approach, making complex concepts easy to understand without requiring an IQ of 120 to grasp or implement them. I'm all about the human-to-human approach, I'm there for the ride for all of my students and love cheering them on every-step of the way.

Q: What are your thoughts on the importance of diversity and inclusion in entrepreneurship?

A: I could talk about this topic for hours! I love that entrepreneurship is no longer the men's club it used to be. Now, people from all walks of life are becoming thought leaders and entrepreneurs. This shift is incredibly important because, regardless of our backgrounds, we all see different gaps in the world. Everyone should have the opportunity to fill these gaps, as it helps others and brings value to the world. Our global diversity is beginning to take flight; however, inclusion must extend to our children and young minds. They need to be taught financial literacy and how to make waves in the world, helping future generations make our world a better place. Young minds need to be taught how to harness failures, successes, resilience, compassion, and risk-taking. Every person can be an entrepreneur; they just need the resources available to help them strategise and grow. It's not about acceptance; it's about self-belief and strapping on your superhero outfit.

Q: Can you share a particularly memorable success story or milestone from your entrepreneurial journey?

A: Funnily enough, when I won an Award for Digital Services at the Ausmumpreneur Awards in 2022, I thought that would be my standout story for years to come. While I was incredibly grateful to achieve that early in my entrepreneurial life, there was no greater feeling than finishing The Business Start-Up Essentials Course, which is the centrepiece of The Business Vault. I started with just a couple of topics in mind, and as I wrote, the course kept growing. It turned into a 200-page workbook, an 8-module course covering over 70 topics. Taking 11 months to write it felt like a marathon; there were many times I wanted to give up. However, I knew it needed to have a place in the world to help people make their dreams a reality. It's an ever-growing course, but finally seeing my vision come to life was one of the greatest moments in my entrepreneurial journey.

ALISHA &
ROCHELLE
Schwartz

Q: Can you share a particular memorable success story or milestone from your entrepreneurial journey?

A: My mom and I work together as The Mother Daughter Dynamic Duo We both come from two different generations her generation was to stay married and suck it up no matter what and give all your power away and stay quiet and don't ruffle the feathers too much or at all.

I was in a movie theater watching the movie Yatel and Barbra Streisand was singing, and I heard her say Pappa I have a voice now and what I received was I have something important to say and share in the world. Because of this experience and finding my voice I was able to then manifest being on the Oprah Winfrey Show.

My story and my journey were challenged with a learning disability and having a verbally abusive father. That experience gave me no self-esteem growing up. I felt insecure, unimportant and that no matter what I said or did I didn't matter. The gifts I've received from this part of my journey lead me into what I do today. I am a gifted healer and bodyworker; I work with my mother, and we are a mother daughter dynamic duo supporting women going through various stages of life. We are speakers and workshop leaders and authors. We are experts in Relationship Coaching and we work with mothers and daughters in healing their relationship.

Q: What advice would you give to other women who are considering starting their own business?

A: First research the business you want to go into to see if that is right for you. It's so important to find a mentor or teacher in whatever business you're looking to go into. Also, networking to meet other entrepreneurs is essential in building relationships which support you in building your business as well as giving back and doing charity work which helps people get to know you and your business which in turn supports you and other people's business thrive and become successful. To become successful, you must be willing to put money into you and your business and ultimately Believe in Yourself and what you're doing.

Q: How do you stay motivated and resilient during tough times in your business?

We have found that if you continue to grow and work on yourself and give yourself the self-care through tough times it allows you to always see a new perspective and have a positive outlook on things even when things aren't always going as we plan. That's when you have the biggest growth. It's so important to have a great outlook on life in general which always transpires into every area of your life, not only business but all areas of your life. Also, it's important to have a great sense of humour and have fun and not take everything so seriously. Meditation, journaling, working out and community and great friends really support your vision and dreams and most importantly your mental health which in turn helps in all aspects of your life.

Q: Can you tell us about your journey as an entrepreneur and what inspired you to start your own business?

A: Going through your own journey of transformation and all its twists and turns and the willingness to look at yourself, led us to the work we do today as a mother and daughter dynamic duo. We both had to be willing to look at ourselves and heal the deeper wounds from our childhood to then be able to coach and support women of all walks of life, Weather that was divorce, toxic unhealthy relationships, family dynamics and issues, learning disabilities, physical and verbal abusive. The most important piece is you must go through and do the inner work to be able to coach someone else and provide each person with a safe place.

Q: What advice would you give to someone who is considering starting their own business?

A: Make sure you do some extensive research on the area in which you want to start your own business. It's so important to have a vision board that excites you and to also make sure you write out the pros and cons of the business you want to start. Be honest with yourself and make sure you surround yourself with other people that are doing inspiring things as well. Make sure you allocate a budget for the business you want to start and you're super organized. It's super important to continue to do the things you love that make you happy and feel fulfilled and balanced. Make sure you also ask for the support you need in the areas you feel you're not strong in, so you become more successful.

Q: Looking ahead, what are your goals and aspirations for the future of your business?

A: Making sure we always implement self-care and continue to grow and evolve and have fun. To be around positive people which includes friends and family and the people we work with and collaborate with and to work on projects that inspire change in the world by giving back and supporting charities that we love and make a difference in the world.

Melissa J. Rubin is a top-ranked Real Estate Advisor at Compass, specializing in Miami properties. As one of the top 1%, she brings expert guidance and local insight to her clients. Founder of National Advisory, Melissa combines her passion for real estate with innovative solutions.

Q: How do you maintain a work-life balance while running your own business?

A: I maintain a work life balance by purposefully planning a business that fits into my life. I create both personal and business plans for the year, breaking them down into 90-day goals. Each day, I block out time on my calendar for both personal and business tasks, prioritizing them based on their urgency.

Q: What strategies have you found most effective for networking and building professional relationships as a female entrepreneur?

A: Successful networking is built on 2 principles, connections and continuity. Connections from hosting in-person dinners in my home, one on one meetings, and being part of networking groups. The real success is found in the continuity of those relationships after the initial interaction. From hand written notes, personal phone calls, and gifts.

Q: How do you approach leadership and team building within your company?

A: My leadership style emphasizes clarity through communication, collaboration, and meeting people where they are. A team is a true collaborative and by involving everyone in the planning and execution of key business activities it creates an environment and culture that promotes growth, ideas, and people being able to share who they are in a team setting.

Q: How do you stay motivated and resilient during tough times in your business?

A: Keep it simple and set clear 90-day goals. Things are always going to be up and down and that is life. Having a plan of action allows me to stay focused on my daily routine, actions, and activities that will get me to my long term goals. After going through several ups and downs I find that just sticking to my plan creates the most confidence and comfort during tough times.

Q: What were some of the biggest challenges you faced when starting your business, and how did you overcome them?

A: Transitioning from fashion to real estate presented a unique challenge: separating my identity from my business. Ego can sometimes hinder progress. This was a valuable lesson for me. Starting over was a humbling experience after representing a big-name watch brand. Recognizing the importance of continuous learning and growth was another significant lesson. To overcome these challenges, I surrounded myself with an amazing circle of people I could lean on for guidance and assistance. This support system remains invaluable to me to this day.

Q: What advice would you give to someone who is considering starting their own business?

A: For those considering starting their own business, my advice is:

- Create a business that is meaningful to you and you find purpose in.

- Embrace the journey and recognize that each lesson learned brings you one step closer to your end goals and the only time you lose is if you quit.

- Remember that the path to success is rarely linear, but the road will always lead you to where you need to be if you continue to stay in a constant state of action.

- Don't compare yourself to others and focus on your journey, your plan, and your goals.

Q: Pink or red lipstick?

A: Red! It's a feminine neutral that makes me feel both sexy and complete. I like red as it is elegant and exudes confidence all at the same time.

Kelly Greenslade is a dedicated Strength Coach and Sports Nutritionist who specializes in Athlete Preparation. With a passion for fitness and nutrition, Kelly helps individuals optimize their performance both in and out of the gym. She also co- hosts the "Queen We Got You" podcast, where she shares insights on health, wellness, and achieving success in athletics.

KELLY
Greenslade

Q: Can you tell me about your journey as an entrepreneur? What inspired you to start your own business?

A: I had always been a corporate girl, told to climb the corporate ladder and secure higher positions in businesses that offered a stable, regularly paying job.

After several different jobs, none of which I held for longer than 2.5 years (I would just get so bored), I started to wonder: what if I did something I loved? I talked to my family and parents at the time and told them I wanted to be a personal trainer. The idea was quickly shut down. "The market is oversaturated," "You won't have a stable income," "You can't grow past your business," and "It's hard." I gave up the idea and continued my miserable existence in the corporate industry.

By the age of 35, I hated who I was, hated everything I was becoming, and couldn't see the point anymore. I hired a coach and started training, learning about nutrition, and eating well. I became stronger, changed my whole life, and became more positive and motivated. I loved it! I also realized that for a majority of my life, I'd been misled about food—how much I should eat and the type of training I should be doing as a woman.

After a year with my coach, I spoke with him and said that I wanted to consider becoming a coach, but I had been told for years that it wasn't a good plan because there are millions of coaches out there. His response was, "There may be a million coaches out there, but very few good coaches." I only needed that one person to believe in me. So I got to work, studied, and became not only a qualified personal trainer but also a sports nutritionist.

I reached the point where I was training people before and after my full-time job. I became an in-demand coach and soon quit my 9-5 to coach full-time. Four years later, I'm now a well-known name on the Sunshine Coast, and I'm aiming to expand globally to help people find themselves, take care of themselves, and live happy, healthy lives without having to restrict all the foods they love. I want to change how we think about training and help people become stronger both physically and mentally.

Q: What are some of the biggest challenges you've faced as a woman entrepreneur, and how have you overcome them?

A: Being a female in the personal training arena can be tough, as it's a male-dominated space. Many people perceive female trainers as 'soft' or think we only know how to teach yoga or Pilates, not how to lift or push clients. Having feminine energy in this space often means taking a different approach to delivering feedback and coaching.

There's a common perception that personal training is all about bootcamp or army-style coaching. While some people respond well to that type of training, it's not the only way to coach. I'm a caring, understanding coach, but I also get the most out of my clients because I'm willing to ask the hard questions when needed. I have great relationships with my clients, and I think that sets me apart—I'm genuine and caring, but I can also push them without yelling.

The feminine approach can often be rejected, but my response is, "How's it been working out for you before?" It's not always helpful to be yelled at; sometimes, you need support and education to create lasting change. I've always been authentically me, and I pride myself on that. I am who I am, and everyone else will adjust!

Q: How do you stay motivated and resilient during tough times in your business?

A: I believe that I'm now in the most important phase of my life with my business. What I'm doing is needed, and my message to a wider audience is so important that it would be a disservice to quit.

When things get hard (which they often do in my business, especially when clients leave and new ones come on at the same time), I remind myself that the universe has my back. The universe gives me the space to create more content, improve my service, change things in the business, or catch up on tasks I always complain about not having time to do. If you really believe in your cause, your purpose, and your business, then just keep going!

Q: What problem or need does your business solve, and what motivated you to address it?

A: For the longest time, I thought it was normal to "diet" constantly, binge-eat on weekends, and regularly drink alcohol. I thought healthy food was for losing weight, and junk food was for celebrating or socializing.

I had been overweight for most of my adult life and went through cycles of losing weight and gaining even more back. I was unhappy and felt that losing weight was impossible for me. As I got older, I began to accept that this was just the way things were.

When I made changes in my life—educating myself on nutrition and exercise and deciding that health isn't just about a number on the scale—that's when my life changed. Now, I want to help others navigate the confusing landscape of social media and false information about health. My purpose is to disrupt diet culture and empower people to take control of their health.

Q: What strategies do you employ to attract and retain customers?

A: Pure honesty! I don't filter myself. I'm open about my life, my struggles, and the fact that achieving health and fitness is hard—but it's also hard to hate yourself and be unhealthy. I set fair and realistic expectations for how we'll get there.

I also focus a lot on mindset through my coaching, taking a holistic approach to health and fitness as a lifestyle that supports happy, healthy minds. My approach is about longevity, not just aesthetics. I emphasize hormone health and a well-rounded perspective that helps clients take care of themselves for the long term.

Lesley Ross, Founder of Power Path Consultancy and Co Founder & Co Ceo of BAM Consultants.

LESLEY
Ross

"Once you recognise that you are your own greatest love, you'll understand why you refuse to settle for anything less than your true value."

Q: Can you tell me about your journey as an entrepreneur? What inspired you to start your own business?

A: Growing up with the belief that a corporate career was the epitome of stability and security, I adhered to this path for many years. However, as I climbed the corporate ladder, I realised that I was yearning for something more fulfilling. The turning point came when I recognised that my passion and potential were being stifled. The decision to venture into entrepreneurship was fuelled by the desire to create something meaningful, where my hard work would directly contribute to my own success rather than someone else's. It was a leap of faith, driven by the resolve to build a legacy without limits.

Q: Have you found any specific advantages or opportunities in being a woman in your industry?

A: Absolutely. Being a woman in my industry has allowed me to leverage the unique perspectives and strengths that women inherently possess. Women have a remarkable ability to connect and empathise, which fosters deeper relationships with clients and partners. This connectivity opens doors to opportunities that might otherwise remain closed. My journey has been about embracing these attributes and using them to create a business environment that is inclusive, innovative, and empowering for other women as well.

Q: Looking ahead, what are your goals and aspirations for the future of your business?

A: One of my primary goals is to pave the way for more women to realise their entrepreneurial dreams. I aspire to build a business that not only achieves financial success—reaching our 7-figure targets annually—but also contributes to societal change by empowering women to pursue their passions. My vision is to create a sustainable business model that serves as a beacon of possibility for future generations.

Q: What problem or need does your business solve, and what motivated you to address it?

A: Our business tackles the barriers that prevent women from reaching their full potential, which often stems from fear and self-doubt. We are committed to dismantling these obstacles by fostering a supportive environment where women can confront and embrace their challenges. Our approach is hands-on and personalised, ensuring that each client feels valued and understood. This personal touch differentiates us from the one-size-fits-all approach of other companies.

Q: What advice would you give to someone who is considering starting their own business?

A: My advice is to prioritise investing in yourself. Seek out a mentor or coach who shares your vision and can provide the guidance and support you need during times of uncertainty. It's essential to have a clear understanding of your goals and a deep knowledge of your product or service. Building a strong foundation from the start will set you on the path to success.

Q: What role do you think mentorship and support networks play for women in entrepreneurship?

A: Mentorship and support networks are crucial for women in entrepreneurship. They provide a safe space to share experiences, gain insights, and receive encouragement. These networks can be instrumental in navigating the unique challenges women face in business, offering resources and connections that facilitate growth and resilience.

Q: Have you encountered any gender-based biases or discrimination in your industry, and if so, how have you addressed them?

A: Yes, I have faced gender-based biases, as many women do. However, I approach these challenges as opportunities for education and change. I address them by confidently asserting my expertise and contributions, while also advocating for diversity and inclusion within the industry. By fostering an environment of respect and equality, I aim to break down these barriers for myself and others.

Q: In your experience, what are some common misconceptions or stereotypes about women in business, and how do you challenge or overcome them?

A: A prevalent misconception is that women are too emotional or lack the authority to lead effectively. I challenge these stereotypes by consistently demonstrating competence, confidence, and strategic thinking. By leading by example, I strive to dispel these myths and inspire others to rethink their biases.

Q: How do you build and maintain a strong team, and what qualities do you look for in potential hires?

A: Building a strong team starts with hiring individuals who share the company's core values and vision. I look for qualities such as adaptability, integrity, and a collaborative spirit. Maintaining a strong team involves fostering an inclusive culture where every member feels valued and empowered to contribute their best work. Open communication and ongoing development are key to sustaining a motivated and cohesive team.

Q: Pink or red lipstick?

A: My lipstick colour preference is pink, a reminder that embracing femininity is a strength, not a weakness, in the business world.

Amanda Lavery CEO of CoCaBee Inc . CoCaBee Inc is free from fillers and toxins and proud to not tested on animals.

Q: Can you tell me about your journey as an entrepreneur? What inspired you to start your own business?

A: My journey as an entrepreneur began with my deep love for animals. I've always believed that we could create body care products using raw and natural ingredients without the need for animal testing. This became a key mission for CoCaBee—to advocate against animal testing while offering high-quality, natural products.

Nature and meditation have also played a significant role in shaping my vision. The earth's natural elements, like essential oils, inspired me to create products that are both sustainable and effective. Our packaging, made from bamboo, reflects our commitment to eco-friendly practices.

Having modeled since I was 16, with experiences in high-end fashion shows and magazines across Paris and Athens, I've gained a deep understanding of skincare's importance, especially when constantly traveling. It was during a small entrepreneurship course that I realized my passion for being my own boss, which ultimately led to the creation of CoCaBee.

Q: How do you maintain a work-life balance while running your own business?

A: I prioritize balance through activities that ground me, like hiking, practicing yoga, and meditating. These practices not only help me relax and clear my mind but also allow me to breathe deeply and recharge. They're essential for maintaining both my physical and mental well-being. I often find that this is also when I get the most creative, which feeds back into my work with fresh ideas and inspiration.

Q:) What advice would you give to other women who are considering starting their own businesses?**

A: My advice is to trust yourself and never lose sight of why you wanted to start your business in the first place. There will be challenges, but staying true to your vision and values will keep you moving forward. It's also essential to maintain balance in your life—whether that's through self-care, hobbies, or simply taking time to breathe. And don't forget to have fun along the way! Building something you're passionate about should be an enjoyable and fulfilling journey.

Q: How do you stay motivated and resilient during tough times in your business?**

A: I stay motivated by reminding myself why I created CoCaBee in the first place—to be a voice against animal cruelty, promote clean, natural products, and support women entrepreneurs. That purpose keeps me grounded and focused when things get challenging. I also believe it's important to surround yourself with great people who uplift and inspire you. Having a supportive network makes all the difference during difficult times.

Q: How did you come up with the idea for your business, and what was the process like from concept to execution?**

A: The idea for CoCaBee came to me after taking a small entrepreneurship course, which sparked my interest in health and wellness. As I started using essential oils and becoming more health-conscious, I realized I didn't fully understand many of the ingredients in the body care products I was using. That inspired me to create my own products using just five natural ingredients.

From there, I wanted to ensure that the packaging aligned with my values, so I chose bamboo for its eco-friendly and recyclable qualities. My friends and family loved the lip balms I made, and that gave me the confidence to turn my passion into a business. That's how CoCaBee was born.

Q: What sets your business apart from competitors in the market?

A: What sets CoCaBee apart is our dedication to simplicity, purity, and sustainability. We focus on using only five natural ingredients, ensuring our products are raw, clean, and safe for our consumers. Our bamboo packaging not only offers an eco-friendly and exotic alternative, but it also reflects our commitment to reducing environmental impact. Additionally, our advocacy for cruelty-free products and ethical practices is central to our brand. We aim to keep things as simple, natural, and transparent as possible, making it easy for consumers to feel confident and connected to what they're using on their skin.

Liahna Cole is the owner of Vitality Vibe Wellness Center.

In July 2020 I opened my own solo practice focused on therapeutic massage. You might be thinking, "She must be crazy! Opening a business touching people at the height of a global pandemic?!" What I've learned is that when you take a risk, there is fear. Fear from your loved ones, friends, and even deep within yourself. But that can be the root of courage.

Someone once told me that if you want to grow your business, grow yourself first, then hire a team to grow with you. At the time I had been struggling financially and an opportunity to rent a small space came on to my radar for a reasonable price. I thought to myself, even if I fail, I can probably get a job and cover the cost of the office. After all, I've raised seven kids, so how much harder could it be to start a business?

It has been a wild ride and such an adventure. Through attending business networking groups, I learned how to market my unique style and niche. By January 2021, which was only the first six months of being on my own, I matched what I had made in a year working for other people. By 2022 my business experienced massive growth and I was fully booked. That's when a business mindset coach entered the picture and Vitality Vibe Wellness was born. It was time to move from a small space and expand.

Running a wellness center was a completely different challenge. I needed systems and contracts and finishings and wall decorations, everything to start a brick-and-mortar business. I enlisted the help of my friends and family to track down all the items I needed for the new space. I hired a total of 3 different coaches during that year to learn what I didn't know I needed to know. One principle became the foundation of Vitality Vibe Wellness. Integrity.

Integrity became the fiber and life blood of the business. Integrity is how my team runs the daily operations, It's how we interact with clients and each other. Integrity is how we conduct ourselves in the community. Integrity has formed a bond of trust and because of it, I am able to balance work and family and so does my team.

I am out to change the industry and elevate massage therapy to a recognized adjunct to traditional health care where clients and therapists are valued and treated with compassion and respect. With a careful blend of humility, gratitude, and passion, we are always growing and learning. Everything we offer at Vitality Vibe Wellness Center is focused on a holistic approach to physical and emotional pain relief.

This journey from the unknown to courage to vulnerability to learning and growth has not happened without challenges and loads of growth, but the right mentor support and team can be powerful tools in success. I'm a pick lipstick gal which I feel symbolizes tenderness, empathy, and my high ambition commitment to self-worth.

Yolanda Gysbers is a licensed REALTOR®, she has achieved her Luxury Homes Certification (LHC), Real Estate Negotiation Expert (RENE), and Accredited Buyer Representative (ABR®) designations. At the time of this publishing Yolanda works with Rimrock Real Estate a boutique real estate brokerage in Edmonton, Alberta, Canada.

YOLANDA
Gysbers

Photo Credit: Headshot by Digital Dreams Media

Q: How do you measure the success and growth of your business?

A: The measurement of success is a personal journey I base on many different metrics. I believe one of the most important factors is client satisfaction, this should be the driving force of any business. The ability to have a thriving business based on referrals and repeat clients is the most favorable compliment one can receive. The importance of having a positive impact on people's lives through the services I provide as well as contributions to my field have allowed me to experience growth both professionally and personally. Reviewing professional goals, accomplishments, and realizing my strengths and weaknesses all play a generous role in how I measure the growth of my business.

Q: How do you maintain a work-life balance while running your own business?

A: The ability to know your own limits as well as determining what works for you both personally and professionally requires some commitment and time. I have a busy family with two children so it can be challenging to manage everyone's schedules. Overextending yourself has negative consequences in all aspects of your life, your family, your business, and your personal /

professional growth. I have found that prioritizing, organizing and re- evaluating has helped me immensely to maintain a work- life balance without compromising family or business.

Q: What strategies have you found most effective for networking and building professional relationships as a female entrepreneur?

A: Strategies I use and have found most effective to network include being present (sounds crazy I know) this day in age with all the devices and technology, it is too easy to lose touch with people leading to insincere interactions. You must socialize, not to talk about your business necessarily, but just to talk to people. Building relationships personally, professionally and engaging in positive conversation is powerful and not to be underestimated. Some strategies I have utilized include joining local business groups, networking events, and surrounding yourself with people who have similar goals and ambitions.

Q: How do you stay motivated and resilient during tough times in your business?

A: In real estate there will always be high and low activity phases in the market. I utilize my downtime committing to continuous learning whether it be researching industry trends or developing new ideas and approaches I can use in my business. Setting clear, achievable goals is just as important as celebrating your successes. You will encounter challenges. I found it essential to adapt and be open to change when I was faced with difficult situations. I often reflect, remembering the many reasons why I decided to make a change and how far I have come since I began my journey. Staying motivated takes energy and commitment, you have to take the good with the bad and remember what you have to offer.

Q: How do you stay innovative and adapt to changes in your industry?

A: To stay innovative and adapt to changes in real estate I am continuously leveraging data analytics, monitoring emerging trends, utilizing educational opportunities and networking. Part of my role as a REALTOR® is to educate my clients and provide information relevant to their needs so keeping up with current market trends and statistics plays an integral role in our industry. With the emergence of technology and social media some trends are user friendly, however also enlisting a company to help you can prove to be very effective. I have had to adapt and learn considerably more forms of technology than ever anticipated. When I have struggled, hiring that portion of work out has been favorable and allows for me to focus on other parts of my business requiring attention.

Q: Looking ahead, what are your goals and aspirations for the future of your business?

A: Looking ahead my goals and aspirations in business remain focused on my clients. By enhancing the client experience and implementing strategies I aim for consistent and sustainable growth. Through innovation and technology I will continue to enhance the overall client journey to build loyalty and satisfaction. I look to strengthen brand presence through marketing, partnerships, and community engagement. My goal is to create a lasting and positive impact. I will continue to strengthen my value and set a high standard while including personalized solutions, and creating memorable interactions. In closing I have always structured my business around the client and exceeding expectations which in turn has enabled me to work with some truly incredible people, and to me that is what it is all about.

Q: Pink or red lipstick?

A: Pink!

Allison Seller is a transformational business strategist, coach, and Amazon #1 Best-Selling author of The Art of Falling Up: From Trial to Triumph, Crafting a Life That is Purpose-Driven. With over 20 years of experience, Allison is on a mission to help entrepreneurs—especially women—break free from the cycle of stagnancy and monetize their expertise. Her programs, The WELLthy Entrepreneur, Becoming WELLthy, and The Winners Circle Mastermind, empower business owners to package their knowledge into scalable, high-value offers so they can achieve financial freedom without sacrificing their personal lives. Through her work, Allison teaches that true success is built not by working harder but by working smarter and aligning your business with your values. Allison's personal journey of trial and triumph, as detailed in her best-selling book, serves as a testament to the idea that setbacks are not failures but stepping stones to greater success. With her expertise, Allison is helping to shape the next generation of women leaders by encouraging them to embrace their unique strengths and create businesses that reflect their worth.

Breaking Free from Stagnancy: Building a WELLthy Business

As a business strategist, coach, and author, my mission has always been to help entrepreneurs break free from the cycle of stagnancy. Throughout my 20-year journey, I've seen countless business owners—especially women—struggle to monetize their expertise and reach the next level. My path was no different. I knew I had the talent and drive, but it wasn't until I shifted my mindset from trading time for money to creating scalable, results-based programs that my business truly transformed. That's where the concept of WELLthy living came in—a combination of wealth and well-being, designed to create financial freedom while honoring the life you want to live.

My programs—The WELLthy Entrepreneur, Becoming WELLthy, and The Winners Circle Mastermind—were born from this realization. They are designed to empower entrepreneurs to package their expertise, price it correctly, and step into their role as industry leaders. These programs teach that the key to business growth is not working harder, but smarter. My clients have turned their businesses around by focusing on what truly matters—monetizing their knowledge, not their time.

The inspiration behind the WELLthy business model came from my own struggle with balancing business growth and family life. I realized that constantly trading time for money wasn't sustainable. I wanted to serve my clients at the highest level without sacrificing what matters most to me—my family and my time. This pivotal moment led me to create a business model that aligned with both my personal and financial goals. Now, I help other entrepreneurs escape that same trap and build businesses that honor both their professional ambitions and personal values.

In my Amazon #1 Best-Selling book, The Art of Falling Up: From Trial to Triumph, Crafting a Life That is Purpose-Driven, I dive deeper into the idea that we are not defined by our failures or setbacks. As women, we often face unique challenges in our entrepreneurial journeys—challenges that can feel like falls. But I've learned, and now teach, that these falls are not signs of failure. Instead, they are stepping stones to something greater. Our falls give us the perspective, strength, and resilience we need to rise even higher.

This mindset is especially important for women entrepreneurs who may feel stuck in their business. Feeling stuck often comes from being misaligned with your business model. Are you constantly working harder but not seeing growth? It may be time to rethink how you're monetizing your expertise. I advise focusing on creating high-value, scalable offers that free up your time while still delivering amazing results for your clients. The shift from selling time to selling results is a game-changer.

The Art of Falling Up is a guide for anyone who has felt defeated, stuck, or unsure of the next step. It's a reminder that success is not a straight line, but a series of rises and falls that craft a life driven by purpose. In the book, I share my own journey of trial and triumph, offering insights into how I turned my setbacks into opportunities. I believe this mindset is critical for women entrepreneurs—your "falls" do not define you; they are what shape you into the leader you are meant to be.

For me, setbacks are no longer something to fear. Instead, I've come to see them as opportunities. In The Art of Falling Up, I talk about how our "falls" aren't the end—they're stepping stones to something greater. Every challenge I've faced has given me a chance to grow stronger and better align with my purpose. Instead of letting setbacks define me, I use them to propel me forward.

To those reading this, my message is simple: You are capable of achieving more than you realize. Focus on your strengths, package your expertise, and don't be afraid to grow. You are not just building a business—you're creating a legacy. And remember, every fall is just another opportunity to rise higher than before.

Tina Aquila-Posteraro is the owner and lead photographer of Oculus Studios by Tina Shoots Boudoir. She believes in empowering all women of all ages and sizes through her work as a Luxury fine art portrait photographer. She also holds women's events at her studio that focus on empowering the "whole" women- body, mind, and spirit. She resides in Vancouver, BC, Canada with her loving husband and two beautiful children.

TINA AQUILA
Posteraro

Q: Can you tell me about your journey as an entrepreneur? What inspired you to start your own business?

A: I created my business as a special sanctuary for women, at a time when I really needed one just like it myself. I had two little ones under three years old, my husband worked 14 hour days and I felt I had lost my tribe as three of my best friends moved away from the city. I was also learning how to accept my new role as a mother, with my changing body, and going at it "alone".

My Boudoir Portrait studio is a place where women can hit the pause button on their every day roles and labels, and reconnect with the divine feminine that lives inside. I want to remind women that they are more than enough – they are powerful, beautiful, and worthy of all their own love and adoration.

As a Luxury Boudoir Studio, Our full day sessions are dedicated to indulging each woman in their feminine magic. We also hold women's events and workshops at the studio, where we empower women through mediation, sound, breath, and host other experts in areas of finance, women's health and more. My mission is empowering the whole woman- holistically.

Q: Have you found any specific advantages or opportunities in being a woman in your industry?

A: Absolutely. As a woman in my 40's, I experience all the growth and change that women face throughout their journey. I know first hand how it feels to learn to embrace our ever changing bodies, how scary it can be to be vulnerable in the process, and how empowering it is when you cross that finish line. While there are many amazing male photographers, I feel that I have a special insight to how delicate this process can be because of my first hand experience.

Q: What do you believe are the keys to building a strong brand identity and reputation?

A: I believe the key is to create a brand that is aligned with your core values, and authentic to what you want to put out in the world. For me, I serve women at every age, stage, and size, who are looking to reconnect with their divine feminine and spend the day indulging in that energy. Staying focused on who I serve, what they need, and how my business solves that need, is at the centre of all my brand and messaging.

Q: Can you discuss a failure or setback your business encountered, and how did you bounce back from it?

A: I have had too many lessons to list! From trusting the wrong people, to investing in things that didn't move the needle, to collaborations that did not fulfill the goal, and more. I think every person in business (and in life!) experiences what they perceive as failures at one time or another. I believe that 'failures' are actually lessons and redirections that point us to where we are supposed to be. They are also a great way to define your own personal boundaries and reminders to stick to them, no matter what. Everything happens for a reason.

Q: How do you balance work-life commitments as an entrepreneur?

A: As a Mom and an entrepreneur, I am still working on this. I tend to be the person that spends most of the day working, then picks up kids for afterschool activities, then dinner and bedtime, THEN flip open my laptop with the intention of working for one more hour and end up working past midnight! While my family and business are my top priorities, I do make time to take in the little joys of life. Whether it is admiring a sunrise or sunset, noticing how beautiful the leaves are, taking a little extra time to hold my children as they fall asleep, or enjoying a cup of hot coffee while admiring the view from my patio. Life is busy these days but taking a minute for gratitude for the present moment is everything.

Michelle Walker is a businesswoman who has achieved more than she ever imagined with so much more to come. Every action is for her daughters - Rochelle, Valentina & Charlize and in the memory of her beloved father Roman Katz.

Q: Can you tell me about your journey as an entrepreneur? What inspired you to start your own business?

A: In 2017 when my older daughters were still little, I was coming home from the office at 7pm and sometimes 9pm. I decided that I wanted to be present for my children and decided to use my 15 years of recruitment expertise at the time to start my own business. My husband used to always tell me wow, I've never heard a recruiter operate at your level and he encouraged me to back myself and make a difference. It was so heartwarming to see my industry friends and community supporting and cheering me on along the way. I now have 3 beautiful daughters, and I will never give up because I know they are watching me. I love them very much and only want them to be proud of me!

Q: What strategies have you found most effective for networking and building professional relationships as a female entrepreneur?

A: It isn't really a strategy, but it is incredibly important for me to build genuine and warm long-term connections. Building relationships is something that I do naturally, and it is never because there is something that I can gain for it. I believe that building genuine relationships is the no1 priority and other opportunities will just come. Sometimes as women we can feel like we're not smart enough or simply just not good enough to belong in a successful crowd. I think that as women we need to keep showing up, keep being consistent and my little strategy is – "It's okay to fake it until you make it, because you're not really faking it – you're just helping it come out", showing the world who you really are and shining and deserving of all the success that comes your way. The key is to not give up but also be authentic in your communication because people want to get to know the real you.

Q: Can you share a particularly memorable success story or milestone from your entrepreneurial journey?

A: Unfortunately, when I was 25 years old my beautiful business minded father had passed away from cancer. Throughout the years I had always missed him being by my side during this special journey. Last year in 2023 I had attended the Australian Ladies in Business Awards, and the screen had flashed to my image as the winner for the next category Professional Service of The Year 2024. This was a special moment because it was a sign that my father has been with me all along and that night, he was celebrating with me!

Q: What advice would you give to other women who are considering starting their own businesses?

A: Starting your own business is invigorating and has been the most exciting thing I've ever done! It gives you the opportunity to take control of your own destiny. It is so incredible that as a businesswoman we can create success on our own terms. Take the plunge… don't be afraid to make your own dreams come true!

Q: What role do you think mentorship and support networks play for women in entrepreneurship?

A: Throughout my entrepreneurship journey I have met women who have become my mentors and support network. Sometimes, when it gets tough juggling all the balls in the air it is so comforting knowing that no matter what you have like minded friends that cheer you on every step of the way! I'm a huge supporter of women in business and always try to guide and share kind words to support others on their journey too!

Q: How do you stay motivated and resilient during tough times in your business?

A: My beautiful daughters are my inspiration to always stay motivated and be resilient in the face of tough times. No matter what I always gather myself, plan and make the most of what I have and work hard to do what I need to do to reach a successful outcome. "Hardships often prepare ordinary people for an extraordinary destiny".

Q: Red or Pink lipstick?

A: Red – because nothing is going to get in my way of success!

Thank you to my husband for supporting me, so I can reach for the stars.

Allison Lee Patton is a naturopathic doctor, mother, business owner and politician who views her path as a spiritual journey of helping others, learning, and growing.

ALLISON
Patton

Q: How do you maintain a work-life balance while running your own business?

A: As a Naturopathic Doctor who is extremely passionate and dedicated to my calling, I have not always done this in a balanced way!! Since my daughter headed to university, it has become more of a realistic possibility. I consider it part of my practice what I preach concept. How can I ask my patients to live a more balanced life if I am not willing to do so?

Q: Can you share a particularly memorable success story or milestone from your entrepreneurial journey?

A: Currently I am looking forward to next year as I will celebrate five years as a solo entrepreneur after many years in partnership with others in business. I plan to celebrate International Woman's Day AND the five year anniversary of Ardour Wellness in one big celebration. I am really looking forward to celebrating with the community and especially to honour my patients at this event.

Q; What advice would you give to other women who are considering starting their own businesses?

A: Go for it. Even if you do not feel ready or confident; you will never feel ready or confident. It all comes as part of the process. If you have a deep passion or calling and a simple business concept, forge ahead. We always regret what we did not do as opposed to what we did do.

Q: How do you measure success for your business?

A: I measure success by the impact I make on my patients' lives—helping them reach their health goals is the ultimate win. When patients trust me enough to refer their friends, family, and colleagues, it's a clear sign that I'm on the right path. I also measure success through growth, whether that's expanding the services and products I offer or reaching more people who need solutions to their health challenges.

Q: What do you think are the most important skills or qualities for a small business owner?

A: Discipline, drive, and patience are key, but in my profession, passion is non-negotiable. I am deeply invested in finding innovative solutions for my patients' health concerns. That balance between relentless pursuit of excellence and the patience to see long-term results is what keeps a business like mine thriving.

Q: How do you acquire new patients and retain existing ones?

A: The best way I've found to acquire new patients is through word of mouth and community connections. I enjoy engaging with people, and when I see an opportunity to offer a solution, I want to be that go-to resource. As for retaining patients, it's about being present and providing ongoing support. I follow up with my patients to ensure they're cared for, and when they need help down the road, they know they can rely on me once again.

Q: How do you approach leadership and team-building within your company?

A: I approach it with a lot of patience, compassion and courage. Leadership is about how your colleagues, staff and patients grow into their best selves not about you and your journey. I have learned this the hard way even though I have an MBA with a specialization in Leadership. The greatest teacher is the school of life lessons and sometimes they are harsh lessons but with perserverance, life is truly beautiful and leadership is wrapped up in this beauty.

Q: How do you stay motivated and resilient during tough times in your business?

A: I always remember that leadership and resilience is not demonstrated when times are good but instead matter most when the floor falls out beneath us. Who are we in those moments? How do we get to the other side of the mountain impasse? I remind myself of this when I want to throw a pity party and then I take a number of really deep breaths and carry on. Once I am through the tough times, I celebrate the wins and feel deep gratitude for the opportunities.

Q: Looking ahead, what are your goals and aspirations for the future of your business?

A: My goal is to be involved in my business for another 20 years and then pass it forward to the next person. I am going to keep learning, growing, changing and helping my patients and I am extremely excited looking ahead to all of the possibilities available to do just that.

Q: Red or Pink lipstick?

A: Burgundy/Red

Jennifer Ratcliffe is a proud mother of four, a devoted wife, and a driven business owner who believes in pursuing her dreams with full force. She is passionate about pushing boundaries, overcoming challenges, and proving that nothing can stop those who refuse to back down. With determination and purpose, Jennifer is committed to inspiring others to fearlessly pursue their goals. She is the owner of Pebble Lane Early Learning, where she brings her vision and dedication to life.

Q: Can you tell me about your journey as an entrepreneur? What inspired you to start your own business?

A: I've always had a passion for providing quality childcare and wanted to create a space where children could learn, grow, and feel nurtured. Starting Pebble Lane Child Care was about building a supportive, safe environment for children, and it's been incredibly rewarding to watch families thrive through our services.

Q: What are some of the biggest challenges you've faced as a woman entrepreneur, and how have you overcome them?

A: One of the biggest challenges has been balancing societal expectations, particularly when it comes to being a mother and a business owner. I've overcome this by staying focused on my goals and surrounding myself with a support network of like-minded women and mentors who encouraged me along the way.

Q: Have you found any specific advantages or opportunities in being a woman in your industry?

A: Absolutely. Being a woman in childcare, I feel like I can deeply understand the concerns and needs of parents, especially mothers. This helps me build trust with clients and create services that truly address the challenges families face.

Q: How do you maintain a work-life balance while running your own business?

A: It's definitely a challenge! I make time management a priority, setting boundaries between work and family time. Delegating tasks to my team has also been key in allowing me to focus on both my business and my family without feeling overwhelmed.

Q: Can you share a particularly memorable success story or milestone from your entrepreneurial journey?

A: Opening the second location of Pebble Lane Child Care has been one of the biggest milestones for me. Seeing how we've grown and being able to expand while maintaining the same quality of care has been incredibly rewarding. It showed me that our approach is truly valued by families.

A: One misconception is that women aren't as capable when it comes to handling business operations or taking risks. I challenge this by letting the success of my business speak for itself and by showing that with determination and the right strategies, we can excel just as much as anyone else in entrepreneurship.

A: Go for it! Don't let doubt or fear hold you back. Find mentors, build your network, and trust in your abilities. It's not always easy, but the rewards far outweigh the challenges if you stay focused on your goals.

A: I believe in leading by example and fostering a collaborative environment. I focus on open communication, mutual respect, and empowering my team to take ownership of their roles. It's important to me that everyone feels valued and motivated.

A: Mentorship is invaluable. Having someone to guide you and offer advice can help you avoid mistakes and navigate difficult situations. For me, having strong mentors and a support network of other female entrepreneurs has been essential to my growth.

A: I remind myself of why I started in the first place—my passion for providing excellent childcare and supporting families. During tough times, I lean on my support network, take things one step at a time, and focus on finding solutions rather than dwelling on the challenges.

A: Yes, I've faced moments where my abilities were questioned simply because I'm a woman. I've addressed this by staying confident in my decisions and demonstrating through my results that I'm more than capable of leading a successful business.

A: Diversity brings new perspectives, ideas, and innovation. It's essential not just for a fair workplace, but for the overall success of a business. I make it a point to foster an inclusive environment where everyone's voice is valued.

A: I'm excited about the growing emphasis on early childhood education and the role of play-based learning. There's also a trend toward creating more eco-friendly and sustainable daycare environments, which I'm interested in exploring more at Pebble Lane.

A: One family has been with us since the very beginning, and their journey with Pebble Lane always stands out to me. I remember when they first enrolled their child—they were apprehensive about finding the right environment. Over the years, we built a strong relationship based on trust, and I had the pleasure of watching their child grow from a shy toddler into a confident, curious learner.

One day, the parents shared how much our care had positively impacted their child's development. They told me that enrolling in Pebble Lane was one of the best decisions they made for their family. Hearing how much of a difference we made in their lives reaffirmed my dedication to providing quality childcare. It's moments like these that remind me why I started this business and motivate me to strive for excellence every day.

A: Red! It's bold and empowering, just like I strive to be in business.

Leah ZsaZsa is a travel expert specializing in luxury and last-minute getaways, corporate travel, and unforgettable group experiences. From dream weddings and family-friendly all-inclusive resorts to immersive retreats and thrilling adventure tours, Leah curates personalized, exceptional journeys. Whether it's arranging private jets and yachts or crafting bespoke itineraries for your next escape, her expertise ensures every trip is seamless, luxurious, and tailored to perfection.

Q: What advice would you give to women considering starting their own businesses?

A: Starting a business as a woman comes with unique challenges and opportunities. Here's some advice tailored for women entrepreneurs:

Believe in Your Vision: Confidence is key. Trust in your ideas, skills, and ability to succeed. Don't let doubts—yours or others'—deter you. Many successful women entrepreneurs started with a vision they fiercely believed in, even when others didn't recognize its potential.

Build a Strong Support System: Surround yourself with people who understand your journey and can offer guidance, encouragement, and support during challenging times.

Find Mentors and Role Models: Look for women who have built successful businesses, whether in your field or others. Their experiences and insights can be invaluable.

Seek Funding Strategically: Women often face difficulties securing funding. Explore women-focused investors, grants, and organizations that support female-led businesses.

Leverage Female-Focused Networks: Many organizations, incubators, and networking groups focus on supporting women entrepreneurs. Use these resources to build connections and grow your business.

Be a Role Model for Others: By believing in your vision, staying persistent, and seeking the right support, you can overcome challenges, build a successful business, and inspire others to follow their own path.

Q: What advice would you give to someone considering starting their own business?

A: Starting a business can be exciting and rewarding, but it comes with its own set of challenges. Here's some advice for anyone ready to take the leap:

Validate Your Idea: Make sure there's a market need for your product or service. Conduct market research, speak to potential customers, and test your concept on a small scale.

Develop a Business Plan: A solid business plan outlines your goals, strategies, financial projections, and how you plan to compete in the market. This is essential when seeking investors or funding.

Know Your Finances: Understand startup costs, cash flow management, and profitability. Create a clear budget and be prepared for unexpected expenses.

Build a Strong Network: Connect with mentors, industry peers, and other entrepreneurs for guidance, support, and potential partnerships.

Focus on Customer Experience: Provide excellent service and build long-term relationships with your customers. A loyal customer base is key to sustaining and growing your business.

Balance Passion with Practicality: While passion is crucial, ensure your business is financially viable. Keep emotions in check when making critical decisions.

Q: What sets your business apart from competitors?

A: What sets my business apart in the travel industry can be summed up in a few key areas:

Personalized Travel Experiences: I specialize in creating customized itineraries tailored to each client's preferences, needs, and dreams. From boutique hotels to exclusive local experiences, my goal is to provide personalized trips that feel unique and one-of-a-kind.

Attention to Detail: I focus on the small details that make a trip special—whether it's surprise welcome gifts, restaurant reservations, or private experiences that clients might not find on their own.

Exceptional Customer Service: I offer 24/7 support during trips, ensuring clients can reach out anytime for help, whether it's dealing with unexpected changes or flight delays. This level of care provides peace of mind many competitors can't match.

Exclusive Partnerships and Perks: Through strong relationships with airlines, hotels, and tour operators, I offer my clients exclusive deals, upgrades, and perks they wouldn't get if they booked independently.

Expert Knowledge and Industry Experience: I have in-depth knowledge of the destinations I recommend, providing clients with personalized insights and insider tips. My expertise ensures they experience destinations like locals, not just tourists.

Long-Term Relationships and Loyalty: I focus on nurturing ongoing relationships with my clients through loyalty programs, exclusive promotions, and personalized follow-up service. Many of my clients return, thanks to referrals and word-of-mouth recommendations.

Q: Looking ahead, what are your goals and aspirations for the future of your business?

A: For the future, I aim to:

Expand Travel Offerings: I plan to specialize in specific types of travel, such as luxury tourism, wellness retreats, or eco-friendly trips, to attract a targeted and loyal clientele.

Develop Loyalty Programs: Building a rewards program for repeat customers will help foster long-term relationships and encourage customer retention.

Provide Superior Customer Service: Continuing to deliver exceptional, personalized customer service is key to maintaining positive reviews, referrals, and growth.

Become an Industry Leader: I aspire to become a thought leader by speaking at conferences, writing for industry publications, and hosting webinars. Being recognized as an expert will boost my credibility and attract high-value clients.

Q: Pink or red lipstick?

A: Pink lipstick is timeless and versatile—it complements many skin tones and personalities!

Leah Corrin, an award-winning medical aesthetician and the founder of Essence of L Medi Spa, has over 20 years of experience in the skincare industry. She created her own line, EOL Skincare, after a long personal journey battling acne. Leah's passion for skin health and her commitment to providing personalized, client-first care have earned her a reputation as a leader in her field.

LEAH
Corrin

Q: Can you tell me about your journey as an entrepreneur? What inspired you to start your own business?

A: My entrepreneurial journey began with my personal struggle with acne, which led me to become a medical aesthetician. Frustrated with products that worsened my skin, I set out to create an acne-safe skincare line that truly works. With guidance from my parents, I developed a solid business plan and launched Essence of L Medi Spa (EOL). My mission was to provide effective, safe skincare treatments and products that empower clients to feel confident in their skin. Twenty years later, I'm proud to offer cutting-edge solutions while maintaining a client-first approach to care.

Q: Can you share a particularly memorable success story or milestone from your entrepreneurial journey?

A: One of the most memorable milestones in my entrepreneurial journey was securing my first loan to purchase laser equipment. After initially relying on my parents' support to start my business, I built enough credit over the years to qualify for a large bank loan on my own. It was a proud moment, knowing I had grown my business to the point where I could independently invest in advanced technology. That laser device opened the door to offering cutting-edge treatments and elevated the services at Essence of L, helping me expand and solidify the clinic's success.

Q: How do you stay motivated and resilient during tough times in your business?

A: I stay motivated by focusing on my passion for helping clients regain their confidence and remembering why I started my business in the first place. Challenges, like when I had to rebuild after my divorce and pandemic closure, reminded me of my strength and adaptability. Surrounding myself with a supportive team and my husband, Matt keeps me grounded. I also believe in continuous learning—staying updated on skincare advancements keeps me excited about what I can offer my clients. Seeing positive transformations in my clients' lives is what truly drives me to push through any adversity.

Q: What are some trends or developments in your industry that you're particularly excited about?

A: I'm excited about the industry shift towards collagen-forward skin health, focusing on rebuilding the skin's natural structure rather than relying solely on injectables. Treatments like Sylfirm X and Sciton's BBL Hero stimulate collagen production, offering natural, long-lasting results by strengthening the skin from within. Clients are now seeking long-term solutions that improve skin health at a cellular level, which aligns perfectly with my philosophy of creating sustainable, acne-safe skincare. This trend promotes skin rejuvenation and anti-aging in a way that enhances natural beauty without augmentation, and I'm thrilled to be part of this evolving approach.

Q: What problem or need does your business solve, and what motivated you to address it?

A: My business addresses the need for effective, acne-safe skincare solutions that also cater to anti-aging and pigmentation concerns. After battling acne for 15+ years and struggling to find products that didn't clog pores or cause breakouts, I was motivated to create EOL Skincare—a line that is both safe and effective for acne-prone skin. Traditional skincare for melasma and anti-aging often triggered more acne for me, so I wanted to develop solutions that could target multiple concerns without compromising skin health. I aim to empower clients to achieve clear, healthy skin with products they can trust.

Q: What sets your business apart from competitors in the market?

A: What truly sets EOL Skincare apart from competitors is our commitment to creating acne-safe products that target multiple skin concerns without causing breakouts. Unlike many brands that may focus solely on one issue, our formulations are meticulously designed to be non-comedogenic while still providing powerful results for overall skin health. My experience with acne and frustration with ineffective products inspired me to build a line clients can trust for clear, glowing skin without worrying about clogged pores.

We also stand out by offering a client-first, personalized approach. Clients receive a tailored skincare regimen supported by professional treatments that suit their unique skin types and goals. Backed by FDA-registered labs with the highest standards of testing and efficacy, we prioritize both safety and results. By combining advanced technology with personalized care, EOL Skincare offers an effective, safe, and client-centric holistic solution, setting us apart in the industry.

Q: Can you share a significant milestone or achievement your business has reached, and what did you learn from it?

A: Reaching 20 years in business has been one of the most significant milestones for Essence of L, especially in a market where many businesses struggle to keep their doors open. This achievement speaks to our resilience, adaptability, and commitment to providing exceptional client care. Over the years, we've faced many challenges, including navigating two economic downturns and the continued impact of the pandemic. Each obstacle taught us the importance of staying true to our values, continuously evolving, and placing clients at the heart of everything we do. I've learned from this milestone that success comes from building strong relationships, staying innovative, and never compromising on quality. Consistency and a client-first approach have been key to earning trust and loyalty over two decades. This achievement is a testament to the dedication of our team and the unwavering support of our incredible clients.

Q: Pink or red lipstick? I love a nude pink lip because it strikes the perfect balance between natural and polished. It enhances my features by creating a soft, sophisticated look that works for any occasion. Nude pink also complements my skin tone, giving me a fresh, effortless appearance while feeling put together.

Taylor Smith is the CEO & Founder of Taylor Smith & Co Ltd, a dynamic business consultancy firm dedicated to partnering with forward-thinking, driven entrepreneurs ready to grow their business into a profit making machine which also gives them the freedom they deserve. Taylor is a seasoned business consultant dedicated to helping female coaches, consultants and entrepreneurs build their freedom business. With a background as a chartered accountant, Taylor can focus on implementing simple yet effective strategies that support entrepreneurs in growing their businesses in a way that aligns with their vision and ensures financial security and freedom.

Q: Can you tell me about your journey as an entrepreneur? What inspired you to start your own business?

A: I actually spent a lot of my career in corporate employment. I qualified as a chartered accountant and worked my way up the corporate ladder. I was promoted to Finance Director of a few UK companies. It was incredible, I learnt so much and was fortunate enough to play a part in growing one of the companies to over £400 million in sales per year. But with that role came a lot of stress and I wasn't getting any freedom to do what I loved most, so I decided enough was enough. I was done with working to someone else's timetable. I was great at growing businesses and I knew I could help other business owners grow their businesses. So I decided to start my own business supporting female entrepreneurs to grow their businesses.

Q: What are some of the biggest challenges you've faced as a woman entrepreneur, and how have you overcome them?

A: The biggest challenge has actually been my own mindset. At the beginning, I questioned myself a lot. I questioned if I had enough qualifications if I could really get results for my clients, and if I was charging too much. I had to do a lot of inner work, to cement my confidence and remind myself that I am incredible at what I do, and I need to start believing in myself rather than questioning myself all the time.

A: I don't believe there will ever be a perfect 50/50 split between work and life. There will be times where I really need to put the work in, so extra hours and long days may be a necessity at that point. Then there will be times where processes and automation are set up, resulting in less input needed from myself, and in those times, I can maximise spending time with my family and doing things I love. As soon as I accepted that and stopped chasing this perfect 50/50 balance, I felt relieved and I could enjoy both work and life without feeling overwhelmed, or feeling like my life was out of balance.

A: DO IT!!!! If you have a passion and you know you can deliver something that will support other people, absolutely do it. Stop waiting for the "right time", because it will never come! You don't need more qualifications or to do another course before you start! Just start! There are so many people ready to support you with the areas you may not be confident in, so go for it. For the areas you know you need support in, ask for support! You don't have to do everything by yourself and it doesn't make you any less of a successful entrepreneur if you do ask for support. In fact, the most successful entrepreneurs all recognise where they need support and they take steps to get that support, so don't fall into the trap or thinking you have to do everything by yourself.

A: My business supports female entrepreneurs to not only make more money in their business but also give them back their time. I support them to build a business that suits their lifestyle and gives them the freedom they want whilst making money. The reason why I decided to focus on this area was because I could see too many female entrepreneurs doubting themselves, not charging enough money and working all hours under the sun as well as running their households, and it's not fair! So I empower women and support them in creating their dream business, so they can live a fulfilling life.

Maintaining resilience can be really tough in the world of entrepreneurship. I have made so many decisions in my journey that have resulted in an outcome that I didn't necessarily want. However, it's important to remember that these "mistakes" are necessary. These are moments of learning which are required to mould you into the person you need to be, to build a successful business. Once you understand this, remaining resilient in those tough times becomes easier. To stay motivated, it was important for me to have a really strong why. Why did I even start a business, what is it I'm actually trying to achieve? For me, my why is my family. I want to be able to spend as much time with them as possible, but I also want to show them that you can lead a much more fulfilling life when you're doing something that you love and you're able to combine that with supporting other people in the world.

Firstly, I have a set of goals that I want to achieve long term, for example over the next 5 years. I then break down the 5-year goal into yearly goals, to get an understanding of what I need to accomplish each year, which will then get me to the result I want in 5 years time. Once I understand my goals for the year, I break this down into milestones, both quarterly and monthly. These include targets and projects I want to focus on, which once accomplished will mean I would have achieved the goal for the year. I use tasks for my day-to-day planning. I have a master task list which lays out everything that needs to be completed for that week, and list them in order of priority. I prioritise based on deadlines for tasks as well as the importance of the task, if something needs to be done quickly or is really important, I will do those tasks first. Once I have my weekly tasks, I plan which tasks will be done each day. My task list for the day will have a maximum of 3 tasks, if I get through those, any additional tasks completed are a bonus.

Aldwyn Altuney is a mass media marketing expert, publicist, speaker, animal activist, host of Media Queen TV, founder of the Mass Media Mastery program, Global Good News Challenge, and Animal Action Events.

ALDWYN
Altuney

Q: Can you tell me about your journey as an entrepreneur? What inspired you to start your own business?

A: I started my business, AA Xposé Photography, in 2002 on the Gold Coast after experiencing a few small car accidents while working late nights with a photography company in Brisbane. During the day, I was a journalist at the Sun Newspapers. When I left that position in 2005, the business evolved into AA Xposé Media as clients began requesting public relations work, copywriting, video production, graphic design, editing, and media training services.

I conducted my first media training workshops in 2003 and received numerous requests for more. In 2005, I invested $7,000 in my first personal development course in the Hunter Valley, NSW. To date, 19 years later, I have invested about $1 million in business and marketing courses, as well as various personal development modalities. This investment has been invaluable for the growth of my business and myself, offering deep insights into the decisions I've made and their meanings.

Career highlights include interviewing stars such as Charlie Sheen, Jewel, Vanilla Ice, Hugh Jackman, Russell Crowe, Cyndi Lauper, and Debbie Harry (Blondie). I have also been featured in over 20 inspiring compilation books, many of which are international best-sellers, and I won the 2024 Global Woman of Influence Award.

Q: What are some of the biggest challenges you've faced as a woman entrepreneur, and how have you overcome them?

A: Navigating a male-dominated industry has been incredibly challenging. In TV, radio, and print media, it was difficult to secure promotions, we were paid less, and I often faced workplace bullying.

I had to toughen up to handle criticism and build my self-worth, which required years of personal development. I learned to advocate for myself, build confidence, and speak my truth at all times, regardless of others' opinions. Over time, I shifted from being a people pleaser to honoring myself, realizing I needed to fill my own cup before I could help others.

Q: How do you stay motivated and resilient during tough times in your business?

A: While business can be tough, I always remind myself that things could be worse. I feel a deep connection and support from my ancestors. Scientifically, we carry the DNA of 14 generations. My great-grandparents were among the 30,000 Kulaks executed by Stalin's men in Ukraine in the early 1930s. They were hanged outside their home on a farm in Kiev. My grandfather, who was in another part of Ukraine, spoke out against the government until friends warned him, "They are coming to kill you." He fled to Turkey, where he met my Greek grandmother.

I was born in Australia as a first-generation Australian, with a resilient European heritage that shaped me. I know my ancestors are supporting me spiritually in helping others stand up and speak their truth.

After experiencing burnout multiple times and several near-death experiences, I developed self-care practices to maintain resilience. These include meditation, yoga, long beach walks, body surfing, saunas, massages, baths, healthy eating, drinking clean filtered water, and breathwork. I also believe having fun is crucial, and I enjoy performing in my comedy duo The Fiddly Gigglers, acting, playing ukulele, singing, and dancing.

Q: What trends or developments in your industry are you particularly excited about?

A: I'm excited about the current mass media landscape, where millions of media outlets exist, and we are all part of the media. In just 20 years since Facebook started, there are now over 5 billion active social media users each month. We shape the media with every post and piece of content we share.

While AI has brought significant advancements, I believe authenticity and speaking from the heart will always have more impact than a machine-generated message when it comes to effective marketing.

Q: What do you believe are the keys to building a strong brand identity and reputation?

A: Building a strong brand starts with clarity in your message, understanding your target market, selecting the right media channels, and knowing how to monetize your efforts. Speaking your truth and being authentic will help you build a loyal following.

There is only one you, and by being born, you've already beaten a billion swimmers to the finish line. Embrace the miracle of life and express yourself at every opportunity, with kindness. Remember, "If you don't stand for something, you'll fall for anything."

Q: Looking ahead, what are your goals and aspirations for the future of your business?

A: My goal is to positively impact over 1 billion people globally with uplifting news stories. I am passionate about promoting good news stories in the mass media to help reduce depression and suicide rates worldwide and boost people's spirits.

I founded Global Good News Day on August 8, 2018, and launched the free monthly Global Good News Challenge in June 2020. Additionally, I am committed to raising awareness and respect for animals. I founded the world's first Animal Action Day on the Gold Coast in 2007, and have since held 18 annual events, generating millions of dollars in free publicity for various animal charities.

My ultimate vision is to inspire a world where people love their lives and live their love—a world where kindness extends to animals, people, and the planet. For this to happen, self-love is essential. World peace starts from within; it happens by transforming one person at a time

Neesha Hothi is an award-winning marketing and communications executive with 17 years of experience and is the founder of Neesh Communications, a boutique firm specializing in entertainment, hospitality and not-for-profits. Based in Vancouver, she has served as Event and Public Relations Manager for the Olympic Superstore of 2010 Vancouver Olympics, Marketing and Communications Director for the Vancouver JUNO Host Committee 2018 and 2025, and PR Chair for the BC Summer Games 2020 and 2024. She is also an avid cultural champion, working to preserve, elevate and highlight South Asian arts, culture and voices.

Q: What are some of the biggest challenges you've faced as a woman entrepreneur, and how have you overcome them?

A: I didn't know what I didn't know and I needed someone to tell me. As women we tend to speak to each about almost everything else, but rarely business. Only recently am I starting to witness women engage with each other about money, investing, financial growth, business development, etc. Whereas men have been having these discussions for eons. We need to be able to share what we know with one another.

I was fortunate to have female mentors when I started my business, both who ran their own businesses at different scales and were willing to tell me what I didn't know. They were also gracious enough to open their contact books and guide me to reliable resources. That type of support early on is invaluable.

My advice is to surround yourself with a strong support network. Men, women, business owners, service providers, clients, industry colleagues, friends – and truly talk to them. You don't have to share every secret, but discuss potential challenges, pose questions and make specific asks. If you want support with something then make the ask, you never know what could happen.

Q: Can you share a particularly memorable success story or milestone from your entrepreneurial journey?

A: When I was asked to serve as the Marketing and Communications Director for the 2018 Vancouver JUNO Host Committee, it came to me through a colleague I had collaborated on a previous project with. Now at that time I had no idea that this person would open these doors for me, I was just truly passionate about the work we were doing together and we struck up a relationship.

When you combine the power of networking and being truly prepared for opportunities when they arise, you are placing yourself at the pinnacle of possibility. I share this story because when this role came to me I had my head down in my lane and was just doing the work. That was enough.

In the months to follow, other firms and individuals asked how this came to be and why they weren't considered. To that I say to remember that what is meant for you will come to you. Your job is simply to do great work, showcase your strengths, be ready, and build relationships.

Q: What advice would you give to other women who are considering starting their own businesses?

A: Know your why. Why do you really want to start a business? Many will say it's to do what they love, but as a business owner you often end up doing less of what you love and more of everything else - the HR, the admin, the accounting, will all take up major chunks of your time.

Are you looking to create a role that doesn't already exist? Are you passionate about a niche that has low market penetration? Are you looking to create an income producing venture that provides you with flexibility in your schedule so you can be there for your family or other obligations? Do you want to be in control of your financial growth potential?

When you know your true why then you can build a business that gives you what you need.

Personally, I wanted to be able to take on the projects that mattered to me, in particular South Asian community projects that other firms weren't going to take on. I wanted the flexibility to be there for my family & friends, and travel as I pleased. I wanted the ability to work from anywhere if I desired and pick up short term roles that interested me. And lastly, I knew I wasn't interested in scaling, but staying boutique and niche. I only needed the business to be strong enough to fund the lifestyle I desired. By the way, it's ok to not want to be the biggest or the baddest around, it's ok for your goals to fit your needs and not the status quo.

Q: What advice would you give to someone who is considering starting their own business?

A: Setup your processes and procedures early. I was given this advice but didn't heed it and ended up paying the price. In the beginning when resources are scarce you feel you don't have the time or money to document everything or hire the right people. That's how I felt and I didn't get a bookkeeper or accountant right away. My accounting always felt daunting to me and then once I got behind or made a mistake, it became that much more overwhelming and difficult to fix. Get ahead of these potential blunders.

Have your accounting systems setup, document your how-tos, and process as much of your business as possible. This will make everything else so much easier at every future step - from financial reporting to onboarding new hires and clients.

Q: How do you balance work-life commitments as an entrepreneur? How do you maintain a work-life balance while running your own business?

A: It is really easy to allow your work to seep into all hours of day. In the beginning you will feel productive, as if you're getting ahead by being on top of everything at a moment's notice, while later on, you'll start to resent the work or clients that are breaching your personal time. It is very important to set boundaries on yourself and those you work with to ensure you have the space required to be fully present for all the other facets of your life. If you don't fill your cup up first, you'll have no capacity left to give to the business.

Limit the hours you'll take meetings, set DND for work emails during family time, setup an email responder as required, have dedicated 'me' time - whatever you need to establish separation between the time you're available to work and the time you're focused on your family, friends and self.

I had a client who would always call me around dinner time because during the day he was so focused on his own clients that he only thought about his marketing during his drives in or out of work. After a while I stopped taking his evening calls but would listen to the voicemail and schedule an email for 9am the next day responding to his thoughts. I was attempting to subconsciously train him to know when he could or could not expect responses from me. Ultimately I had to fire him as a client as we couldn't find a way to work within the boundaries I had set for myself.

Q: Pink or red lipstick?

A: Both! I love various shades of both, and use them to compliment my attitude for the day. Whether it be your lipstick or your outfit, it's a form of self-expression and can signal so much to those around you. Use it to your advantage ladies!

Valerie Mrakuzic, Registered Holistic Nutritionist, is a graduate of the Canadian School of Natural Nutrition and has also studied at The Quantum Academics using the Indigo Biofeedback System. She is passionate about helping her clients attain their optimal well-being through holistic health and nutrition. Valerie has dedicated her practice to identifying the root causes of your health concerns and developing a personalized eating plan that suits your needs.

VALERIE
Mrakuzic

Q: How does technology contribute to the success of your business?

A: Technology is the cornerstone of my practice as a Nutritionist, I rely on advanced tools to assess imbalances affecting my clients' health. Many imbalances arise from nutrient deficiencies, food sensitivities, hormonal disruptions, organ dysfunction, toxin accumulation, and emotional stress.

Central to my approach is a Class II medical device called a Bioresonance Biofeedback machine, which precisely identifies nutritional imbalances. By leveraging this advanced technology, I provide personalized care that goes beyond traditional methods, uncovering subtle issues that might otherwise remain hidden. Bioresonance therapy operates on the principle that our bodies emit electromagnetic frequencies. By detecting and addressing disruptions in these frequencies, this innovative approach provides crucial insights into my clients' overall well-being.

I integrate this high-tech analysis with a comprehensive review of symptoms to develop personalized, targeted recommendations that directly address each client's unique health concerns. This approach of combining advanced technology with expert nutritional knowledge allows me to achieve remarkable outcomes for my clients, which in turn drives the success and growth of my business.

By offering this level of personalized, technology-enhanced care, I not only improve my clients' health but also set my practice apart in a competitive field, ensuring both client satisfaction and business prosperity.

Q: Could you share your journey as an entrepreneur? What inspired you to start your business?

A: They say that "overnight success" can take years, and that has certainly been true for me. My own health challenges inspired me to launch my business. For a long time, I struggled to uncover the root cause of my autoimmune condition and came to realize that nutrition, along with my body's ability to absorb nutrients, played a crucial role in my well-being. When I was introduced to the Bioresonance Biofeedback device, everything changed; I finally understood how subtle imbalances were linked to my health issues. With this technology, I was able to heal and eliminate symptoms that had plagued me for years.

Recognizing its transformative potential, I knew this tool could be a game changer in helping my clients achieve life-changing results. Building a business through referrals is incredibly powerful, and it all begins with delivering exceptional service and fully supporting each client on their journey to optimal health.

Q: What strategies do you use to attract and retain customers?

A: I prioritize making my clients feel genuinely heard, understood, and aligned with our shared goals. My primary objective is to enhance each client's health, helping them feel better and significantly improving their overall quality of life. Satisfied clients are more likely to refer others, so ensuring they are happy with my recommendations and support is essential for attracting new clients through word-of-mouth. I also maintain strong connections through consistent follow-ups, ensuring that clients continue to feel well and addressing any ongoing issues. This approach not only builds trust but also fosters lasting relationships that are vital to my practice's success.

Q: Can you share a memorable customer experience?

A: What truly inspires me is witnessing my clients fully embrace their personalized programs and healing journeys once they're equipped with the right tools and guidance. One client's story particularly stands out. She came to me during an incredibly stressful period in her life, having gained five dress sizes in just a year and grappling with debilitating pain and inflammation. Her dedication to following her tailored program and commitment to every recommendation was unwavering. The results were nothing short of remarkable—within a mere few months, her pain and inflammation subsided dramatically, and she shed an impressive 40 pounds. Today, she continues to thrive, armed with the knowledge and resources to maintain her health and vitality. This transformation not only changed her physical well-being but also restored her confidence and zest for life. Stories like hers fuel my passion and reinforce the profound impact of personalized, holistic nutrition care.

Q: What do you believe are the keys to building a strong brand identity and reputation?

A: For me, everything stems from a core belief: understanding and meeting each person's unique nutritional needs has the power to transform health. Knowing and staying true to your "why" is essential in entrepreneurship. Every business owner has a unique purpose, and that purpose shapes the brand identity they project to the world.

A strong reputation is built on the quality of work and the results you deliver for clients. Positive reviews and referrals can spread rapidly—but so can negative ones. By consistently giving your best effort and staying aligned with your vision, your passion and dedication will naturally shine through, creating a lasting impact on those you serve.

In the realm of nutrition and wellness, this commitment to individualized care and unwavering quality not only helps clients achieve their health goals but also establishes trust and credibility in a competitive field. It's this combination of purpose-driven work and tangible results that forms the foundation of a thriving, respected practice.

Q: Can you discuss the role of networking and partnerships in growing your business?

A: Attending wellness and health shows throughout the year is invaluable for networking with companies and meeting new clients. There's simply no substitute for face-to-face interaction. While virtual meetings offer convenience, in-person connections foster deeper relationships and genuine bonds with clients and business partners. Building these connections, as well as reconnecting with existing clients, has been essential to my success, creating strong foundations for lasting partnerships. These personal interactions not only enhance trust but also open doors to new opportunities, enriching both my practice and the experiences of those I serve.

Q: Looking ahead, what are your goals and aspirations for the future of your business?

A: My vision is to alleviate unnecessary suffering for as many people as possible. To achieve this, my team and I are currently developing an online course designed to provide clients with valuable insights that can help them start or enhance their health journeys. Additionally, I aspire to write a series of books to share this knowledge more broadly, reaching individuals who could greatly benefit from it. Through these initiatives, I aim to empower others with the tools and understanding they need to improve their well-being and lead healthier, more fulfilling lives.

Robin Sandhu is the founder of Get Toned by Robin and a leading expert in the field of EMS (Electrical Muscle Stimulation) training. With a deep passion for health, wellness, and fitness, Robin specializes in helping clients achieve their goals and transform their lives through tailored EMS sessions. What sets Robin apart is her commitment to empowering women, guiding them to reclaim their self-confidence and discover their true potential.

Q: Can you tell me about your journey as an entrepreneur? What inspired you to start your own business?

A: I was tired of working a 9-to-5 job that offered no growth opportunities aligned with my future goals. The idea of being my own boss had always been a dream of mine, especially since I disliked being micromanaged. After experiencing EMS treatments myself, I realized this service had significant potential, as very few people were aware of it.

I noticed that many women were dealing with various issues leading to weight gain, and this became a common topic among my friends and colleagues. Taking these conversations into account, along with my own positive experiences with the service, I decided to capitalize on this opportunity—and that's exactly what I did.

The journey was challenging, filled with setbacks and many sleepless nights, but I remained focused and worked towards my goal every day. Reflecting on that experience now, I can proudly say it was all worth it.

Q: Have you found any specific advantages or opportunities in being a woman in your industry?

A: The majority of my clients are women facing challenges such as muscle damage from pregnancy, stubborn fat, or chronic pain related to various diagnoses. My personal experiences with similar issues enable me to relate to them on a deeper level, fostering a comfortable environment during our sessions. Since the treatment requires women to be in their undergarments, being a woman myself is a significant advantage, helping them feel more at ease throughout the process. Dealing with body image issues myself, I understand the profound impact this can have on mental health, particularly for women. Because of the similarities I share with my clients, I strive to create a supportive environment where women feel safe to be vulnerable, free from judgment or shame.

Q: How do you maintain a work-life balance while running your own business?

A: Achieving a work-life balance has always been a challenge for me, as work ranks among my highest priorities. However, I start my day by spending quality time with my son before dropping him off at school. I also make it a point to take breaks to pick him up from school and strive to have dinner as a family most evenings. Additionally, I prioritize family trips, which allow me to physically disconnect from work and focus on creating lasting memories with my family.

Q: What role do you think mentorship and support networks play for women in entrepreneurship?

A: Mentorship and support networks are extremely crucial and play a vital role for women in business. The more we network, the more awareness we create about our business and its existence. Seeing other women succeed has always been a powerful motivator for me. Stepping into a mentorship role myself and reinforcing that success is achievable has been both gratifying and rewarding.

Q: What advice would you give to other women who are considering starting their own businesses?

A: Starting a business is a significant commitment and a long journey full of successes and obstacles. It is essential to believe in yourself and the opportunity you are pursuing. Once you make the commitment, it's important to persist and learn at every turn. Embrace failure, as every failure comes with a lesson, and remember to celebrate even the small wins. Take advantage of every networking opportunity that comes your way to capitalize on growth. Lastly, surround yourself with supportive people who will encourage you and share your drive in life.

Q: Can you share a story about a particularly memorable customer interaction or experience?

A: I have many success stories about assisting clients with their treatment needs, but one in particular stands out. About four years ago, a woman visited one of my locations after receiving a referral for EMS from her family doctor. She had been involved in multiple car accidents, which led to persistent chronic pain and a need for muscle rehabilitation and pain relief.

I recall her arriving at the first appointment with a noticeable limp, struggling with pain and stiffness from the accidents. By the time she completed the recommended treatment plan, she was able to walk 5 km daily. She referred to me as her "lifesaver" as a way of expressing her gratitude. Eventually, she purchased a unit herself to provide this remarkable treatment to her clients, family, and friends. We have kept in touch to this day.

Elizabeth Oates is a global executive, bestselling co-author, and co-founder of the multi-million-dollar family of companies, Global Leader Group. Her superpower is building bridges, with the belief that achievement is best when celebrated in humility, knowing that greatness is a journey, not a destination.

ELIZABETH Oates

Q: Can you tell me about your journey as an entrepreneur? What inspired you to start your own business?

A: My work ethic became my ladder to success. Starting as a bank teller while putting myself through college solidified my belief — there were no shortcuts, only dedication. This philosophy propelled me from teller to global bank executive, leading diverse teams across continents. It was in this context that I uncovered my values: generosity, excellence, empowerment, authenticity, and integrity.

In 2019, a crossroads emerged. Yearning to be present for my family, I took a courageous step with a career sabbatical. During that time, I connected with my future co-founder, Jonathan, who ignited a new spark. Inspired by his vision for a boutique learning and consulting firm, we joined forces alongside his brother Joe to start Global Leader Group. What began as a single consulting role has blossomed into a thriving ecosystem. Today, Global Leader Group boasts a family of companies with partners worldwide, and offices spanning the US, Canada, UK, Europe, Asia and the Middle East.

Q: What problem or need does your business solve, and what motivated you to address it?

A: Our business focuses on helping leaders reimagine their human potential. This can be different for each individual, but we know that such perspective challenges you to be more than you can often see in a moment – or in yourself.

Q: How do you approach leadership and team-building within your company?

A: We approach it through weaving our values into how we model every day. Leadership is less about training and more about creating authentic growth with changed behavior. Each team gathering, we ask our team members to recognize one another where they have seen our values come to life and to express gratitude. We also invite EBI's: Even Better If's. One of our values is to get better every day and, in that spirit, we openly solicit feedback as a regular practice where it is seen as a positive versus how it can sometimes be viewed as judgemental or negative. This has fostered a courageous listening culture.

Q: What advice would you give to other women who are considering starting their own businesses?

A: Don't be afraid to take the risk. We often can tell ourselves all the reasons WHY NOT to do something instead of focusing on all the reasons to just move FORWARD. Moving forward doesn't have to look perfect, but it does require a plan. When you form a plan that is based on a new idea, it's important to forecast success through facts and data. I encourage all women to decide what success looks like for them both professionally and personally, then apply that lens to the plan to ensure you will meet your baseline of what winning is to you. Successful businesses all need structure and systems; build those as fast as possible – without them it can be hard to grow.

Q: What role do you think mentorship and support networks play for women in entrepreneurship?

A: Community is key to keeping your JOY and FOCUS factors. Having a network who surrounds and supports your goals is very grounding. They can cheer you on and remind you of who you are in those moments when you may feel lost. As I have grown my businesses, I have participated in multiple supportive communities – both formal and informal – including a female entrepreneur's group for the last several years where, together, we give, receive, mentor and encourage one another. I always suggest for women to look for a diverse range of perspectives that are outside of their comfort zone while simultaneously being surrounded by those that truly know you.

Q: How do you maintain a work-life balance while running your own business?

A: In my experience, balance is not just elusive, it's an illusion. One of my mentors shared with me years ago, that there is no such thing as BALANCE, only good CHOICES. In that spirit, I have operated knowing that I must decide: what is the good choice for today? Some days it will be to prioritize the roles of wife and mom, other days it will be to lean into the work priority. The great news is that these are both good choices – and there are many more. Choosing one doesn't mean the other is not good, but I have the next day to recalibrate on the GOOD choice for that new moment in time.

Q: How do you stay motivated and resilient during tough times in your business?

A: I remind myself about what I have already overcome and remember all the times where I didn't see a path, but the path emerged. In those moments, anxiousness and disappointment turn quickly to gratitude. I believe in the power of prayer and the realization that I cannot do all things in my own strength.

Q: Can you share a significant milestone or achievement your business has reached, and what did you learn from it?

A: It was a significant milestone when I had my first company hit the million-dollar revenue mark – a moment where it felt like all the sacrifice had paid off but, most importantly, it validated our decision to create business in partnership. I reflected on how it may have taken me much longer on my own, but through trusted relationships the path was accelerated. The most valuable learn for me was not only in the achievement, but what it would mean after...how to maintain it. This level of success would require a rigorous plan to be kept in repeatable cycle to achieve. Never underestimate the maintenance!

Aldwyn Altuney

aaxpose.com

P. 214-215

Amanda Da Saliva

@amanda.da_silva

P. 2-3

Alexis Gail Ellis

@alexis777cdn

P. 44-45

Amanda Lavery

@amandajlavery

P. 192-193

Coach Rochelle

Alisha & Rochelle Schwartz

rochelleschwartz.com

P. 184-185

Amber Hill

@behaviourinterventionwithamber

P. 96-97

Allison Patton ND

ardourwellness.ca

P. 204-205

Anita Cotton

@monocoreplus

P. 62-63

Allison Seller

healthacademyinc.com

P. 198-199

Ann Lindholm

KeyofDavidConsulting.com

P. 180-181

Allyson Matos

allyfotografy.com

P. 38-39

ASHIKA LESSANI

Ashika Lessani

ashikalessani.com

P. 122-123

Allyson O'Brien

@aobwellness

P. 60-61

Ashleigh Kirsten

akconsultantsandhealthcare.com

P. 108-109

Alyson Jones

alysonjones.ca

P. 100-101

Barbara Morandi

@barbaramorandi_connectendo

P. 152-153

Bec Bucci

@sexologistbecbuccigspotlovedoc

P. 116-117

Christine Daer

linktr.ee/PowerinAging

P. 18-19

Becky Mary Kehoe

mindful-hypnosis.ca

P. 106-107

Cindy Van Arnam

cindyvanarnam.com

P. 128-129

Belinda Djurasovic

@brass__village

P. 64-65

Clarke Cornwell

fountainofyouthau.com

P. 174-175

Beth Chisholm

@kamiyah_coaching

P. 12-13

Daina Gardiner

theenergizedwoman.com

P. 88-89

Billie Aadmi

@billie.irei

P. 142-143

Dana Kovacic

@danapaigekovacic

P. . 114-115

Brooke Abel

@mymahimind

P. 6-7

Daniela Fisher

naturallygiven.com

P. 72-73

Cathy Cena

@cathycena

P. 10-11

Danielle Duncan

@thegoodandthebad11

P. 70-71

Christina Bonnor

@studioshe.hairextensions

P. 48-49

Dawn Chubai

kingwillowmanagement.com

P. 14-15

 DeeAnn Lensen

advancedspatech.com

P. 120-121

 Erica Paynter

myvbk.com

P. 144-145

 Diane Rolsten

dianerolston.com

P. 80-81

 Erin Sample

simplyimmaculatehomes.com

P. 40-41

 Dorela Iepan

relatiaperfecta.ro

P. 178-179

 Estrellita Gonzalez

myskinsalon.com

P. 78-79

 Dr. Avi Charlton

@dr_charlton_low_carb_gp

P. 56 -57

 Geeta Dayal

bycharleymadison.com

P. 22-23

 Dr. Divi Chandra

@drdivi

P. 16-17

 Genicca Whitney

genicca.com

P. 66-67

 Elie Kamankesh

neshuny.ca

P. 104-105

Heidi Morrison

exhalo.ca

P. 32-33

Elizabeth Oates

globalleadergroup.com

P. 222-223

Heidi Nordlund

namaskarhealing.com

P. 28-29

 Erian Baxter

deepcovekayak.com

P. 82-83

 Jai Harvey Yin

howcanihelpbiz.com

P. 170-171

Jaina Jordan

jainajordan.com

P. 24-25

Jessica Bouchard

@crystaltherapy.ca

P. 150-151

Jaishri Hall

coachjaishrihall.mobirisesite.com

P. 94-95

Kamal Atwal

@keep.ingupwithkamal

P. 20-21

Jasmine Daisy

@jasmine_d_corbet

P. 58-59

Karen Dosanjh

@karendosanjh

P. 46-47

Jasmine Tella

jasminetella.com

P. 160-161

Karen Kobel

kahlena.com

P. 112-113

Jennifer Dawn

@sagittariuscoach

P. 30-31

Katrina Thompson

katrinathompsonphotography.com

P. 156-157

Jennifer Ratcliffe

pebblelane.ca

P. 206-207

Kelly Greenslade

@kelly_greenslade

P. 188-189

Jenny Krahn

@jennykrahn7

P. 110-111

Kelly Graham Tick

@/kellygrahamtick

P. 34-35

Jessica Rae

@artistjessicarae

P. 172-173

Kerri Anne Kedziora

kedziorasystems.com

P. 146-147

Kim Mowatt

resetfromstresstohappiness@gmail.com

P. 136-137

Lillian Nejad

drlilliannejad.com

P. 52-53

Krystal Stephens

theworksource.com.au

P. .162-163

Lily Ahonen

@blondvagabond

P. 8-9

Laura Gindac

omnirisetraining.com

P. 90-91

Lindsay Maheu

@vigoradvantage

P. 132-133

Leah Corrin

glowskinshop.ca

P. 210-211

Lisa Huppée

@justlikefamily.ca

P. 102-103

Leah Zsa Zsa

obtravel.com

P. 208-209

Lise Parton

liseparton.com

P. 140-141

LeiLani Kopp

sweetleilani.com

P. 36-37

Lynda Honing

@theurbanoasisblooms

P. 98-99

Lesley Ross

powerpathcoaching.co.uk

P. 190-191

Lynda Moffatt

@artist.lynda.moffatt

P. 134-135

Liahna Cole

@VitalityVibeWellness

P. 194-195

Magdalena Gulda

thesoundhealinginstitute.com

P. 92-93

Marcie Gregorio

oneworldwidetitle.com

P. 130-131

Maria Lyons

lifewave.com/1989689

P. 126-127

Marika Wessels

marikawessels.com

P. 154-155

Marilyn Wilson

oliobymarilyn.com

P. 42-43

Melissa Rubin

mjrgroupe.com

P. 186-187

Michelle Walker

katzrecruitment.com

P. . 202-203

Nassreen Nadat

naturaffinity.com

P. 4-5

Neesha Hothi

neeshcommunications.ca

P. 216-217

Paige Freeman

thebusinessvault.com.au

P. 182-183

Ralitza Spassova

authenticitymd.com

P. 166-167

Randi Winter

thep2plife.com

P. 26-27

Rani Sanghera

wellnesswithrani.ca

P. 176-177

Renee Lodge

@reneemoneymatters

P. 84-85

Robin Lipnack

rllmarketinggroup.net

P. 124-125

Robin Sandhu

@get_tones_by_robin

P. 220-221

Sabine Deans

heidentravelverse.com

P. 50-51

Saireen Neilsen

menopausitivity.ca

P. 138-139

Tanya Steele

tanyasteele.ca

P. 164-165

Sandra Flora

sandraflorahomedesign.ca

P. 74-75

Taylor Smith

taylorsmithandco.com

P. 212-213

Shelly Smee

integritygrp.ca

P. 148-149

Tina Aquila Posteraro

@tinashootsboudoir

P. 200-201

Stephanie Lehr

stephanielehr.com

P. 118-119

Valerie Mrakuzic

eatingtolivewell.com

P. 218-219

Susan Sheehan

sc7international.com

P. 168-169

Vicky Theunissen

@etsmakemiraclestrue

P. 158-159

Susie Ford

letsjustbefabulous.com.au

P. 76-77

Virginia Ede

ambiencewellnesscentre.com.au

P. 68-69

Talia Beckett

@taliadavispr

P. 54-55

Yolanda Gysbers

@yolandagysbersrealestat

P. 196-197

Tanya Benlow

@tanyabenlow

P. 86-87

Printed in the USA
CPSIA information can be obtained
at www.ICGtesting.com
CBHW082224271124
18130CB00030B/609